COMMUNICATIVE SYLLABUS DESIGN

*A sociolinguistic model
for defining the content of purpose-specific
language programmes*

COMMUNICATIVE SYLLABUS DESIGN

A sociolinguistic model
for defining the content of purpose-specific
language programmes

JOHN MUNBY

CAMBRIDGE UNIVERSITY PRESS

Cambridge
London · New York · Melbourne

Published by the Syndics of the Cambridge University Press
The Pitt Building, Trumpington Street, Cambridge CB2 1RP
Bentley House, 200 Euston Road, London NW1 2DB
32 East 57th Street, New York, NY 10022, USA
296 Beaconsfield Parade, Middle Park, Melbourne 3206, Australia

First published 1978

Printed in Great Britain
at the University Press, Cambridge

Library of Congress Cataloguing in Publication Data
Munby, John.
Communicative syllabus design.
Bibliography: p.
Includes index.
1. Languages, Modern — Study and teaching.
2. Curriculum planning. 3. Competence and performance
(Linguistics) 4. Sociolinguistics. I. Title.
PB36.M85   407   77-90216
ISBN 0 521 22071 8

CONTENTS

PREFACE

It is arguable that the most crucial problem at present facing foreign language syllabus designers, and ultimately materials producers, in the field of language for specific purposes, is how to specify validly the target communicative competence. At the heart of this problem is a reluctance to begin with the learner rather than the text, and the lack of a rigorous system for finding out the communication needs that are pre-requisite to the appropriate specification of what is to be taught. Once this is done, the next part of the problem is how to convert needs into syllabus content. This book attempts to provide a contribution to the solution of this problem.

In the preparation of this book I was influenced at the macro-level by the sociolinguistic writings of Dell Hymes and Michael Halliday, and at a more micro-level by the work of, in particular, Henry Widdowson, David Wilkins and Christopher Candlin. To many others, especially Roger Hawkey and my other colleagues in English Language Consultancies Department of the British Council, and to Jo Barnett, Roland Hindmarsh and Lilian Munby, I would like to express my appreciative thanks for their most active interest and support. In particular I am indebted to Peter Strevens and Terry Culhane whose unfailing encouragement, understanding and wise guidance in a work of this nature has been invaluable and much appreciated. Finally I would like to acknowledge the fact that this work would not have been possible without the financial support and encouragement of the British Council.

January, 1978   J.L.M.

INTRODUCTION

1. The upsurge of interest in the content of the language syllabus, following the concern with communicative competence generated by Dell Hymes, reflects inter alia a feeling that we ought to know much more about what it is that should be taught and learnt if a non-native is to be communicatively competent in English. Broadly speaking the post-war mainstream of language teaching (and testing) seems to have been concerned more with methodology, with *how* rather than *what* to teach, but syllabus design and content has in the present decade been receiving an increasing amount of attention. There has been a movement away from grammatical syllabuses, and then situational syllabuses, to what are variously described as notional, functional,[1] or communicative[2] syllabuses. A major factor here has been the work of Trim and his colleagues, especially Wilkins, in the Council of Europe Programme for a unit/credit system for adult language learning. Another line of development in this movement has been strongly influenced by the work in discourse analysis (written and oral) of Widdowson, Sinclair, Candlin, Trimble and their colleagues.[3] However, the area of syllabus design which requires more systematic attention is the communication needs of the learner, especially the derivational relationship of syllabus specification to such needs. In terms of designing courses in English for specific purposes (ESP) this seems to us to be of crucial importance.

In recent years ESP has become a major developmental focus in the area of what may now be called communicative syllabus design and materials production. Adult language institutions, publishers, planners and writers have responded with alacrity to the increasing demand for ESP programmes. However, a look at many of the resultant courses and materials prompts the vital question: what *system* (if any) is being used to arrive at the specification of the English deemed appropriate for different purposes? If it does not exist, there is

1

clearly a need for a model that takes account of all the potentially significant variables and systematically applies them to achieve an appropriate specification.

2. It is necessary to define here what is meant by the term ESP.[4] ESP courses are those where the syllabus and materials are determined in all essentials by the prior analysis of the communication needs of the learner, rather than by nonlearner-centred criteria such as the teacher's or institution's predetermined preference for General English or for treating English as part of a general education. There should be important differences in the English course for a non-native requiring English in order to study medicine in his own country as opposed to England; or when the language of instruction is the learner's mother tongue as opposed to English (when, for example, he might need English only for reading medical texts). Similarly, a course for someone who needs English in order to do his job must take account of, inter alia, the environment and social relationships obtaining between him and his interlocutors. The two major categories of ESP are [A] where the participant needs English to perform part or all of his occupational duties, e.g. working in civil aviation or tourist hotel management (appropriately labelled English for occupational purposes — EOP, for short); and [B] where the participant needs English for educational purposes, to pursue part or all of his studies, the major subcategory of which is discipline-based study, e.g. in agricultural science or chemical engineering (often referred to as English for academic purposes — EAP, for short). These categories subdivide, and in Chapter 3 below we show Strevens' (1977a) classification of ESP.

At this point an explanation should be given of the use of the word 'specific' rather than the more usual 'special' in the term ESP. The word 'special' is contentious in that the statement that a purpose is special seems to imply that it is not ordinary, but this is not necessarily so, and in any case the antonymous characteristic that should be intended by the phrase 'special purpose' is that it is not *general*. Furthermore, 'Special English', which is associated with some of the earlier examples of materials in this field, focuses on distinctive features of the language, especially vocabulary, that are most immediately associated with its restricted use, e.g. technical terms in agriculture. ESP, on the other hand, should focus on the learner and the purposes for which he requires the target language, and the *whole* language programme follows from that. It is this that is new about ESP, together with a much more rigorous approach to the whole subject of course design, using insights and findings from socio-linguistics, discourse analysis, and the communicative approach to language learning. The phrase English for Special Purposes, therefore, would convey its intended meaning more accurately, and avoid the confusion and doubt it sometimes causes, especially on first acquaintance, if it were changed to English for Specific Purposes. This is now the preferred use of the term among an increasing number of scholars, practitioners and institutions.

3. There are a number of reasons for the rapidly growing need for ESP programmes. One of the most significant is the spread of higher and further education with the concomitant need to gain access to the required knowledge that is available, either exclusively or most readily, in English. This is the case with the high-demand area of English for science and technology (EST), from the pioneering work in Chile[5] in the mid 1960s to the projects in Saudi Arabia[6] in the mid 1970s. The science students' need for English to pursue their studies in an English-medium situation, at the University of Zambia, is described, together with illustrations of the different exercise types used, by Wingard (1971). The same type of requirement, but in a non-English-medium situation, at Tabriz University (Bates and Dudley-Evans, 1976),[7] is discussed by Dudley-Evans, Shettlesworth and Phillips (1975).

It has also been observed that in countries where there is a change in the status of English from medium to subject, standards of English are considered in quite a number of cases to be dropping. A third reason for the growing demand for ESP programmes is the obvious attraction to the client or learner of custom-built courses in the English that will enable him to do his job[8] or pursue his studies,[9] rather than the uniquitous course in General English or general literary English whose irrelevance becomes apparent sooner or later.

4. In spite of all the considerable ESP activity that is going on (a lot of which is ESP in name only, being poorly disguised General English courses), this area of communicative syllabus design as yet lacks a rigorous system for deriving appropriate syllabus specifications from adequate profiles of communication needs. This book is an attempt to solve this problem by designing a dynamic processing model that starts with the learner and ends with his target communicative com-

petence. It is the detailed syllabus specification, the target communicative competence, which constitutes the essence of what should be embodied in the course materials. The model does not deal with materials production and so no more than an indication is given of the implementational constraints on the syllabus specification, e.g. the number of trained teachers available, quantity of instruction, the expectations of the institution, traditional strategies of learning, etc. It is pointed out (in the Epilogue, and elsewhere, e.g. page 40) that such variables, although important in the modification of syllabus specifications and the production/selection of materials, belong to the subsequent stage of course design and should not be considered before the syllabus specification has been obtained.

5. In this communicative approach to syllabus design, Chapter 1 is a discussion of some theoretical issues which form the backdrop, as it were, to the designing of the model that is needed, an overview of which is provided in Chapter 2. The next six chapters then go into detail on each part of the model.

In Chapters 3—6 the variables involved in the communication needs of learners of a foreign language are identified and organised as the parameters of the 'communication needs processor'. In this first sector of the model a detailed profile of needs is produced for the particular learner-participant or category of participant.

In Chapters 7—8 the profile of needs is interpreted in terms of the required micro-skills and micro-functions marked for attitudinal-tone. The meaning units may then be realised as appropriate language forms. The result is a syllabus specification systematically derived from the profile of needs.

The model is set out as an operational instrument (i.e. for actual use) in Chapter 9; and to exemplify its application, two very different participant types requiring English for their specific purposes are processed through it in Chapter 10.

6. Advice to reader. The intended (and recommended) order for reading this book is, as can be seen from Section 5 above, straight through from beginning to end. Some readers, however, especially those who are unfamiliar with the subject matter of Chapter 1, may find it preferable to leave Chapter 1 to the end or even to approach the book as follows: begin with Chapter 2 and then go on to Chapters 9 and 10; after this, read Chapters 3—8, the Epilogue, and then finish with Chapter 1.

NOTES

1 e.g. the programmes devised by Jupp and Hodlin (1975); Morrow and Johnson (1975).
2 See Shaw (1975).
3 e.g. the Doctor—Patient Communication Skills materials produced by Candlin, Bruton and Leather (1976a), or the *English in focus* materials designed by Allen and Widdowson (1974 et seq.).
4 cf. Strevens (1977b) on defining ESP, including a discussion on the difference between 'general' and 'special' purposes, and the bandwagon effect of the latter on course organisers and educational administrators (and publishers).
5 Ewer and Latorre (1967 and 1969).
6 Reported by Mountford (1976) and Chamberlain (1976).
7 This programme is now published by Longman as the *Nucleus* materials.
8 e.g. the Mobil Oil course for prospective technicians on the Arun Gas Field, Indonesia, reported by Knowles (1975); or 'English in Flight', a course for air hostesses prepared by ELTDU/OUP (1973).
9 e.g. the materials developed by Moore et al. (1977) at the University of Los Andes; or the University of Malaya project, reported by Cooper (1975).

1

COMMUNICATIVE COMPETENCE AND
A THEORETICAL FRAMEWORK

In trying to design a model for specifying the communicative competence of a foreign language participant, it would seem inappropriate to work within one particular linguistic theory. It may well be the case that a theory of linguistics (in the sense of formal linguistics) is neither the necessary nor the sufficient basis for such a study. 'There is no guarantee that generative transformational grammar, or for that matter any other linguistic theory, will be able to account for all the facts about language which native speakers possess' (Jakobovits, 1970). Furthermore, some of the ideas or activities with which this study is concerned may not be dealt with by such existing theories.

It is proposed, therefore, to operate within a theoretical perspective or framework, which will be derived from a particular view of the concept of competence. This is discussed in this chapter. A theoretical framework will ensure that, in the designing of our model, we ask appropriate questions from a consistent standpoint. Such a procedure should also have the incidental advantage of allowing the model to accommodate developments without sacrificing the underlying philosophy.

Central to the formation of our framework is the concept of the language user's competence and its relation to knowledge and communication, to which we now turn.

KNOWLEDGE AND COMMUNICATION

This topic area is full of statements or comments on the nature of competence and performance. What may be regarded as seminal positions and some important related viewpoints will be briefly examined and evaluated in terms of appropriateness for the purpose of this book.

6

1. Chomsky

I accept Chomsky's rejection of Skinner's behaviourist model as inadequate to account for the complexity of human language and the
creativity of the speaker-listener, though it should be noted [1] that
a stimulus—response model can probably explain *some* of the facts of
language behaviour (Lyons, 1970), and [2] that the equation of this
creativity with the ability to produce and understand an infinite number of novel sentences, with the theoretical possibility of infinite
length of sentence, does not bring out the important point that in the
majority of cases this novelty lies not in the grammar, lexis, or phonology, but in a novel concatenation of non-novel meaning components (Hasan, 1971). In this discussion the major drawback of
Skinnerian theory's refusal to consider anything that is not observ-
able is its inability to handle the now generally accepted notion of
two levels of language, one underlying the other.

Chomsky's view of what it means to know a language is reflected
in his distinction between linguistic competence and linguistic performance. (This distinction has a psychological orientation and is not
the same as de Saussure's 'langue' and 'parole'.) In *Aspects of the
Theory of Syntax* (1965) Chomsky writes: 'Linguistic theory is concerned primarily with an ideal speaker-listener, in a completely
homogeneous speech community, who knows its language perfectly
and is unaffected by such grammatically irrelevant conditions as
memory limitations, distractions, shifts of attention and interest, and
errors (random or characteristic) in applying his knowledge of the
language in actual performance.' The perfect knowledge referred to
here is the mastery of the abstract system of rules by which a person
is able to understand and produce any and all of the well-formed
sentences of his language, i.e. his linguistic competence. The actual
use of language, affected by what he terms grammatically irrelevant
conditions, and identified with the criterion of acceptability, not
grammaticality, is the domain of linguistic performance.

Two major problems arise from the foregoing. These concern [1]
two different interpretations or claims that Chomsky makes for
competence and [2] his line of demarcation between competence
and performance.

Neutral and stronger definitions of competence
Greene (1972) points out that Chomsky makes both a weaker, or

neutral, and a stronger claim for linguistic competence, with very different implications. The neutral interpretation refers to the knowledge of a system of rules (a generative grammar) that in some explicit and well-defined way assigns structural descriptions to sentences. This is purely descriptive, and is not intended to say anything about the way in which the speaker-hearer actually constructs the output of such a system of rules (1965, pp. 8–9). But when Chomsky (1970) says: 'A person who has learned a language has acquired a system of rules that relate sound and meaning in a certain specific way. He has, in other words, acquired a certain competence that he puts to use in producing and understanding speech', he has moved to the stronger claim that the rules of grammar are internalised in the head of the speaker and provide the basis for his understanding of linguistic relations (Greene, 1972). This is also reflected in Chomsky (1965) where he says that a generative grammar 'attempts to characterise in the most neutral possible terms the knowledge of the language that provides the basis for actual use of language by a speaker-hearer'. And, as Greene says, it is this stronger claim, that the system of rules (the underlying linguistic competence) is put to use in producing and understanding speech, that needs to be empirically tested.

Although some kind of competence may underlie the actual use of language, it does not necessarily follow that this consists of the rules of transformational grammar, at least not as formulated in the Standard Theory. Chomsky's neutral definition of competence is not at issue here since it is purely descriptive; we are concerned with his stronger definition since it is offered as the basis for a theory of cognitive processes — for the actual use of language. As has been observed, such a claim must be subject to empirical validation, and insofar as there seems little evidence at present that the rules of TG (Standard Theory) represent how the mind operates, and, given that on the contrary such a process seems implausible in that the human mind appears to operate heuristically rather than algorithmically, any 'stronger' definition of this underlying linguistic competence must refer to a system of rules that has a form and is organised in a way that has psychological reality. Lockwood (1972) seems to be saying much the same thing when he writes to the effect that Stratificational Grammar starts from the premise that any model of competence must be plausible in terms of the principle that it must interact with performance.

Demarcation of competence and performance

'Although a distinction of this kind is undoubtedly both a theoretical and a methodological necessity in linguistics, it is by no means certain that Chomsky himself draws it in the right place. It can be argued that he describes as matters of "performance" (and, therefore, as irrelevant) a number of factors that should be handled in terms of "competence" ' (Lyons, 1970). Hymes, Jakobovits, Campbell and Wales, Widdowson, Cooper and others, all reject Chomsky's restricted view of competence.

Hymes (1971) points out that Chomsky's category of competence provides no place for competency for language use but neither does his category of performance, despite his equating language use with performance. This omits almost everything of sociocultural significance, concerning itself with psychological constraints to do with memory and perception, etc, rather than with social interaction. Also Chomsky's notion of performance seems confused between actual performance and underlying rules of performance (e.g. stylistic rules of performance) which Hymes considers part of underlying competence. Jakobovits (1970) argues that social context selection rules are as necessary a part of the linguistic competence (non-Chomskyan sense) of a speaker as those in syntax with which we are familiar. Campbell and Wales (1970) accept Fodor and Garrett's (1966) one clear sense of the distinction between competence and performance, i.e. 'in which competence in any sphere is identified with capacity or ability, as opposed to actual performance, which may only imperfectly reflect underlying capacity'. But they point out that Chomsky's competence omits by far the most important linguistic ability: 'to produce or understand utterances which are not so much *grammatical* but, more important, *appropriate to the context in which they are made*', and they continue 'by "context" we mean both the situational and verbal context of utterances'.[1]

One could go on, but the message is clear. 'There are rules of use without which the rules of grammar would be useless' (Hymes, 1971), so the notion of competence must be enlarged to include contextual appropriacy. As empirical evidence from sociolinguistics, psycholinguistics, neurolinguistics (cf. Laver, 1970 and 1973), and any other relevant discipline, indicates that the constraints they provide can be formalised as rules, one should extend or recast the concept of competence as performance-constrained competence, to include them —

9

perhaps eventually to cover all rule-governed language behaviour.

The restriction of competence to perfect knowledge in a homogeneous speech community independent of sociocultural features is inadequate to account for language in use, for language as communication. These points are made and others taken up by Dell Hymes (see below) in his concept of communicative competence; but first mention should be made of a different conception of this term, as used by Jurgen Habermas, a leading social theorist interested in sociolinguistics, before turning to consider a different approach to the problem, that of Michael Halliday, who rejects the distinction between competence and performance as either misleading or irrelevant.

2. Habermas

Habermas (1970) preserves Chomsky's distinction of competence and performance but criticises his conception of competence as a monological capability, on the grounds that it provides an inadequate basis for the development of general semantics and because it fails to take account of the essential dimension of communication (in a highly idealised sense). Let us look very briefly at these two points in turn.

Habermas argues that 'universal meanings, which return in all natural languages, neither precede automatically all experience, nor are they necessarily rooted in the cognitive equipment of the human organism prior to all socialization. The universal distribution of meanings and even meaning components is not a sufficient criterion for the a priorism and monologism of general semantics strived for by the Chomsky school of linguistics.' Habermas differentiates between 'semantic universals which process experiences, and semantic universals which make this processing possible in the first place (i.e. a posteriori/a priori)', and also between 'semantic universals which precede all socialization, and semantic universals which are linked to the condition of potential socialization (monologic/intersubjective)'. He shows the four resultant classes as below.

Semantic universals

	a priori	*a posteriori*
intersubjective	dialogue-constitutive universals	cultural universals
monologic	universal cognitive schemes of interpretation	universals of perceptive and motivational constitution

He illustrates the four classes: for example, dialogue-constitutive universals include personal pronouns, formations for question, imperative, negation, certain classes of performatory speech acts (cf. Searle, 1969) etc; cognitive schemes of interpretation include causality and substance, space and time; cultural universals are exemplified by the system of kinship words; universals of perceptive constitution by the system of colour words.

As to his second criticism, that Chomsky's monologic competence takes no account of the intersubjective dimension, Habermas argues that

> it is not enough to understand language communication as an appli-
> cation — limited by empirical conditions — of linguistic com-
> petence. On the contrary, producing a situation of potential ordi-
> nary language communication belongs by itself to the general
> competence of the ideal speaker. The situation . . . depends on a
> structure of intersubjectivity which in turn is linguistic. This struc-
> ture is generated neither by the monologically mastered system of
> linguistic rules nor by the language-external conditions of its per-
> formance. On the contrary, in order to participate in normal dis-
> course, the speaker must have — in addition to his linguistic com-
> petence — basic qualifications of speech and of symbolic interaction
> (role-behaviour) at his disposal, which we may call communicative
> competence. Thus communicative competence means the mastery
> of an ideal speech situation

(it should be noted that this mastery is not to be equated with production). A little later he continues

> Above all, communicative competence relates to an ideal speech
> situation in the same way that linguistic competence relates to the
> abstract system of linguistic rules. The dialogue-constitutive uni-
> versals at the same time generate and describe the form of inter-
> subjectivity which makes mutuality of understanding possible.
> Communicative competence is defined by the ideal speaker's
> mastery of the dialogue-constitutive universals irrespective of the
> actual restrictions under empirical conditions.

From the foregoing one can see that Habermas' conception of competence is pitched at a higher level of idealisation than Chomsky's. His view of communicative competence as comprising knowledge of the universal formal features of language that make human communication possible has more in common with Halliday at the latter's

most idealised level of theorising. Habermas sees his initial ideas for
a theory of communicative competence as providing the kind of basis
he thinks necessary for developing general semantics, and he is
interested in the possible application of such a theory for social
analysis. One can leave him now with the question, to be answered
later, whether a perspective resulting from such a socio-philosophico-
semantic approach is appropriate for our purpose.

3. Halliday

Deriving from Firth, Halliday is interested in language in its social
perspective and so he is concerned with language use to account for
the language functions realised by speech. As Sinclair, Forsyth,
Coulthard and Ashby (1972) point out, these language functions are
defined in terms of formal features of language which enable communication to take place — which enable the *sine qua non* relations
or universals of Habermas' communicative competence to be
expressed. In this sense Halliday's macro-language functions relate to
Habermas' communicative competence, and the approach is at the
same very high level of idealisation. But his approach is not always so
general or idealised (social theory requiring a much lower level of
idealisation), and he is also concerned with the very low level as
when describing the grammar of the clause.

Halliday's approach to the question of the language user's competence is different from the others discussed in this chapter in the
important sense that he rejects the distinction between competence
and performance as being of little use in a sociological context.

> Here we shall not need to draw a distinction between an idealized
> knowledge of a language and its actualized use: between 'the code'
> and 'the use of the code' or between 'competence' and 'perform-
> ance'. Such a dichotomy runs the risk of being either unnecessary
> or misleading: unnecessary if it is just another name for the dis-
> tinction between what we have been able to describe in the gram-
> mar and what we have not, and misleading in any other interpret-
> ation [1970].

One may agree with the reason he gives for rejecting such a dichotomy
as unnecessary but it is difficult to see that *any other interpretation*
should be misleading (see, for example, Hymes et seq. below). However, let us see what he advocates in its place.

In recent writings (1971, 1972) Halliday has developed a sociosemantic approach to language and the speaker's use of language. At the heart of this approach is his language-defining notion of 'meaning potential', the sets of options in meaning that are available to the speaker-hearer. This meaning potential relates behaviour potential to lexico-grammatical potential: what the speaker can do → can mean → can say. These stages display systematic options at the disposal of the speaker. That is, a social theory determines behaviour options (what the speaker can do) which are translated linguistically as semantic options (what he can mean) which are encoded as options in linguistic forms (what he can say), the options at each stage being organised as networks of systems. 'The study of language as social behaviour is in the last resort an account of semantic options deriving from the social structure' (1971).

Halliday points out that his notion of meaning potential is not the same as Chomsky's notion of competence: what the speaker can do, in the special linguistic sense of what he can mean, is not the same as what he knows. Halliday's 'can do' interacts with 'does' in a simple and direct relation as potential to actualised potential; whereas Chomsky's 'knows' is distinct from his 'does', with a far from clear interaction, which requires a separate theory of performance to account for the 'does'.

Halliday says that his meaning potential 'is not unlike Dell Hymes' notion "communicative competence", except that Hymes defines this in terms of "competence" in the Chomskyian sense of what the speaker knows, whereas we are talking of a potential — what he can do, in the special linguistic sense of what he can mean — and avoiding the additional complication of a distinction between doing and knowing' (1971). This appears to be a misleading representation of Hymes (whose criticism of Chomsky's demarcation of competence and performance is summarised above and below) in that although Hymes does retain the notion of competence, he completely recasts it to include much more than Chomsky's 'knows' (see next section), so that the resultant communicative competence is in fact not unlike the notion of meaning potential, as Halliday remarks before severely qualifying his statement. And as Hymes' recast notion of performance is not the same as Chomsky's, it does not follow, as might be construed from Halliday's statement above, that Hymes retains Chomsky's 'additional complication of a distinction between doing and knowing'.

13

The interactional aspect of Halliday's notion of meaning potential has clear pedagogic possibilities, one of which will be indicated below. Although he himself cautions about the limited applicability of his sociosemantic networks — 'We would not be able to construct a socio-semantic network for highly intellectual abstract discourse, and in general the more self-sufficient the language (the more it creates its own setting, as we expressed it earlier) the less we should be able to say about it in these broadly sociological, or social, terms' (1972) — one should note the insights it provides for the language learning experience.

4. Hymes

Summarised above is Hymes' (1971) criticism that Chomsky's categories of competence and performance provide no place for competency for language use, i.e. the theory fails to account for a whole dimension, the sociocultural. It is interesting to note that some Transformational-Generative grammarians now claim that the theory will eventually deal with sociocultural rules of use (perhaps as part of performance-constrained competence) but they insist that that time is still well over the horizon. Hymes, however, points out that the Standard Theory's failure to provide an explicit place for sociocultural features is not the result of such a scientifically justifiable simplifying assumption, since no mention to that effect was made. The reason, he claims, is to be found in an ideological aspect to the theory (a 'Garden of Eden view') which also affects its view of performance. He criticises this view of performance because of its implicit ideological identification with the imperfect state resulting from the fall of the perfect speaker-hearer from grammatical competence, and also draws attention to Transformational-Generative Grammar's generally disparaging attitude to performance as a residual category for the theory (what we might call the 'dustbin view') essentially concerned with memory and perceptual constraints and ignoring social interaction. He also points out that Chomsky's notion of performance, as used in *Aspects*, seems confused between actual performance and underlying rules of performance ('stylistic rules of reordering'). As these latter look like rules of use (Chomsky does not develop this notion), one would agree with Hymes that this should be part of competence.

The Chomskyan restriction of the concept of competence to the perfect knowledge of an ideal speaker-listener, in a homogeneous speech community, unaffected by sociocultural or psychological constraints, cannot account for the communicative function of language. Applied linguistics needs a theory that, in Hymes' words, 'can deal with a heterogeneous speech community, differential competence, the constitutive role of sociocultural features', that can cope with phenomena such as White Thunder (a forty-year old Menomini (cited by Bloomfield) who spoke no language tolerably), relativity of competence in two, three or four languages (e.g. a Western Nigerian Muslim who speaks Hausa, Arabic and English as well as his mother-tongue Yoruba), contextual styles etc., etc. Hymes does not under-estimate the vast scale of the task for research but points out that linguistic theory itself needs such a theory for its foundations to be secured — for example, one needs to study the rules of speech acts, discourse units, since 'they enter as a controlling factor for linguistic form as a whole' — and he suggests that the key may be provided by the notion of competence itself, which he recasts as communicative competence, as follows.

If an adequate theory of language users and language use is to be developed, it seems that judgements must be recognized to be in fact not of two kinds (grammaticality and acceptability) but of four. And if linguistic theory is to be integrated with theory of communication and culture, this fourfold distinction must be stated in a sufficiently generalized way . . . :
1. Whether (and to what degree) something is formally possible;
2. Whether (and to what degree) something is feasible in virtue of the means of implementation available;
3. Whether (and to what degree) something is appropriate (adequate, happy, successful) in relation to a context in which it is used and evaluated;
4. Whether (and to what degree) something is in fact done, actually performed, and what its doing entails.
Hymes observes that a normal member of a community has both a knowledge of and a capability with regard to each of these aspects of the communicative systems available to him. Those four sectors of his communicative competence reflect the speaker-hearer's gram-matical (formally possible), psycholinguistic (implementationally feasible), sociocultural (contextually appropriate) and de facto (actually occuring) knowledge and ability for use. The fact that the grammatical sector is only one of four parameters of communicative competence shows the extent of this recasting of Chomsky's notion

of competence, which consisted only of grammatical competence.

It may help here to clarify Hymes' use of the terms competence, knowledge and ability for use. He says

I should take *competence* as the most general term for the capabilities of a person . . . Competence is dependent upon both (tacit) *knowledge* and (ability for) *use. Knowledge* is distinct, then, both from competence (as its part) and from systemic possibility (to which its relation is an empirical matter) . . . Knowledge also is to be understood as subtending all four parameters of communication just noted. There is knowledge of each. *Ability for use* also may relate to all four parameters. Certainly it may be the case that individuals differ with regard to ability to use knowledge of each: to interpret, differentiate, etc. The specification of *ability for use* as part of competence allows for the role of non-cognitive factors, such as motivation, as partly determining competence.

He also states that 'in speaking of competence, it is especially important not to separate cognitive from affective and volitive factors, so far as the impact of theory on educational practice is concerned'.

Of *performance*, Hymes says that this now refers to actual use and actual events, with certain reminders and provisos.

The 'performance models' studied in psycholinguistics are to be taken as models of aspects of ability for use, relative to means of implementation in the brain, although they could now be seen as a distinct, contributory factor in general competence . . . Here the performance of a person is not identical with a behavioural record, or with the imperfect or partial realization of individual competence. It takes into account the interaction between competence (knowledge, ability for use), the competence of others, and the cybernetic and emergent properties of events themselves.

In sum, the goal of a broad theory of competence can be said to be to show the ways in which the systematically possible, the feasible, and the appropriate are linked to produce and interpret actually occurring cultural behaviour [Hymes 1971].

5. Some related viewpoints

Cooper's (1968) view of communicative competence is very like Hymes' although he is concerned only with the sociolinguistic and grammatical parameters. He reinforces Hymes' point that effective communication requires more than linguistic competence: 'To communicate effectively, a speaker must know not only how to produce any and all grammatical utterances of a language, but also how to *use* them appropriately. The speaker must know *what* to say, with *whom*, and *when*, and *where*.' Cooper talks about two grammars or sets of rules, the speaker's linguistic and contextual competencies, as comprising the two components of communicative competence. With reference to second language testing, where the two sets of competencies may be acquired disjunctively, he points out that since both components are a necessary condition for communicative competence, though neither is sufficient, one cannot assume that information gained from testing one will necessarily tell us anything valid about the other. Existing testing frameworks, concentrating as they do on linguistic competence, do not necessarily assess a person's communicative ability. Knowledge of the target language may not be sufficient for effective communication to take place in that language, and our ability to predict communicative competence depends upon the test content being based upon the specific communication requirements of the particular category of learner. Cooper further points out that the social situations in which the second language speaker is to participate may require more than one variety of the language, i.e. he will need a linguistic repertoire (in Gumperz's (1964) sense) from which to select appropriately. In this case it will be no good constructing a test within a framework of the target language 'as a linguistically undifferentiated, single code'.

Another linguist with an essentially Hymesian view of communicative competence, although deriving more from rhetoric and discourse analysis, is Widdowson (1971 and 1975). He disagrees with the Chomsky/Katz and Postal view of performance as a residual category for everything unsystematic and therefore not accountable under competence, since some of their so-called performance features are in fact systematic and should therefore be regarded as part of a person's competence. A speaker's competence includes knowing how to recognise and how to use sentences to perform what he calls rhetorical acts — e.g. defining, classifying, promising, warning, etc. This is knowledge of the rules of use in particular social situations, which is what Widdowson means by communicative competence, and which he distinguishes from the rules of grammar, the speaker's grammatical competence, both components being involved in a speaker's competence. He makes the important point that for learners outside the European cultural tradition such rules of use need to be carefully taught, which means, among other things, giving as much attention to communicative competence as to grammatical competence. Of course, in order for rules of use (rhetorical rules) to be taught they must first have been described, and the current sparsity of our knowledge of discourse represents an obvious impediment to immediate and widespread implementation. But it should be emphasised that this is only temporary — rules of use can be, and are being, precisely described[2] — for 'there seems to be no reason why rhetoric as the description of communicative competence should not achieve similar standards of precision as grammar has in the description of grammatical competence'. Widdowson also provides an interesting insight when he says 'My guess is that the best way — perhaps the only way — of characterising different language registers is to discover what rhetorical acts are commonly performed in them, how they combine to form composite communication units' (e.g. a scientific report), 'and what linguistic devices are used to indicate them.' This is illuminating not only of possibly the most significant distinguishing characteristics of register but also of the important place of discourse, and the rules and characteristics of its units like the speech (or rhetorical) act and the speech event, in communicative competence.

Jakobovits, whose reasons for rejecting the Standard Theory view of (linguistic) competence accord broadly with Hymes, Cooper and Widdowson, specifies four aspects of knowledge that he considers part of a person's communicative competence (1970). These concern paralinguistic, kinesic, sociolinguistic, and psycholinguistic factors. Although Jakobovits' view is wider than Cooper's or Widdowson's, and includes the psycholinguistic aspect, his set of parameters is not the same as that of Hymes, the most important difference being his omission of grammatical knowledge from communicative competence. This must necessitate his retention of linguistic competence, in the restricted sense of grammatical competence, in addition to the concepts of communicative competence and performance. Hymes' formulation is to be preferred since, by incorporating grammatical competence under communicative competence as one of its parts, it emphasises the all-important *relationship*, rather than the pedagogically less relevant contrasts, between the grammatical and the sociocultural and psycholinguistic aspects of a person's competence. Also, Hymes' set of parameters of communicative competence seems notionally a little more substantial (at least for our purposes). It further avoids two possible and misleading conclusions that might arise from separating grammatical competence and communicative competence: (i) that grammatical competence and communicative competence should be taught separately, or in that order (this actually happens); and (ii) that grammar is not an essential factor in communicating through language, or that it is somehow not related to communicative ability. It must be stressed that Jakobovits himself, a leading advocate of the cause of communicative competence in teaching, does not draw any such conclusions, and his discussion makes it clear that he would disavow them — in fact he expressly condemns the first on more than one occasion.[3] The point is just that Hymes' formulation, apart from the merit of its interactional goal, logically does not admit of such conclusions.

Jakobovits makes some important points about the relation of communicative competence to language testing. In discussing the inadequacy of the discrete-point approach (still the major one today) to language testing and teaching, he points out that experience has shown that 'performance on these language tests and the ability to make use of the language for communicative purposes are not necessarily related, indicating that the former is not a good measure of the latter'. In view of the importance of the latter, and the current lack of a clear and comprehensive answer to the question of what it is to know how to use a language, he suggests the pragmatic strategy of making detailed definitions of 'specific communicative goals and of assessing the extent to which an individual is capable of meeting these goals'. He also recognises that there are different levels of communicative competence and, like Hymes, allows for less than native language competence in the specification that should be made of the different levels of proficiency that are relevant to a second language learner.

SUMMARY

It can now be seen that, from views of knowledge and communication as discussed in this chapter, it is possible to derive insights for the formation of a theoretical framework. Such insights stem from views of competence (in the broad sense) that are motivated by the same basic concerns, and it is therefore possible to describe the resultant orien-

19

tation as predominantly linguistic, psycholinguistic, sociolinguistic, etc. (see Figure 1). One should perhaps stress the word predominantly, since it is of course possible to have an orientation that is socio-psycholinguistic, but the comprehensiveness of this term blurs the focus which a theoretical perspective is intended to provide. The question is one of emphasis rather than synthesis or antithesis. When Campbell and Wales state (1970) that communicative competence is the primary goal of the psychology of language, one should remember that they are two cognitive psychologists for whom communicative competence is central in the study of language acquisition, with which they are concerned. Therefore, the environmental factors, which consist of both psycholinguistic and sociolinguistic features, will be considered from the point of view of language acquisition. Hymes, on the other hand, an anthropologist and sociolinguist, whilst including a psycholinguistic component in his conception of communicative competence, is mainly concerned with the fact that a language user's competence entails judgements and abilities related to, and interdependent with, sociocultural features. Communicative competence is central to such sociolinguistic study, and so will be looked at from such a viewpoint. Some environmental or contextual factors may be common to both conceptions of communicative competence, but they may have different implications and receive different emphases depending on whether the fundamental concern is sociolinguistic or psycholinguistic in nature.

The Chomskyan position has already been evaluated above and an attempt made to show that the basically linguistic orientation, with his psycholinguistic extensions, that stems from Chomsky's conception of competence is inappropriate here. This is important, for Chomsky's unique contribution has been to revitalise theoretical lintuistics, and without his having done this we might not now be in a position to appraise the problem as we can. Basically, however, his notions of competence and performance do not, or cannot, handle the sociocultural dimension that is essential to any study concerned with the communicative aspects of language.

Nor will a perspective resulting from the socio-philosophico-semantic approach of Habermas be appropriate for our task. Habermas is concerned with an ideal speech situation, eschewing the constraints of the real world as does Chomsky's view of competence, which he considers inadequate. His introduction of the intersubjective and a

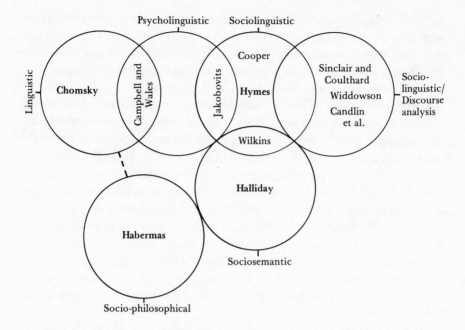

Figure 1 'The competence constellation'

posteriori dimensions into his conception of semantic universals provides insights into studying the prerequisite features of human communication, but it is of little practical use to restrict the concept of communicative competence to the ideal speaker's mastery of dialogue-constitutive universals and to ignore actual speech situations. Despite his concern with communication, his decontextualised view of communicative competence is too idealised.

What is needed is a theoretical framework that stems from a sociolinguistic view of knowledge and communication, where the contextual or environmental factors which constrain competence, or are involved in the development of communicative competence or in the realisation of meaning potential, are predominantly sociocultural. This brings us to Halliday and to Hymes.

At a very high level of idealisation, Halliday's language functions are concerned with the same issues as Habermas' conception of communicative competence, which is very different from Hymes' conception. But at a lower level of idealisation Halliday and Hymes are similarly concerned with language in use. At this lower level Halliday

21

is more detailed than Hymes but within a smaller area, whereas Hymes explores an overview, indicating what a broad theory of communicative competence ought to cover. Hymes' sociolinguistic view emphasises the interactional aspect of a person's competence that is necessary for actual communication, a theoretical proposition that has important pedagogic significance, as has the interactional aspect of Halliday's notion of meaning potential. Here it should again be mentioned that this important concept of meaning potential seems closer to Hymes' communicative competence than is maintained by Halliday.

Hymes' retention of competence and performance, albeit completely recast enables his approach to affect and be affected by developments in major theoretical fronts such as Case Grammar and Generative Semantics – providing, hopefully, a much needed socialisation of such grammatical theory. One might argue that Halliday can do just this, but his rejection of any distinction (in a non-trivial sense) between competence and performance makes his theory to that extent less accessible to the desired two-way influence possible with Hymes.

Both contribute major insights for the formation of our theoretical framework. In particular, Hymes spotlights the vital factor of contextual (sociocultural) appropriacy and Halliday brings out the sociosemantic basis of linguistic knowledge. Both these features have important pedagogic implications, as may be seen below.

One other point is worth noting here. This concerns discourse. Although Hymes includes discourse within the context to be covered by a theory of communicative competence, he has not got beyond suggesting lines of investigation;[4] and Halliday, concerned as he is with intersentential cohesion, has restricted his actual analysis of language in use to the level of the clause.[5] For insights into discourse as a central factor in competency for use, it will be necessary to turn to other sources (Sinclair and Coulthard, 1975; Widdowson, 1977a and b; Candlin, Leather and Bruton, 1974, 1976a and b).

CONSTITUENTS OF A THEORETICAL FRAMEWORK APPROPRIATE TO THE SPECIFICATION OF A PERSON'S COMMUNICATIVE COMPETENCE IN A SECOND LANGUAGE

I am concerned with a second language participant whose proficiency in the second language has to be specified for some particular pur-

pose. To guide consideration of the parameters which will comprise
the model that needs to be designed for this purpose, the following
theoretical framework is proposed. It consists of three major constituents and their parts. These will be presented in outline form only,
since some discussion has already taken place and it is the purpose of
the succeeding chapters to go into the detail that results from their
influence on different parts of the model.

1. Sociocultural orientation

1.1 Competence and the community
As Hymes points out, one is not dealing with perfect competence
in a homogeneous speech community but the reality of differential
competence, and relativity of competence, in a heterogeneous
speech community. This needs to be borne in mind when considering matters such as the nature of communication needs and the
establishing of target levels that are relevant to them.

1.2 Contextual appropriacy
Knowledge about the target language, in the sense of knowing
whether and to what extent something in that language is sys-
temically possible, may not be sufficient for effective communication. Hymes, Cooper, Widdowson and others have drawn attention to the equally important factor of contextual appropriacy:
'There are rules of use without which the rules of grammar would
be useless'. Therefore we should teach the rules of use and language
features appropriate to the relevant social context. It follows that
in specifying communicative competence which, as we have seen,
subsumes both grammatical and contextual competence, dealing
with one component alone will usually not be valid.

A word needs to be said about the concept of 'language variety',
in the intra-lingual sense as used and clarified by Gregory (1967)
and Crystal (1971). Although it is clear that in a language such as
English there is a great deal of stylistic variation, the difficulty is
in the assumption that a putative variety exists, i.e. that the
specific situation really does have a necessary and sufficient set of
distinctive forms and rules of use to warrant the term variety. In
this sense it seems unlikely that 'Diplomatic English', for example,
is a variety of English except at so high a level of abstraction as to

23

have little practical use; on the other hand, it is possible to specify the English required by diplomats for specific diplomatic purposes. Whether that is a variety or not might then be said to be irrelevant. Where the concept of language variety is required, however, it is perhaps best characterised by its selection and use of linguistic forms for its constitutive communicative acts or functions, neither the forms nor the functions necessarily being situation-specific since they usually occur across social situations.

1.3 Communication needs

A sociocultural orientation focuses on the social function of language and displays a learner-centred approach. Before deciding what to teach the learner one wants to know his requirements in terms of, for example, communicative mode and activities, and the relationships between him and his interlocutors. In other words, the specification of communication requirements or needs is prior to the selection of speech functions or communicative acts to be taught. By drawing up a profile of communication needs one can more validly specify the particular skills and linguistic forms to be taught.

2. Sociosemantic basis of linguistic knowledge

2.1 Language as semantic options deriving from the social structure

Halliday's concept of meaning potential draws attention to the sociosemantic basis of linguistic knowledge and indicates the central and metamorphosing role of the semantic options (available to a person) in translating options in behaviour into options in linguistic form. At each stage these options are organised at networks of systems. At present, the significance of this for pedagogic purposes lies not in attempting to construct such system networks for the diverse social contexts with which our categories of learner are concerned (Halliday, who is concerned with understanding the language system, himself warns about the limited amount of adult speech that is accessible to this approach (Halliday, 1972)), but in the theoretical support it gives to programme designers, materials producers, teachers and testers, to approach linguistic form in a different way, i.e. from the standpoint of meaning, *ab initio*.

2.2 A communicative approach

Wilkins (1972) advocated a semantic or notional approach to the specification of language to be taught, which ensures the consideration of the communicative value of such content. He later called this a communicative approach (1974).[6] In this, one starts from the notional categories which a learner needs to handle (the things we use language for) and then selects, from the sets of linguistic forms for encoding the categories or sub-categories, those that are appropriate to his level and requirements. This is much more relevant to the development of the communicative competence of the learner, and therefore less wasteful, than the commonplace grammatical syllabus where one starts from the linguistic forms themselves, which are regarded like Everest, to be taught because they are there (or accorded the status of scientific truths that must be taught), and where the problem is thereafter seen as one of sequencing according to the competing criteria of relative simplicity and high functional load. The communicative syllabus has potentially wider applicability, and is less likely to omit appropriate items, than the situational syllabus of recent times whose basic problem has been that not all of a person's language needs are relatable to situation* or predictable from an analysis of situational needs. Wilkins' framework, which will be considered later, involves three sets of notional categories and their sub-categories (with no claim to be exhaustive), of which his categories of communicative function are especially important.

3. Discourse level of operation

There is a need here, perhaps, for a terminological note. Discourse is written as well as spoken, and terms like *speech act, speech event, speech situation* should be understood to apply to both media of communication. Sinclair et al. (1972), in their seminal work on discourse analysis, postulate discourse as the level between grammar and non-linguistic organisation. Hymes (1972) puts it another way when he says that 'the level of speech acts' (which we understand him here to mean a communicative unit at the level of discourse) 'mediates immediately between the usual levels of grammar and the rest of a speech event or situation in that it implicates both linguistic form

*The term 'situation', as used in the context of the situational syllabus, should be interpreted to mean 'setting'.

and social norms'. It is possible to relate these terms. For example, if we take the system of analysis set up by Sinclair et al. for classroom discourse,[7] their discourse unit lesson (not necessarily the same as the pedagogic unit period) might be regarded as the speech situation since it also is apparently not rule-governed. That is, there are no rules of occurrence for the transactions that comprise a lesson. On the other hand, the different transaction types seem to operate at the level of the rule-governed speech events that exist within speech situations. Transactions are made up of different types of exchange, which could be regarded as operating at the same level as Hymes' speech acts that are embedded within speech events. Speech acts have formal features and rules of occurrence; so do exchanges, which consist of different types of move and act,[8] and rules of occurrence state how the acts combine to form moves and how the moves combine to form exchanges. Whatever the terms used, the concern here is with units of communication, distinct from and generally above the level of the clause, units which have formal characteristics and are governed by rules of occurrence.

It seems clear that communicative competence includes the ability to use linguistic forms to perform communicative acts and to understand the communicative functions of sentences and their relationships to other sentences. This happens at the level of discourse and involves, inter alia, knowledge of the rhetorical rules of use that govern the patterning of such acts, the interpretative strageties of the language user (Widdowson, 1975), and also what Candlin (1976) has described as the contextual meaning of an utterance (the value derived from its positional significance in the discourse). These discourse units (rhetorical acts, speech acts, speech functions) have characteristics and formal rules of occurrence that can be and need to be made explicit. More analyses and descriptions are needed, such as those provided by Sinclair et al., Candlin et al. (1974), and, on a smaller scale, Ervin-Tripp (1972).

The implications for the model include the following:

3.1 Selecting communicative units, such as speech functions or rhetorical acts, rather than grammatical elements in the specification of a syllabus, takes place at the level of discourse.

3.2 Rhetorical rules and contextual meaning are as important as grammatical rules and referential meaning, so they should be taught as appropriate to the required acts and functions.

3.3 A concern with communicative competence indicates the need for redefining the dimensions of syllabus specification to take account of the communicative value of discourse level units.

NOTES

1 Campbell and Wales note that Chomsky (1965) allows that part of this ability belongs properly to linguistic competence: 'an essential property of language is that it provides the means for . . . reacting appropriately in an indefinite range of new situations'. But he fails to provide for this in his theory.

2 e.g. conditions on the performing of speech acts like commanding (Labov, 1969), or promising (Searle, 1969).

3 The same criticism and a similar defence also seem to apply to Widdowson for his division of competence into grammatical and communicative. In his case, however, the problem seems to be terminological, and can be met by relabelling his components with Cooper's terms, i.e. linguistic (or grammatical) competence and contextual competence as parts of communicative competence.

4 Hymes, 1972.

5 Quoted in Sinclair, Forsyth, Coulthard, Ashby, 1972.

6 See, however, Widdowson (1977a).

7 Using the following rank scale of discourse units: *lesson, transaction, exchange, move, act*.

8 Not the same as Austin/Searle or Widdowson terms.

2

DESIGNING THE MODEL:
PARAMETERS AND PROCESS

The theoretical framework outlined above affects the kind of model that we need for specifying communicative competence. In this chapter the parameters of such a model will be postulated, and an outline given as to how the components interact to process a given input into an appropriate output.

1. INITIAL IDEAS AND PROBLEMS

In the first approach to designing a model the problem was considered in terms of a set of hierarchically ordered parameter maps, the first layer being an abstract or general representation of what were taken to be the salient features, the second showing the constituents of the parameters, given a specific type of learner.

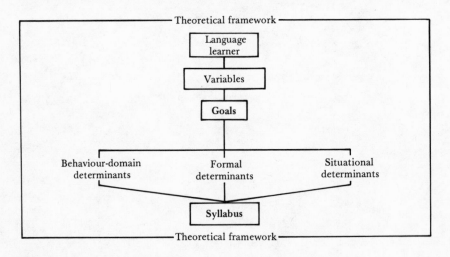

Figure 2 Parameter map: Layer 1 (general)

In Figure 2, variables, of the kind influenced by the adoption of a particular theoretical perspective, operate as constraints on a language learner to identify his goals. Three potential dimensions of syllabus specification, seen as behaviour-domain determinants, formal determinants, and situational determinants, will then reflect the goals.

In Figure 3, a specific category of second language participant has specific communicative objectives which are achieved by controlling particular communicative behaviours. There was then a third layer where all the appropriate realisations take place.

The thinking here reflected the first constituent of the theoretical framework, viz. sociocultural orientation. The learner's goals were seen to be dependent on variables which looked like categories of communication needs, and the target syllabus specification appeared to take account of the importance of contextual appropriacy. In so doing, it was necessary to reject Carroll's (1961) two-dimensional grid for specifying language behaviour in terms of the cells formed by the intersection of skills and language aspects, because it took no account of contextual constraints, and, for the same reason, Valette's (1971) table of specifications for second language instruction, and

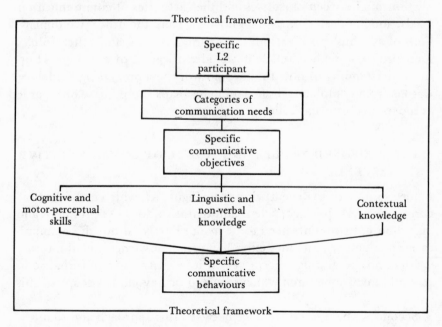

Figure 3 Parameter map: Layer 2 (specific)

other decontextualised frameworks such as Kingsbury's (1971). The redefinition of the dimensions of syllabus specification to include contextual knowledge was influenced by Cooper's (1968) three-dimensional elaborated framework for language testing, although context was taken to be the third dimension rather than an extension of the horizontal axis. It seemed that the question as to which language varieties constituted the learner's linguistic repertoire (Cooper's third dimension) could be more appropriately handled in the model as a variable constraining the specification of his objectives, leaving the third dimension, in the specification of the language behaviours to meet those objectives, to contextual knowledge. Here, therefore, would be specified the appropriate rules of use and characteristic features for the previously identified varieties.

There were problems, however, with this putative 'model'. Firstly, these parameter maps took insufficient account of the second of the constituents in our theoretical framework, viz. the sociosemantic basis of linguistic knowledge, or at least did not make its presence explicit. Secondly, the nature of the processing between the top and bottom halves of the maps was not clear. Thirdly, the dynamic relationship between objectives and the categories of communication needs, and between contextual knowledge and the other two dimensions of syllabus specification, was opaque. At this stage, therefore, some progress had been made in the identification of parameters but the understanding of how they would work in a processing model was far from complete. These parameter maps should now be regarded as superseded by what follows.

2. THE PROPOSED PROCESSING MODEL OF COMMUNICATIVE COMPETENCE

Before turning to the eventual model (Figure 4), which embodies current answers, both confident and tentative, to those problems and many more, two points need to be made. Firstly, although communicative competence includes extra-linguistic knowledge and abilities, we shall not be dealing, except very briefly, with the non-verbal code. It would involve research which seems to be beyond the scope of this work.

Secondly, there is a difference between this approach and that of a variety analyst or stylistician. A stylistician starts with the text

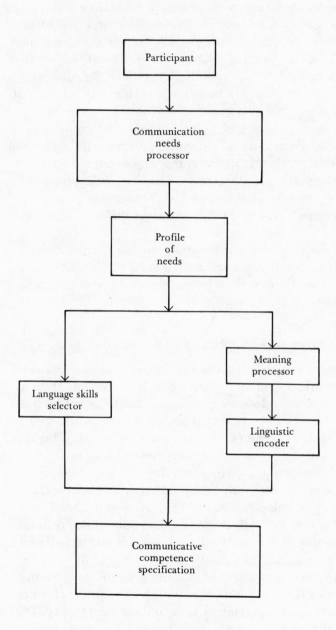

Figure 4 Model for specifying communicative competence

(spoken or written) that is representative of the putative variety and investigates features according to the descriptive linguistic and stylistic categories of his analytical framework. Distinctive characteristics of formal distribution, frequency of occurrence, etc, are noted and such features, formulated as descriptive statements or rules of use, are then postulated as the markers of the hypothetical variety. By contrast, here one starts with the person (a language participant or category of participant) and investigates his particular communication needs according to the sociocultural and stylistic variables which interact to determine a profile of such needs. This profile is eventually translated into the ESP specification that indicates the target communicative competence of the participant. The stylistician's analytical framework and the proposed processing model of communicative competence are therefore bound to be different since different things are being done.

In this model the output, the appropriate specification of communicative competence, is processed from a profile of language communication needs which must itself be systematically arrived at, and to which sub-model we now turn.[1]

3. COMMUNICATION NEEDS PROCESSOR

In the Communication Needs Processor (CNP) we take account of the variables that affect communication needs by organising them as parameters in a dynamic relationship to each other (Figure 5). These parameters are of two kinds, those that process non-linguistic data and those that provide the data in the first place; or, put another way, one set of constraints (a posteriori) that depend upon input from another set of constraints (a priori) before they can become operational. There are reasons too, which should become clear, for the sequential ordering of individual boxes. The parameters, therefore, are ordered in this way for both theoretical and operational reasons. (This possibly reinforces the contrastive point made above, between communicative competence specification and variety analysis, since there is apparently no theoretical ordering between the dimensions for stylistic analysis (Crystal and Davy, 1969).) The a priori parameters are: purposive domain, setting, interaction, and instrumentality. The a posteriori parameters are: dialect, target level, communicative event, and communicative key.

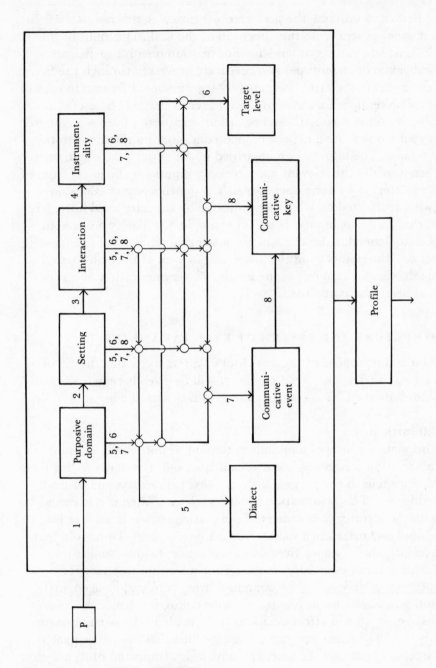

Figure 5 Communication Needs Processor

Before considering the parameters themselves, it is necessary to comment generally on the operation of the CNP. The input to the CNP, which consists of base-line information on a L2 participant (individual or stereotype) is successively processed through the first four boxes in the order indicated by the numbered arrows. In each of these boxes questions are answered in terms that will be useful as input to other boxes. Therefore this information is both stored here for subsequent use and passed on as conditions on the input to the next box. The information identified in the upper band of parameters then provides the relevant and necessary inputs for the lower band of parameters to become operational. The dependency relationships (what is affected by what) are indicated by the numbered lines, 5 to 8, that carry the inputs. Thus, for example, the dialect box can be seen to depend on input from purposive domain, setting and interaction. The results from the processing in each of the eight parameters are written out as the profile of communication needs for that particular participant.

STRUCTURE AND SYSTEM OF EACH PARAMETER

As it is the purpose of the next four chapters to go into the detail of each parameter, only brief comment will be given here in order to show how the CNP works, beginning in fact with the input.

3.0 Participant

This input consists of a minimum amount of potentially relevant information concerning identity and language. The data relating to *identity* tells us the participant's age, sex, nationality, and place of residence.[2] This information becomes relevant when it is matched with the identity of members of the participant's role set (see interaction) and placed in a spatial context (see setting). To be told that a participant is twenty-five years old, female, English, and from London, is not especially revealing; but if we find that this person, or category of person, will be communicating with middle-aged, male, northern Nigerians, *in* Nigeria, we have culturally significant information which will affect decisions to be made in the communicative key box. The data concerning *language* identifies the participant's target language and the extent, if any, of his command of it, his mother tongue, and any other languages that he knows, including the extent of such command. The information on the last point may prove to be irrelevant in some cases but helpful in others.

3.1 Purposive domain
In this parameter one first establishes the *type of ESP* (English for Specific Purposes) involved and then specifies the *occupational* or *educational* purpose for which the target language is required. After the ESP type has been identified as, for example, occupational: post-experience,[3] questions are asked which establish the general occupational classification, the specific occupation, the central and other duties. If the purpose is educational, questions are asked which identify the specific discipline, central area of study, etc. A suitable term to indicate the nature of this higher-order sociocultural constraint that will identify the communicative purpose in such terms is purposive domain (it is preferable not to use the term role unless focusing on relationships).

3.2 Setting
This parameter deals with features of both physical and psychosocial setting. In including both categories under setting one is following Hymes (1972) rather than other authorities. Questions are asked on the spatial and temporal aspects of the *physical* setting in which the target language is required for use. This includes place of work and study settings, as applicable. Then a selection has to be made from a list of *psychosocial* settings (see Chapter 3) which are seen as different environments in which the target language is to be used. Examples of such environments are noisy, demanding, culturally different, aesthetic, unfamiliar. This information, besides operating as constraints on the original input, provides input to the boxes below, the information on physical setting, for example, being relevant to dialect and communicative event, that on psychosocial setting to communicative key.

3.3 Interaction
This is the variable where one identifies those with whom the participant has to communicate in the target language, and predicts the relationships that may be expected to obtain between him and his interlocutors. In this parameter one first states the participant's *position*, i.e. in which he enacts a particular role, by reference to

purposive domain. Then, taking account of constraints from physical setting, one identifies the participant's *role-set*,[4] i.e. the different people with whom he will interact in English in the enacting of a particular role. The *role-set identity* is also specified here in terms of the size of participation, age-group, sex, and nationality of its members. The interaction of the participant's position with a member of his role-set produces a *role relationship*, e.g. assistant master — headmaster. Although interaction relationships tend to be expressed in terms of role relationships, here they will be specified in terms of the *social relationships*, e.g. subordinate—superior, which are implied by the role relationships and the other relevant features so far obtained in the profile of needs. It is the social relationships which will be more significant for determining attitudinal constraints when we come to communicative key. A fuller discussion of this point will be found in Chapter 4, where an inventory of social relationships, from which to make appropriate selections, is provided and explained.

3.4 Instrumentality

Here one is concerned with identifying constraints on the input in terms of the medium, mode, and channel of communication. One needs to know if the required *medium* of communication is spoken or written or both, and if the type of command is receptive or productive or both. Distinctions concerning the nature of the participation between the parties to the communication enable us to specify whether the *mode* of communication is, for example, 'monologue, written to be read' (e.g. books of non-fiction) or 'monologue, written to be spoken' (e.g. news bulletins). There is a set of such subcategories of communicative mode from which to select as appropriate. The third aspect of instrumentality concerns the *channel* of communication that is required. This ranges from the commonly required print and face-to-face channels (both unilateral and bilateral) to the rarer radio contact for navigators and the police. The precise meaning of all the features of instrumentality will be found in Chapter 4 where we discuss each category of this variable in detail. These constraints, either individually or in combination, provide information relevant to the further processing of the input.

3.5 Dialect

Given the constraints of physical setting, role-set, and purpose, one is now in a position to process the input for dialect, e.g. to specify whether it is British or American English, or a regional variety of either, that is more appropriate for the participant to produce or understand. The main dimension of dialect with which we are concerned is the regional/non-regional (discussed in Chapter 5), although matters of social class and temporal dialect are also dealt with here.

3.6 Target level

At this stage of the CNP, the participant's target level of command should be stated in terms that will guide the further processing through the model. Enough input information has been identified in the upper band of parameters for a specification to be made in such terms. The system of target level specification which we have devised for this purpose is set out in Chapter 5.

It is important not to confuse the identification of the target level with the specification of the particular language behaviours for which the target language is required. Level is a determinant, not an objective.

3.7 Communicative event

This parameter is concerned with *what* the participant has to do, either productively or receptively. It first identifies communicative events that result from the interaction of relevant inputs deriving from the prior identification of the participant's purposive domain, physical setting, role-set, and instrumentality requirements. The events thus systematically arrived at are what might be regarded as macro-activities, such as 'waiter serving customer in restaurant' or 'student participating in seminar discussion at university'. The parts, such as 'attending to customer's order' or 'introducing a different point of view', which make up these events, can then be regarded as micro-activities or simply activities.

Events consist of communicative activity and subject-matter. The term *activity* is to be distinguished from the various uses of the terms *act* and *function* (discussed below, pages 44—6 in §5 on the Meaning Processor). The term communicative activity as used here is the unit of communication that results from analysing an event into component parts that facilitate sociosemantic processing or skills selection (see below). Trim's instances of his language activities (1971 and 1973) are generally of the kind for which appropriate language skills could then be selected. In the occupational context our activity is similar to many of the 'communicative purposes', such as seeking advice, stating difficulties or objections, understanding diagrams, which Strevens (1977a) suggests as a set of categories that seem to apply in the technical work-place. The reason for saying many, rather than all, is that some of these communicative purposes, such as agreeing/disagreeing, seeking confirmation, and stating unwillingness, are lower order units which will be handled later on in the model, through the meaning processor. This use of 'activity' is partly similar to Bung's 'operation'. Bung's study of a waiter serving food in a restaurant enabled him to analyse this event (he calls it a function) into eighteen operations (1973b). However, these operations are the product of a very detailed analysis for the purpose of module construction, where a 'must-precede relation' applies in the writing of the materials, which is a different purpose from ours. Without the benefit of Bung's description, this introspective analysis would probably have resulted in a less detailed breakdown, perhaps into only five or six activities. With an event like this, where the tasks are highly predictable, these six activities would probably subsume his eighteen operations. It may be the case that for many events the most viable level of analysis is one that is neither too delicate nor too gross. When analysing on the basis of introspection the criterion should be that the resultant communicative activities will facilitate the subsequent processing into meaning units and the determination of the subject-matter. As indicated above, the term activity includes discoursal activities, such as 'note-taking from lectures' or 'writing up an experiment', from which specific language skills derive and for which such skills are required. Events, then, are broken down into their constituent activities. In academic study contexts, there might be events which are less susceptible to this treatment, in which case an event can be passed intact for interpretation in the skills selector.

The subject-matter of an event consists, initially, of topics or referential vocabulary categories for the communicative activities, thus acting as the central generator of the lexical items that the participant has to be able to understand or produce.

3.8 Communicative key[5]
This parameter is concerned with *how* (in the sense of manner) one does the activities comprising an event (the *what* one does). Its categories derive from different sources from those for events. The prior

identification of the participant's identify, role-set identity, social relationships, the psychosocial setting, and the nature and size of the participation, enables us to specify the likely attitudes or keys that need to be produced or understood in connection with an event. One needs a taxonomy of such features from which to make appropriate selections to mark each communicative act, features which will eventually affect the choice of linguistic realisations. This has led therefore to the construction of an attitudinal-tone index (see Chapter 6) which consists of a set of continua, each one labelled with a superordinate pair of *keys* in a relation of antonymy to each other, e.g. courteous — discourteous. The more likely *attitudinal-tones* for each continuum are indicated, these being co-hyponyms of each of the two antonymous parts of the superordinate term.

The postulation of a continuum indicates that the attitudinal-tones on each side of the continuum are not polarised as independent qualities but are in a 'more than' and 'less than' relationship to some relevant implicit norm (Lyons, 1968). For example, a person who says 'Take off your shoe', with a high fall intonation pattern, is polite rather than impolite (or at least not impolite) with respect to the norm relevant for a doctor—patient interview, but impolite rather than polite with respect to the norm relevant for the shop assistant — customer situation. A continuum also allows for a central position (should this ever be significant) for an attitudinal-tone that is neutral with respect to the extremes of its continuum.

Given the relevant inputs, our procedure is first to predict from the index the likely keys for each communicative activity. This marking is done here in the CNP. The specification of the appropriate attitudinal-tones is done at the stage of sociosemantic processing. The differentiation of a superordinate into its hyponyms varies between individuals as a result of their communication needs, and the initial decision to be more general or more specific is based on the particular needs of different participants.

A profile has now emerged of the communication needs of a particular participant or category of participant. This profile has been systematically arrived at, having been processed through the eight parameters of the CNP. The necessary sociolinguistic variables have been taken into account so it can be said that the profile is contextually or situationally constrained (where context means social context, and situation embraces all the variables and not just that of setting). Guidance in the design of this component of the model was given by the first constituent of the theoretical framework, namely a socio-cultural orientation towards communication.

It should be noted that the profile is a detailed description of particular communication needs without containing any specification of the actual language forms that will realise those needs. The CNP, therefore, operates at the pre-language stage in the specification of communicative competence. In trying out this part of the model on a group of teachers of ESP, it was noticeable how some of them, in their questioning, kept on trying to make the CNP deal with the language itself. This is indicative of both a widespread failure to understand the nature of communication needs (or to distinguish between them and their linguistic realisations) and also a premature insistence on getting down to the target language specification. Syllabus specification in ESP can only take place after the prior and necessary work has been done on needs, or it will not be known whether or to what extent the specification is appropriate. Misunderstanding the nature of communication needs also shows itself when matters of logistics or pedagogy are included as variables in the consideration of the participants' communication needs. For example, the number of teachers available, the intensity or length of the course, financial considerations, the learner's attitude to teachers, and his previous learning methods, are all important factors for consideration in the organisation of the programme and the construction of the materials, but they are irrelevant to the specification of what the learner needs the target language for, which *is* what comprises his communication needs.

4. LANGUAGE SKILLS SELECTOR

In this parameter of the overall model, the profile of needs is interpreted in terms of the specific language skills that are required to realise the events or activities that have been identified in the CNP. It has already been indicated what is meant by communicative activity, as distinguished from different uses of the term act (see section 5 below), and it is now necessary to establish the use of the term language skill. The term skill, as with function, is used both as a macro and as a micro concept. It is commonplace to see statements

about the four skills of listening, speaking, reading and writing. Syllabus designers, as well as writers of books on the teaching of English
as a second language, regularly divide up their subject into aural
comprehension, oral production, reading comprehension, and written
production. All of us are familiar with specification grids which have
these four macro-skills along one axis and linguistic components or
language aspects along the other (e.g. Carroll, 1961), or with similar
two-dimensional grids where the skills axis is divided into psycho-
motor and cognitive skills which are still expressed in macro-level
terms such as 'ability to produce utterances or patterns conveying
the desired explicit meaning' (Valette, 1971). Bung (1973a) uses the
term communication skills as a macro-concept, despite their being
the output or end-product of his model for specifying objectives in
module construction. Kirkwood (1973a) exemplifies and typifies the
use of the term at both macro and micro level when he lists listening
comprehension as a linguistic skill needed for the lecture situation,
which he then points out includes the ability to comprehend rapid
speech and different accents. These in turn presuppose, respectively,
awareness of the phonological rules governing elision and assimilation
and of the phonemes and allophonic variants of the particular
language. It is these latter which are the linguistic skills, rather than
listening comprehension. It is proposed here to use language skill as a
micro-concept, finding that global skills such as listening comprehension are better described as activities.[6] A study of the language
activities listed by Trim (1971 and 1973) would seem to support this
view. Taking another example from Kirkwood, note-taking at lectures
would be regarded as a communicative activity (of the discoursal
type) while abilities such as using rules governing abbreviation and
omission, differentiating major and minor points, etc., are language
skills required for the realisation of that activity.

In the model, macro-level abilities such as 'reading agricultural
journals for information on crop protection' will be identified as
activities in the Event parameter of the CNP, where it will already
have been established from the Instrumentality box that one is dealing with the receptive command of written monologue. The task of
the Language Skills Selector, then, is to select the specific skills for
that activity from a taxonomy of language skills, which has here
been tentatively drawn up (see Chapter 7). In this example, one of
the many resultant skills would be understanding relationships of

41

thought across sentence boundaries through logical connecters. In selecting the skills, recourse is had both to introspection and to any relevant stylistic information available (see §6 below).

In the case of some occupational-type activities, it may be found that sociosemantic processing will be more fruitful than skills selection, the essential instrumentality features such as the medium and mode in which the functional subcategories are to be handled having already been specified in the CNP.

5. THE MEANING PROCESSOR

In the first chapter a theoretical framework was postulated for the designing of this model, the second constituent of which was the sociosemantic basis of linguistic knowledge. In this component of the model, parts of the socioculturally determined profile of communication needs are converted into semantic subcategories of a predominantly pragmatic kind, and marked for attitudinal-tone. Here one must consider the kind of semantic unit that needs to be handled and the nature of the conversion, and the argument for such processing in the first place.

The present system is to characterise communicative events and their keys as units of meaning before their linguistic realisations are specified. Given this aim, one is not concerned with a view of meaning as found in traditional semantics or with the kind of semantic categories to be found in componential analysis, as exemplified by Frake (1961) or Lyons (1968). One is not, in fact, concerned with assigning distinctive or criterial features to verbal forms in order to account for their use, as with Frake's attempt to understand the complex and totally different way that the Subanum of Mindanao subcategorise the disease category of sores, or in order to account for semantically anomalous sentences like 'My teapot is dancing with your kettle.' We are concerned with a different level of meaning, and for the purpose of predicting forms, not describing them in terms of their ultimate semantic components nor accounting for their use.

Candlin (1976) (following Candlin, Kirkwood and Moore, 1975) suggests that there are four possible levels or layers of meaning for an utterance, which are described as *notional, referential, sociolinguistic*, and *contextual* meaning. The notional layer consists of the basic meaning categories of grammar, such as those of quantity, time and case, which Wilkins (1972) classifies as semantico-grammatical categories and their subcategories. The referential meaning of the utterance is its literal, objective, propositional value, described by Austin (1962) as the locutionary force of an utterance. The sociolinguistic meaning of the utterance is its pragmatic value, described by Austin as the illocutionary force of an utterance, which derives from the social context in which the utterance is placed. For example, the referential meaning or locutionary force of the utterance 'Are you going to bed now?' is contained in an open-ended question concerning the immediacy of the addressee's departure to bed, but the utterance also has the illocutionary force of suggestion, complaint, order, request, or threat, depending on social context constraints such as the identity and age of the interlocutors, the social relationships between them, the time of day, etc. At the fourth layer of meaning, the utterance's contextual meaning consists of its positional significance in the text or discourse. That is, part of its meaning derives from what it precedes and what it follows. Candlin et al. (1975) clarify this when they say, referring to the utterance 'This seems acceptable but we must take X into account,' that 'the *this* and the *X* have contextual meaning in the *textual* sense in that the string is inexplicable without anaphoric reference, while the entire string has contextual meaning in the *discoursal* sense in that it exemplifies the giving of a tentative opinion after the citing of evidence and before the making of a conclusion'. This level of meaning, then, is concerned with both the discoursal coherence of the utterance and its textual cohesion which, as pointed out by Halliday and Hasan (1976), is a semantic relation. Of these layers of meaning the most significant for our purpose are the third and fourth.

Converting events into their meaning units at the first layer, i.e. into conceptual categories, is unlikely to be significant for subsequent encoding. Bung (1973a) shares this doubt as to how fruitful such a procedure would be. The fact that notional meaning such as present time, amount, indefiniteness, place, etc, are found in the basic semantic categories of English grammar suggests that they do not need separate specification for each activity in order for appropriate linguistic encoding to take place, as seems to be the case with semantic categories of the functional or pragmatic kind. It should be pointed out here that there is a difference between the set of semantico-grammatical categories postulated by Wilkins, and appar-

ently intended by Candlin as exemplars of this layer of notional
meaning, and the larger set of concepts found at this level by Leech
and Svartvik (1975); the latter's four layers are not strictly the same
as Candlin's except at the fourth.

For Leech and Svartvik the first layer of meaning includes concepts such as cause, purpose, condition and comparison, which are
handled by Wilkins in one of his categories of communicative function. For present purposes such items are regarded as more suitably
located at layer one. The types of meaning handled by Leech and
Svartvik at their second layer (information, reality, and belief) as
categories of logical communication, which are treated by Wilkins in
his categories of modal meaning and communicative function, do
concern us here, as do their third layer of meaning (mood, emotion
and attitude). For a diagrammatic summary of these positions and
their relation to each other, see Figure 17 (p. 134). The fourth layer
of meaning is handled in the Language Skills Selector. Finally it
might be noted that in spite of a preference for operating at layers
which are not decontextualised, 'it seems more productive to consider the indexicality [the fact that the meaning of a term varies with
its context of use] of meaning as a matter of degree ranging from
meanings totally free from a given context to meanings which are
completely context bound' (Giglioli, 1972).

The characterisation of communicative events as meaning subcategories considered from the standpoint of pragmatics can therefore be described as essentially sociosemantic processing. The complex question of what qualifies as a meaning unit of this kind is made
more opaque by the different and often interchangeable uses of terms
like 'function' and 'act'.

The term function is used in both a macro and a micro sense.
Halliday's ideational, interpersonal and textual functions of language
are clearly macro-functions, as are Jakobson's (1960) set, and lists
such as Robinson's (1972) which derive from one or the other. On
the other hand, Wilkins' categories of communicative function, such
as suasion and argument, or rather their subcategories as exemplified
by *threat* and *agreement* respectively, are micro-functions, as are the
speech functions such as *elicit* and *interrogate* to be found in the
analysis of doctor—patient communication by Candlin, Leather and
Bruton (1974, 1976a and b). Candlin uses the term in both senses
when he says 'Thus we can say that the utterance "I'll fix you" can

44

be seen to realise an act termed *threat* and *threatening* is associated
with the function of language we have called social control' (1976).
Here, threatening is a micro-function and social control a macro-
function. As he describes threat as an act, presumably in the Austin/
Searle sense of speech acts, one can see that act and micro-function
are synonymous here, and in many other instances where act is not
restricted to this concept of the speech act. As for the term act, one
must distinguish the speech act of Austin (1962) and Searle (1969),
where it is used for the illocutionary force of an utterance, from the
rhetorical act of Widdowson (1971), from the discourse unit 'act' of
of Sinclair and Coulthard (1975). The latter's twenty-two acts, operating at the lowest rank in their scale of discourse units, include items
such as elicitation (whose function is to request a linguistic response),
directive (whose function is to request a non-linguistic response), and
loop (whose function is to return the discourse to a previous stage).
As they say, 'We are interested in the function of an utterance or part
of an utterance in the discourse and thus the sort of questions we ask
about an utterance are whether it is intended to evoke a response,
whether it is a response itself, whether it is intended to mark a bound-
ary in the discourse, and so on.' Widdowson's use of the term rhetorical act covers speech acts such as promising and ordering as well as
acts such as defining and classifying. In this he and Wilkins are alike,
in that the latter includes all these in his third set, of which he
additionally says 'They include some categories needed to handle
cases where there is no one-to-one relation between grammatical category and communicative function and others involving expression ·
of the speaker's intention and views' (1972). Wilkins points out that
his framework is largely ad hoc and seems to anticipate the unease
that some of us feel in finding comparison and condition in the same
category (rational enquiry and exposition) as definition and classification. There is a sense in which they are of a different order, rather
in the way that promising is of a different order from an act such as
defining. One can say that an utterance is a 'promise' (has the communicative value of promising) by looking at its *social context*, so
functions/acts like this are of the order of *sociolinguistic meaning*.
One can say that an utterance is a 'definition' (has the communicative value of defining) by looking at its *discoursal context*, so
functions/acts like this are of the order of *contextual meaning*.

In spite of problems of categorisation and classification, however, we can draw the following conclusion. For our purpose in this sector of the model we are concerned with *micro-functions* as exemplified by Wilkins' subcategories of communicative function (but not all of them – see pages 139–40) or Widdowson's rhetorical acts, both of which subsume illocutionary acts. Every such function or act will be called a micro-function. This is to be distinguished from what we call a communicative activity (activity, for short), which is a higher order unit at the behavioural level of communicative event. The potentially useful term 'communicative act' will be avoided because it is too easily confused with other uses of the term act, and because it has been used as a catch-all term which conflates the distinction it has been felt necessary to make between behaviour and meaning. These micro-functions, therefore, are units of meaning operating as an inter-level between events and their formal realisations. 'Doctor giving advice on treatment to patient' is an activity whose socio-semantic constituents may include one or more of the micro-functions persuasion, warning, invitation, advice, urging, etc., together with subcategories from argument, rational enquiry and exposition, etc. For example, in this activity the doctor does not simply need to know how to produce *advice* (e.g. I strongly suggest that you take a holiday) but also *warning* (e.g. If you don't take a holiday, you will have a nervous breakdown); and it may well be necessary to lead up to the actual advice through *explanation* of the *cause* (e.g. You're getting these headaches because you don't get enough sleep) or *disproving* a *supposition* and presenting a more plausible *conclusion* (e.g. Let us suppose, as you say, that _____. In that case, how do you account for _____? Isn't is more likely that _____?).

If we look at the list of language functions in Jupp and Hodlin (1975), some of these are what have been termed activities here, such as 'describing mechanical processes' and 'understanding and dealing with embarrassing situations'. The functions taught by Morrow and Johnson (1976) are a mixture of micro-functions, such as 'interrupting' and 'contradicting', and activities, such as 'describing people and places'. These examples have been taken from two texts with much to commend them, rather than from material with less merit, since the purpose here is to illustrate and not to criticise. The point is that, whereas a micro-function (suitable contextualised) is ready for verbal or non-verbal realisation, an activity is not. The latter needs to be processed into micro-functions before any decisions about utterance realisations can be made.

What has been considered thus far is the kind of semantic unit that needs to be handled and how an activity is converted into such units. It now remains for us to consider the argument for such socio-semantic processing in the first place. The direct encoding of a communicative event as lexico-grammatical realisations is not a feasible proposition. For example, how would one select direct from the host of linguistic forms which may feature in an event such as 'doctor attending to patient in his surgery'? It seems necessary first to do an analysis of the event into its activities where the communicative value can then be specified. Then it might be argued that one should go direct from the specification of the activities to the selection of forms for encoding or realising each activity, without sociosemantic processing. There are, however, pragmatic and theoretical reasons for resisting such a course. Firstly, not all events subdivide as clearly into activities as does 'waiter serving customers in restaurant', and where they do not the selection of sufficient as well as appropriate linguistic forms is at least questionable. Secondly, and following on from the first reason, the processing of an activity into its micro-functions allows consideration of the optimal generalisability that may be desirable from the linguistic encoding, i.e. one would normally not select an utterance of restricted or no generality where one with wider applicability exists (given that they are both appropriate). Thirdly, such processing ensures that those forms that realise the less obvious but equally possible micro-functions for an activity are not omitted by default, as might be the case with direct encoding of activities. Fourthly, communicative competence involves semantic as well as linguistic control, so one should be interested in the participant's ability to handle functional subcategories. However, this concern is not with functions in vacuo but with micro-functions as the semantic content of activities constrained by particular communication needs. The functional analysis of communicative activities ensures that the sociosemantic aspect of communicative competence is given systematic and due attention in the learning of linguistic (and extra-linguistic) forms.

Sociosemantic processing, then, characterises events in terms of micro-functions which are marked for attitudinal-tone. It has already been stated how potential keys for each activity are indicated in the

47

communicative key parameter of the CNP. Now each micro-function of an activity is mapped against the applicable continuum in the attitudinal-tone index and a decision is made as to whether to mark the function with the superordinate term for the applicable half of that continuum or with the most appropriate hyponym. The full index is shown and discussed below (Chapters 6 and 8), but as an illustration let us take one of the micro-functions, *suggestion*, from the activity 'attending to customer's order' (in the event 'Head waiter serving customers in restaurant'), and map it against those continua which have previously been identified in the CNP as applicable[7] to the activity:

caring . . . . indifferent	
concerned, interested, enthusiastic, eager, keen, personal, anxious, worried, curious, fascinated	uncaring, unconcerned, uninterested, lukewarm, impersonal, unenthusiastic, incurious, nonchalant, apathetic, perfunctory

respectful . . . . disrespectful	
deferential, reverential, obsequious, dutiful	lacking in deference, familiar, cheeky, impertinent, brash, presumptuous, irreverent

inducive . . . . dissuasive	
persuasive, encouraging, provocative, inciting, urging, seductive, recommendatory	discouraging, damping, intimidating, cautionary, deprecatory, threatening, ominous

This would give us the following result:

suggestion [+ personal] , [+ deferential] , [+ encouraging]

The selection of these particular attitudinal-tones is made on the basis of the prior identification of sociocultural features in the CNP. Now, bearing in mind the full context produced by the profile of needs, one is in a good position to proceed to the next stage, which is the selection of appropriate forms to realise the attitudinally marked micro-functions.

6. LINGUISTIC ENCODING

In the discussion of communicative competence the crucial import-

48

ance was established of the dimension of contextual appropriacy, in both the sociocultural and discoursal senses of context, which is reflected in the constituents of the theoretical framework. As has been seen, the model being designed takes clear account of this in the profiling of communication needs and the subsequent sociosemantic processing. Now that the encoding stage has been reached in this preliminary discussion of our processing model, where the selection of the actual verbal realisations for the micro-functions and subject-matter is made, one has to face the problem of the criterion for our decisions as to appropriacy. That is, does one decide on matters of language variation in a particular context of use on the basis of introspection and one's own subjective judgement as a native speaker as to what is stereotypical, or is there an objective yardstick such as a 'dictionary of use' to which one can turn? Although there is no such reference compendium, the answer lies, it would seem, in applying both criteria, beginning with the objective.

While one may accept Crystal's caveat about the problems in analysing varieties of English (1971), and bearing in mind the embryonic state of discourse analysis, sufficient evidence is to be found of both the quality and the increasing quantity of stylistic description to suggest that a bank of stylistic information is gradually accumulating. For example, there are large-scale descriptions such as those by Candlin, Leather and Bruton (1974, 1976a and b) on doctor—patient communication in casualty departments of hospitals, Sinclair and Coulthard (1975) on the English used by teachers and pupils in classroom discourse, Jupp and Hodlin (1975) on the English for immigrants working in industry; small-scale descriptions such as those by Brown and Gilman (1960), Brown and Ford (1961), and Ervin-Tripp (1972) on forms and rules of address, and the investigations by Crystal and Davy (1969) into the language of conversation, newspaper reporting, etc.; and the approach of Allen and Widdowson (1974) to the English for science and technology, which concentrates on the discoursal characteristics of such written text. There has recently appeared a new kind of grammar, *A communicative grammar of English* by Leech and Svartvik (1975), which focuses on the uses of English grammar in everyday (i.e. generalised, rather than specific contexts) speech and writing. This is of considerable interest, though it is not a dictionary of use. This means, then, that we should take account of the gradually increasing amount of stylistic information on what forms or utterances are appropriate in a particular social context and how they cohere rhetorically in a particular discourse context. Recourse is had then to any available stylistic information at the outset of the realisation stages, to see if there is any objective information on distinctive features, rules of use, co-occurrence and distributional characteristics, which relate directly or indirectly, wholly or partly, to the micro-functions and language skills under consideration. If there is, it is used; if there is no relevant information in the 'bank', then one proceeds on a subjective basis and decides on the appropriate realisation(s) from a combination of one's own intuition, the intuition of suitable informants, and, where necessary, a standard reference grammar[8] and dictionary. It should be noted that such subjective decisions can always be empirically validated.

To conclude this chapter, here is an illustration of the linguistic encoding, subjectively made, of a contextually constrained micro-function, using the example reached at the end of the previous section. That is, in the particular social context being assumed for the head waiter, the following micro-function, marked for attitudinal-tone, was processed:

suggestion [+ personal] , [+ deferential] , [+ encouraging]

The following is a list, non-finite and in no particular order, of possible verbal realisations for suggestion:
1. I suggest (that you try) the _____.
2. May I suggest (that you try) the _____.
3. If I may make the suggestion, the _____ is popular here.
4. Why don't you try the _____?
5. How about the _____?
6. Let's _____.
7. Would you care to try the _____?
8. Some people like the _____.
9. What do you feel about the _____?
10. You could try the _____.
11. You might like the _____.
12. What about the _____?
13. Have you thought about the _____?
14. Suppose you try the _____.
15. Another possibility would be the _____.
16. I wonder if you fancy the _____.

17. Perhaps the _____ appeals to you.
18. Would you consider the _____?
19. Can't we _____?
20. Well, there's the _____.
(each with different possible intonation).

This is a list which we as educated speakers of English can recover quite readily from our own internalised grammar, and augment or check out, if necessary, from a standard work of reference. Now, given the particular features of setting, social interaction, etc., which have previously been identified in the profile of needs and on which the attitudinal-tone markings are based, one can proceed to linguistic encoding by selecting numbers 7 and 2 as being possibly the most appropriate utterances for this particular context.

NOTES

1 In the past decade and a half, work by, for example, Joos (1961), Ervin-Tripp (1964), Gregory (1967), Crystal and Davy (1969), Hymes (1972), Richterich (1972), Candlin, Bruton and Leather (1976b), has produced various sets of descriptive and analytical categories directly or indirectly relevant to the study of communication needs. Richterich's work is a pioneering attempt at a model for defining adult language needs. In Chapters 3 to 6 we hope it will become clear why it is operationally inadequate for our purpose.
2 The question of role, which may come to mind here as a sociological attribute of participant (see Ervin-Tripp, 1964, or Richterich, 1972) is not part of this input. Role involves relationships which are a feature of social interaction in a particular setting, and is therefore dealt with later in the CNP. It would be premature to specify such relationships before taking account of the variables which affect them.
3 See Chapter 3 for a taxonomy of ESP courses (Strevens, 1977a).
4 A concept introduced by Merton (1957). The term *role*, and our approach to it, is discussed at the beginning of Chapter 4.
5 The term 'key' is taken from Hymes (1972); this seems the most suitable cover term for the type of constraint handled here.
6 cf. Wilkins (1977) who favours this term, activities, while feeling constrained to keep the traditional label.
7 For the purpose, solely, of this illustration.
8 Especially Quirk, Greenbaum, Leech and Svartvik (1972).

3

COMMUNICATION NEEDS: PURPOSIVE DOMAIN AND SETTING

Each parameter of the Communication Needs Processor (CNP) will be considered in detail over the next four chapters. This chapter will provide an analysis of the structure and an exposition of the working of the first two of the a priori variables, i.e. purposive domain, and setting. First, however, an input to the CNP is needed.

0.0 PARTICIPANT

The input to the CNP is a foreign language participant, potentially a specific category of such participant. It may, therefore, be an individual or the stereotype of a category of participant.[1] Following Hymes (1972), the term participant is preferred to alternatives such as speaker-hearer, the use of which is ambiguous as to its inclusion or exclusion or reader-writer. As Hymes says 'The Common dyadic model of speaker-hearer specifies sometimes too many, sometimes too few, sometimes the wrong participant.' A participant is someone who takes part in an act of communication involving a foreign language, and the term does not indicate the communicative mode or status of the person requiring the foreign language or the number of persons involved in the communication. Such features will come to light in proceeding through the CNP. Participant, then, is a suitably unmarked term for our input, which consists of the person (individual or stereotype) and what can be regarded as the relevant base-line data on the person, viz. identity and language. This information is obtained under the following headings.

0.1 Identity
    0.1.1 Age   [specify either exactly or in broad terms]
    0.1.2 Sex
    0.1.3 Nationality

0.1.4 Place of residence

Age can be exact or it can be expressed in more general terms, e.g. child, adolescent, adult. Place of residence is included for two reasons, to cover instances where this is different from nationality, e.g. an American living in Italy, in which case one would expect the place of residence to have some effect upon the nationality; and because it may be significant in itself, e.g. a person from London is likely to have some different attitudes from someone from Barnsley. It may be noticed that occupation is not included under this heading (cf. Richterich, 1972). The occupation, per se, of the participant is irrelevant unless he needs the target language for the purposes of his occupation, in which case this crucial information is obtained in the first parameter of the CNP.

The information about the participant's identity is only potentially relevant at this stage, since it has to be matched with the identity features of the other people involved in the communication and placed in a particular setting before its significance can be evaluated. To the example given in the previous chapter, another will be added. If one matches the following identity features

0.1.1 45 years 0.1.2 male 0.1.3 Turkish 0.1.4 Eastern Anatolia
with the following interlocutors (identified later in the Interaction parameter)

mid-twenties, female, English, lecturer in economics
in the following setting (identified later in the Setting parameter)

England, university, seminar, culturally different environment
it is clear that information has been provided which will help to identify features of communicative key which have to be understood and produced.

0.2 Language

0.2.1 Mother tongue (L1)

0.2.2 Target language (TL)

0.2.3 Present level/command of the TL:
zero/false beginner/elementary/lower intermediate/upper intermediate/advanced

0.2.4 Other language(s) known (L2)

0.2.5 Extent of command (in broad terms) of L2.

The identification of the participant's present level of proficiency in the target language (not his target level, which is identified later) is made in general terms, by selecting as applicable from the alternatives listed at 0.2.3. It is unnecessary to be more detailed than this since the model aims to specify what constitutes the target communicative competence, not to assess the present deficiencies. This information, when matched later against the target level, will obviously be required by the materials producers who have to convert the output of our processing model into pedagogically viable learning units.

The L1 and L2 data may or may not turn out to be relevant. For example, the information that a participant, with Kiswahili as the TL, has English as his L1 and elementary French as his L2, is unlikely to be significant at any stage in the process of specifying the communicative competence required here. On the other hand, knowing that a person has French as his L1 and elementary Italian as his L2 may prove useful where the TL is Spanish. Sometimes the L1 will only be spoken, as with many African languages, in which case the L2 is likely to be the one used for writing and there may even be another L2 for some other purpose, e.g. a Kanuri (the main vernacular of the North Eastern State of Nigeria) speaker who writes and also speaks in Hausa and prays in Arabic. If such a participant has as his TL another Nigerian language, the information about his L1 and L2s may well be significant. Where English is the TL (as it will be henceforward in this book), the information that a Spanish L1 participant has Italian as an L2 is unlikely to be useful, whereas French as his L2 would be relevant.

This potentially relevant information concerning the participant's identity and language is all that is required as base-line data comprising the input to the CNP. The first constraint on this input is specified in purposive domain.

1.0 PURPOSIVE DOMAIN

Gregory (1967) uses 'purposive role' as the situational category related to field of discourse in order to endorse the point that an intelligible purpose is revealed by participants in speech events. In other, more oblique treatments of this area, Trim (1971) writes of 'user roles' and Richterich (1972) uses 'the role of the adult in this field' as a criterion in defining types of adult learning a foreign language. As stated earlier, the term 'role' is preferred when focusing on relationships (see interaction for a discussion of role) and here this is not the case. Here, what one wants to specify is the occupational or educational purpose for which the target language is required. A suitable term to indicate the nature of this a priori determinant operating initially on the input to the CNP would seem, therefore, to be purposive domain. Fishman (1971) uses the term domain for a macrolevel sociolinguistic category. Although the term is not being used identically, it is also being used as a higher-order sociocultural category, from which particular activities derive.

The first question that might be asked in this parameter arises from the basic distinction that can be made between purposes that are occupationally or professionally motivated and those that are not, while allowing for the fact that both kinds can apply to the same participant. Trim sees this distinction as professional/personal (or social), Richterich as socioprofessional/sociocultural, and Gregory as specialised/non-specialised. In dealing with ESP, however, one is not centrally concerned with non-specialised or broadly sociocultural purposes such as travelling or performing everyday routines. One might try to do what is possible in specifying for such broad and relatively unpredictable purposes, but the main interest here focuses on the basic division of ESP into the occupational and educational dimensions.

Strevens (1977a) has proposed a taxonomy of ESP courses, one half of which classifies the different types of ESP as in Figure 6.

The rationale for his initial distinction between EST and all other types of ESP course is not clear. The fact that EST (and non-EST) can appear in the subdivisions of either the educational or occupational categories, depending for example on whether the participant needs English to study engineering science or to do his job as an engineer, suggests that it is an exponent of a category rather than a category in itself. For this reason, too, it would be preferable to regard the 'teachers' conversion' heading as an exponent of the post-experience sub-category. With this proviso, it is proposed to use this helpful classification of the types of ESP from which to answer the first set of questions to be asked in purposive domain.

1.1 ESP classification
Is the purpose for which English is required occupational or educational?

    1.1.1 If *occupational*, will it be pre-experience or post-experience ESP?

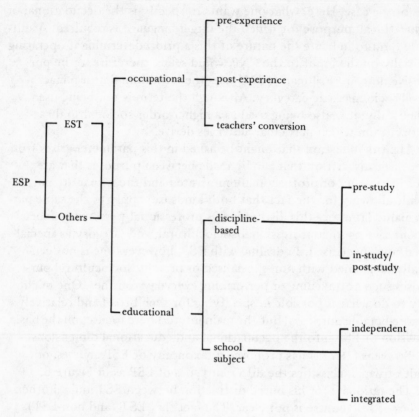

Figure 6 Types of ESP (Strevens, 1977a)

1.1.2 If *educational*, will it be discipline-based or school subject ESP?

    1.1.2.1 If discipline-based, will it be pre-study of in-study ESP?

    1.1.2.2 If school subject, will it be independent or integrated ESP?

Examples of English for occupational purposes are: English for air traffic controllers, hotel employees, international banking, civil engineering, doctors in general practice. An Indonesian learning English for working in an oil field at the same time that he is being instructed in the job itself is an example of pre-experience ESP; whereas the Pakistani doctor learning English in order to communicate with his patients in surgery is an example of post-experience ESP. Examples of English for educational purposes are English for studying medicine, engineering, economics, general science. A Turkish student in the preparatory department of the Middle East Technical University, who is studying English before going on to study engineering in English, is an example of pre-study, discipline-based ESP. A Mexican student in the faculty of veterinary science at the National University of Mexico, who is studying English in order to read books and articles on his subject that are written in English, is an example of in-study, discipline-based ESP.[2] Independent, school subject ESP may occur where the English syllabus, though separate from the other subjects in the curriculum aims to service the study of one or more of those subjects. An example of this is the 'Learning Through Language' course (Isaacs, ed., 1968) written in Tanzania to facilitate the transfer from studying in the L1 to studying in English in the first year of secondary education. Integrated, school subject ESP is exemplified by the Singapore Primary Pilot Project (described by Newberry in *ELT Documents*, No. 4, 1974) which closely combines the learning of English with the parallel learning of mathematics and elementary science, something similar to which was attempted in the mid 1960s in parts of East Africa (the Peak Course).

What has been established so far is the type of purpose in terms of ESP classification. The information required will now be specified under either the occupational or educational headings.

1.2 Occupational purpose

1.2.1 *Specific occupation*
State the occupation for which English is required.

1.2.2 *Central duty*
Identify the central duty of that occupation (if different from 1.2.1).

1.2.3 *Other duties*
Identify other known duties, if any, for which English is needed.

1.2.4 *Occupational classification*
Using the framework provided, classify the occupation by matching, as appropriate, the type of worker on the vertical axis with the field of work on the horizontal axis (e.g. technical officer in industry).

So, if the specific occupation (1.2.1) for which English is required is that of motor vehicle engineer, for which the central duty (1.2.2) is identified as service department foreman, the occupational classifi-

Field of work

Type of worker	commerce/industry	public administration	liberal professions	science	armed forces	entertainment/the arts	utilities/services	?
	[i]	[ii]	[iii]	[iv]	[v]	[vi]	[vii]	[viii]
[a] manual worker: skilled/semi-skilled/unskilled								
[b] clerical officer/ administrative assistant								
[c] technical officer/ technical representative								
[d] manager/ senior administrator								
[e] professional practitioner								
[f] officer								
[g] artiste/sportsman								

Figure 7 Occupational classification framework

cation (1.2.4) will be: technical officer in services. If, however, the participant needs English for working as a motor vehicle mechanic for which the central duty is to carry out standard servicing, the occupational classification will then be: skilled manual worker in services. It should be noted that the question mark on the horizontal axis allows for a field of work which cannot be subsumed as an exponent of one of the categories [i] to [vii] to be treated as a field in itself and listed at [viii].

It may be helpful to give some examples of the occupational classification for specific occupations:

e.g. garage mechanic/air stewardess/restaurant
employee = [a] in [vii]
travel agency clerk/director's secretary = [b] in [i]
airport announcer/immigration officer = [b] in [ii]
local authority inspector/air traffic controller = [c] in [ii]

sales manager/company director/international banker	= [d] in [i]
news editor/college principal/senior diplomat	= [d] in [iii]
teacher/doctor/nursing sister/broadcaster	= [c] in [iii]
nuclear physicist/research chemist/civil engineer	= [e] in [iv]
air force navigator/naval rating	= [f] in [v]
detective inspector/police constable	= [f] in [ii]
music director/actor/singer/footballer	= [g] in [vi]
factory foreman/travelling salesman	= [c] in [i]
nurse/compositor	= [a] in [iii]
inland revenue accountant/local government councillor	= [e] in [ii]

The main reason for doing the occupational classification is that it summarises the answers concerning the specific occupation and central duty in such a way as to help in the determination of the social relationships between the participants. Also, in terms of stylistic reference it may help in indicating where to look when no information exists on the specific occupation.

An example of the other duties for which English is needed (1.2.3) would be the occasional interviewing done by a television broadcaster, whose central duty was reading the news.

1.3 Educational purpose
1.3.1 *Specific discipline*
State the specific discipline or subject for which English is required.
1.3.2 *Central area of study*
Identify the central area of study in which the participant will be engaged.
1.3.3 *Other areas of study*
Identify the other areas of study for which English is needed.
1.3.4 *Academic discipline classification*
Select, as appropriate, from the following: mathematics/physical science/humanities/social science/biological science/medicine/ engineering/education.

An example of answers at these sub-headings would be:
1.3.1 veterinary medicine
1.3.2 animal pathology
1.3.3 anatomy, animal physiology
1.3.4 medicine

The generalisation of 1.3.4 needs explaining. There is going to be overlap between the language skills and micro-functions required for one discipline or area of study and those involved with another where the two have stylistic features in common. The exact nature and extent of the overlap can be verified by discourse analysis of the areas concerned. Meanwhile, it seems reasonable to suggest that disciplines that come from the same academic family will have more stylistic features in common, requiring the same language skills for managing them, than those that do not. Therefore, stating the general academic classification in terms of a macro-discipline may enable one, when it comes to language skills selection and sociosemantic processing, to draw on what is collectively known about that macro-discipline, especially when there is no information available on the specific discipline required.

2.0 SETTING

The next variable that has to be taken into consideration when drawing up a profile of a participant's communication needs is Setting.

Setting is the situational variable that refers, inter alia, to the time and place of the communication, i.e. the physical circumstances in which the language will be used. Hymes (1972), while distinguishing setting from scene, the types of which he regards as 'psychological setting', sees the two as linked components, labelled Setting as the unmarked term. Richterich's (1972) categories of time and place are mainly concerned with physical setting; he does ask in what 'surroundings' the language is most often used, but the list of elements for this subcategory and the lack of any detail for the following subcategory of 'environment' indicate either uncertain or insufficient attention to this aspect. Ervin-Tripp (1964) uses setting in the physical sense of time and place (which she calls 'locale') and in the sense of situation, as exemplified by a family breakfast, a faculty meeting, and a date. In this latter sense she seems to be using setting to cover the occasions or events that result from the interaction of two or more variables, which is inconsistent with its use as one of the variables that collectively constitute a situation. The converse use of situation to mean setting is equally unhelpful, in that the former term is then no longer available (or should not be, if ambiguity is to be avoided) in its more normal sense, where it is the superordinate which includes setting as one of its parts. Here one is following Hymes in positing physical setting and psychosocial setting[3] as the two categories of this parameter.

Physical setting consists of spatial and temporal subcategories. The spatial subdivides into the location and the actual place, including their extent, where the participant needs to use English. The temporal subdivides into the point of time, duration and frequency of the participant's use of English. This categorisation of physical setting can be shown as in Figure 8.

Information is sought through the following questions at each of these sub-headings, as follows.

2.1 Physical setting: spatial
2.1.1 *Location*
2.1.1.1 *Country*
In what country does the participant need to use English?
2.1.1.2 *Town*
In what town does the participant need to use English?

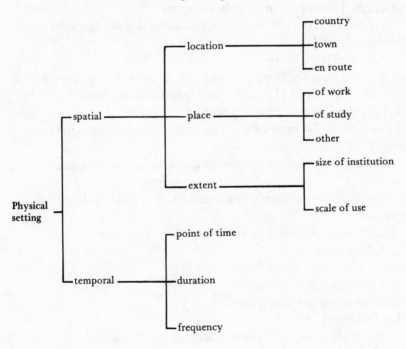

Figure 8 Subcategories of physical setting

61

2.1.1.3 *En route*

If English is required while en route, specify the appropriate setting:

in flight/on board ship/in train/on bus/in car.

2.1.2 *Place of work* (occupational)

In what occupational premises will the participant need English?
Specify, as appropriate, from the following list, supplying the item where necessary:

2.1.2.1 hotel, restaurant, inn, cafe . . .

2.1.2.2 department store, shop, showrooms, market . . .

2.1.2.3 factory, workshop, work site, power station, laboratory . . .

2.1.2.4 company office, government office . . .

2.1.2.5 airport, docks, railway/bus station, post office . . .

2.1.2.6 school, university, research institute, conference room . . .

2.1.2.7 hospital, surgery, law court, church, bank . . .

2.1.2.8 barracks, camp, police station

2.1.2.9 theatre, hall, recording/broadcasting studio, sports arena, night club . . .

2.1.2.10 private house . . .

and give the name of the place of work, if known (e.g. Ford Motor Company Halewood Plant, Istanbul International Airport).

2.1.3 *Place of study and study setting*

Give the name and type of the educational institution where the participant needs English:

2.1.3.1 university/college/institute/secondary school/primary school

For which of the following academic study settings is English required:

2.1.3.2 lecture room/theatre

2.1.3.3 classroom

2.1.3.4 laboratory/workshop

2.1.3.5 seminar/tutorial

2.1.3.6 private study/library.

2.1.4 *Other places*

In what other places will the participant need English?

2.1.5 *Extent: size of institution*

Is the place where English will be used: small/medium/large?

2.1.6 *Extent: scale of use*
Does the participant need to use English:
    internationally/nationally/locally?

2.2 Physical setting: temporal
2.2.1 *Point of time*
When is English required most?
2.2.2 *Duration*
For approximately how many hours per day/week is English
required?
2.2.3 *Frequency*
Is English required regularly/often/occasionally/seldom?
These subcategories and the questions asked on them need little comment, but comparison with Richterich's treatment (1972) will help
to avoid any misunderstandings. Richterich's questions on geographical location (p. 39) ask about the country of origin, country of residence, and professional or non-professional purpose of the participant.
The information on the first two of these elements is not necessarily
relevant to the location where the participant needs to use English,
and is in any case base line data that is more appropriately obtained
as part of the participant's identity. The information on the third
element can hardly be said to concern physical setting. Another
anomaly is the way all his questioning on the subcategory of place is
modified for frequency, while his questions on the subcategory of
frequency are focused on the participant's familiarity (or lack of it)
with his interlocutor, an aspect which relates to psychosocial rather
than physical setting. Richterich's subdivisions of place into 'out-
doors', 'indoors', and 'means of transport', and then indoors into
'private life', 'public life', and 'work', is more useful for general
English than ESP, for which our treatment of place should be more
fruitful. 'Extent' is included as a spatial subcategory, since the information that the school or hotel is a small one may well affect the
relationships between the participant and his interlocutors and the
activities expected of him; and the information that the participant
needs English for international use will affect matters of dialect and
the choice of accent.
    Psychosocial setting refers to the environment in which the target
language will be used. The different types of environment postulated
in section 2.3 are predictable from the profile of needs so far obtained,

in that they are objectively specifiable as corollaries of the physical setting previously identified. In the case of the last three on the list, however, a local informant may be necessary. The list is not finite; rather, an attempt has been made to produce a detailed inventory of relevant types. Here, relevance consists in providing the kind of information which, when joined with the subsequent specification of social relationships (in the interaction parameter), will assist in the derivation of the 'communicative keys' that affect the language the participant has to understand or produce. The inventory is set up as a number of continua so that one can modify, as appropriate, the selected element on any continuum, e.g. semi-intellectual, very noisy. Information on this category of setting is sought as follows.

2.3 Psychosocial setting

What is the psychosocial setting in which the participant will use English? Using the inventory of psychosocial environments, on each applicable continuum select the appropriate element, modifying as necessary (e.g. non-intellectual, usually noisy, fairly demanding).

Inventory of psychosocial environments

2.3.1	culturally similar	— culturally different
2.3.2	age/sex discriminating	— age/sex non-discriminating
2.3.3	intellectual/thinking	— non-intellectual/unthinking
2.3.4	aesthetic/refined	— non-aesthetic/unrefined
2.3.5	ethical*	— non-ethical
2.3.6	sporty/recreational	— non-sporty
2.3.7	religious/ritualistic	— secular
2.3.8	political	— apolitical
2.3.9	professional	— non-professional
2.3.10	educationally developed	— educationally undeveloped
2.3.11	technologically sophis- ticated	— technologically unsophis- ticated
2.3.12	urban	— rural
2.3.13	public	— private
2.3.14	familiar physical	— unfamiliar physical
2.3.15	familiar human	— unfamiliar human
2.3.16	quiet	— noisy
2.3.17	demanding	— undemanding

*By 'ethical' is meant constrained by moral considerations.

2.3.18 hurried	— unhurried
2.3.19 formal	— informal
2.3.20 hierarchic	— non-hierarchic/egalitarian
2.3.21 authoritarian	— unauthoritarian/laissez-faire
2.3.22 entertaining/festive	— serious
2.3.23 aggressive/argumentative	— conciliatory/harmonious
2.3.24 reserved	— unreserved
2.3.25 sympathetic	— unsympathetic

Information previously gathered about the participant's identity, communicative purpose, and especially physical setting, points to the types of environment that apply in the particular case. For example, let us take a mid-twenties, female, Mexican air stewardess working for Mexicana, who needs English for communicating with English-speaking passengers in flight. The psychosocial setting that derives from this specification would be:

2.3.3 non-intellectual 2.3.4 occasionally aesthetic

2.3.13 public 2.3.14 familiar physical 2.3.14 unfamiliar human

2.3.17 fairly demanding 2.3.18 hurried 2.3.19 generally formal.

'Hurried' refers to an environment where there is little or no time for reflection when using the target language; 'occasionally aesthetic' refers to occasions when she is asked to advise on places to visit, local art and craft to sample, national dishes to try. None of the other types of environment appear to be relevant here. A different example would be a Saudi Arabian female student in a university faculty of medicine, who needs English for academic study purposes. The relevant environments that derive from this input would be:

2.3.2 sex discriminating 2.3.3 intellectual

2.3.4 non-aesthetic 2.3.7 religious 2.3.9 quasi-professional

2.3.13 private and public 2.3.14 familiar physical

2.3.15 familiar human 2.3.16 fairly quiet 2.3.17 demanding

2.3.18 mainly unhurried 2.3.19 semi-formal

2.3.21 authoritarian 2.3.22 very serious.

The first continuum (2.3.1) is only going to apply where the participant needs to use English in a country other than his own. For a Western European in England the environment is culturally similar, whereas for a Middle-Easterner in England it is culturally different, while culturally fairly similar might apply to metropolitan Mexicans in England or the United States. 'Refined' (2.3.4) would derive from, for example, diplomats or cabinet ministers receiving their opposite numbers, while 'aesthetic' (2.3.4) would apply to a visiting Russian conductor rehearsing the mainly British singers and orchestra for a performance of Boris Godunov at Covent Garden. Quasi-ritualistic (2.3.7) might be used to refer to settings where a lot of the communication follows a prescribed formula, e.g. in weather reports on the radio, or even in telephone switchboard operating. 'Urban' (2.3.12) refers to the non-physical aspects of this environment; and 2.3.14 and 2.3.15 focus on the familiarity of the environment, not the objects or people in it. 'Hierarchic' (2.3.20) would apply to settings involving the civil service, for example, and the armed forces. It should be noted that the last three continua refer to the environment and not to the participant. 'Unsympathetic' (2.3.25) refers to a setting that is, for example, impersonal or hostile or difficult, e.g. immigrant workers in factories in large urban conurbations especially when there is a lot of unemployment.

In the next chapter the third and fourth of the a priori variables will be considered.

NOTES

1 One must beware of setting up broad types as if they applied in all contexts, a conclusion that may be drawn from Richterich (1972: 27). Each broad type or participant category must still be processed each time so that the variables are always checked out. Even a broad type is bound to be situationally constrained.

2 It is difficult to see what would constitute post-study, discipline-based ESP, since the purpose for learning English would almost certainly be occupational, e.g. a practising heart surgeon needing to attend conferences held in English or to keep up to date on the literature in his field.

3 This term is preferred to Hymes' 'psychological setting' or scene. Psychosocial better describes the non-physical features of the environment, and scene is a term normally used to refer to physical setting.

4

COMMUNICATION NEEDS:
INTERACTION AND INSTRUMENTALITY

3.0 INTERACTION

The input to the CNP now reaches the parameter here known as
Interaction. This is the situational variable that identifies the other
participants with whom the input communicates in the target
language and the relationships that may be predicted as obtaining
between them.

In any discussion of social interaction the term *role* inevitably
appears. Although role has for some time been a key concept in
sociology, its adequacy as a theoretical concept in general role theory
has in recent times come under considerable fire (see, for example,
Jackson, ed., 1972, especially the paper by Coulson). In discussing its
difficulties from an ethnomethodological standpoint, Cicourel (1972)
argues that 'the social analyst's use of abstract theoretical concepts
like role actually masks the inductive or interpretative procedures
whereby the actor produces behavioural displays which others and
the observer label "role behaviour".'[1] We are not, however, directly
concerned with problems such as its lack of precision or clarity as an
analytical tool in sociology;[2] or with the question of its range of
applicability, where its normative nature reduces its suitability for
handling the less structured areas of social interaction. On the other
hand the sociologist's problem of defining a particular role in the
absence of role consensus is of general concern. Role has obvious
utility as a reference term for an important conceptual area that
sociolinguists have to concern themselves with, and its deficiencies as
an analytical tool should not obscure the de facto reality of role
relationships, and the wider social relationships that they imply,
which are important matters in the study of communication needs.

Therefore, one must state what is understood and meant by the term in any use made of it.

Here, one is not concerned with the classification of roles (as variously treated by Linton, Southall, Nadel and Banton, and described by the last named in Banton, 1965) but a working definition of the concept is needed. Banton provides a basis when he says:

> It is agreed that behaviour can be related to a position in a social structure; that actual behaviour can be related to the individual's own ideas of what is appropriate (role cognitions), or to other people's ideas about what he will do (expectations), or to other people's ideas about what he should do (norms). In this light a role may be understood as a set of norms and expectations applied to the incumbent of a particular position.

But, as Worsley et al. (1970) point out: 'It is important to note that we are dealing with relationships here; a role exists only in relation to other roles. Thus . . . the role of doctor implies the role of patient.' Further, Banton's definition does not address the problem where there is a lack of role consensus, in which situation it seems realistic to recognise the variability of role conformity. The necessity of working with stereotypes is accepted here. A role, then, is an expected, normatively defined, dynamic pattern of social behaviour associated with a particular position, implying a relationship with other roles, and to which behavioural pattern individuals are likely to conform in varying degrees.

Worsley et al. also draw attention to the pressures that arise when status considerations affect role relationships, or when there is conflict between different roles that a person plays, or when there is conflict within the role-set[3] (see below). Where such *role conflict* is predictable one may be able to handle in some measure the communicative implications of such role relations. This may be done by specifying the 'communicative key' for particular events where the prior identification of certain social relationships, which is done in this parameter, predicts role conflict.

In this parameter one starts with the participant's *position*. This is the sociological concept of the term, i.e. position in the structure of society, the typical incumbent of which enacts the role associated with that position, and examples of which might be 'doctor' or 'university student'. This information is provided by purposive domain, and together with other constraints on the input enables us to ident-ify the participant's *role-set*. The role-set, a very useful concept to handle role-audiences introduced by Merton (1957), comprises the different people that the participant will interact with in the playing of one particular role or by virtue of a particular position. For example, the role-set for an assistant master in a typical secondary school will probably include the pupils he teaches, other pupils in the school, other teachers, principal, departmental head, non-teaching staff, visiting educationists, and parents. This role in relation to these *role-others* may be represented as in Figure 9. In the model one is concerned with the *target language role-set*, i.e. only those members with whom he has to communicate in English. For example, a Spanish-speaking teacher of English in a technical school in Mexico would have a target language role-set consisting only of the pupils he teaches and foreign visiting educationists. However, in the Anglo-Mexican institutes[4] in that country the TL role-set for this same par-ticipant may well be enlarged to include other teachers, i.e. non-native Mexicans whose Spanish is less than fluent.

The next step is to establish the *role-set identity*. For each mem-ber of the role-set, specifications are given as to the size of partici-

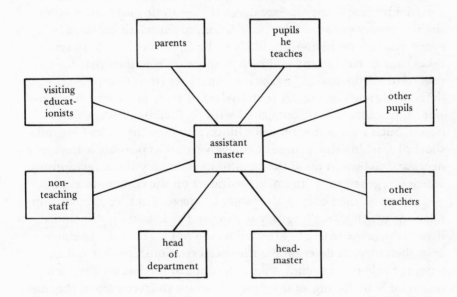

Figure 9 Example of a role-set

pation, age-group, sex, and nationality. This will be in general terms, such as 'mostly British, some American', when a role-other is hetero-geneous.

A statement of *role* relationships, e.g. assistant master — head-master, can follow directly from the identification of the role-set. Interaction relationships tend to be expressed in terms of the roles of the participants. However, it is proposed to specify the *social* relation-ships, e.g. subordinate—superior, which are implied by the interaction of the participant with each member of his role-set. A social relation-ship is more significant than a role relationship for determining atti-tudinal constraints when considering communicative key. The role relationship itself does not necessarily imply one particular social relationship, i.e. there is no automatic one-to-one correlation between a role relationship and a social relationship. The features so far obtained in the profile of needs enable one to determine a particular social relationship as, for example, subordinate—superior rather than, say, primus inter pares or colleague—colleague, the relationship that may be the case in a small, two-teacher primary school with an informal atmosphere. The assistant master—headmaster *role* relation-ship in itself may imply any of these three *social* relationships, or others (given a different input). One needs to know which obtains in a particular case if appropriate decisions are to be made when con-sidering communicative key. In addition, social relationships, a synchronic phenomenon, are likely to be (i) stable, i.e. the stereotype takes time to change and is therefore more reliable than that for a role relationship, and (ii) a relatively small set (the concept is self-defining through listing). A tentative set of sixty-one social relation-ships is postulated here, compared with role relationships which are legion. Such a set is theoretically finite, although the claim here falls short of this. In attempting as exhaustive a list as possible it has been necessary to bear in mind the need to include only those relationships which can generate attitudinal constraints on the communicative activities, and then only in the target language. Thus, certain kinship relations which affect language use in the Far East are not included here because the language affected would not be English. The pro-cess, therefore, of determining the social relationships that follow from the role relationships, taking account of setting, etc., is made manageable by having an inventory to which to refer such as the one given in section 3.4.

Here follows the instructions for processing the required information through the four components of this parameter.

3.1 *Position*

State the participant's position (i.e. in which he enacts a particular role) by reference to §1.2 and §1.3 above.

e.g. university lecturer/teacher

3.2 *Role set*

Identify the target language role-set (i.e. the different people with whom he will interact in English, by virtue of his 'position'), taking account of the physical setting, especially location and place of work/study.

e.g. students he teaches
other teachers (expatriate)
visiting educationists (foreign)

3.3 *Role-set identity*

Identify particulars for each member/group of the target language role-set in terms of the following:

3.3.1 *Number*

Select as appropriate from: individual/small group/large group/mass

3.3.2 *Age-group*

Select as appropriate, modifying for degree or quantity if necessary, from: elderly/adult/adolescent/child/mixed

3.3.3 *Sex*

State: male/female/mixed, modifying if necessary (e.g. mostly male)

3.3.4 *Nationality*

State nationality, modifying if necessary (e.g. mainly British)

3.4 *Social relationships*

From the inventory of social relationships, determine those that are implied by the role relationships (the interaction of 3.1 with each member/group of 3.2), taking account of identity, domain, and setting.

e.g. instructor – learner (from/for teacher – students)
adult – adult (from/for teacher – students)
colleague – colleague (from/for teacher – other teachers)
professional – professional (from/for teacher – other teachers/
visitors)
native – non-native (from/for teacher – other teachers/visitors)
stranger – stranger (from/for teacher – visiting educationists)

Inventory of social relationships

Asymmetrical		Symmetrical	
3.4.1 superior	— subordinate	3.4.38 equal	— equal
3.4.2 senior	— junior	3.4.39 insider	— insider
3.4.3 'primus'	— 'pares'	3.4.40 colleague	— colleague
3.4.4 chairman	— member	3.4.41 group member	— group member
3.4.5 winner	— loser		
3.4.6 evaluator/judge	— applicant/ contestant	3.4.42 team-mate	— team-mate
3.4.7 authority	— offender	3.4.43 professional	— professional
3.4.8 government	— opposition	3.4.44 native	— native
3.4.9 official	— public	3.4.45 competitor	— competitor
3.4.10 employer	— employee	3.4.46 enemy	— enemy
3.4.11 management	— worker	3.4.47 neighbour	— neighbour
3.4.12 investigator	— subject	3.4.48 intimate	— intimate
3.4.13 mentor/supervisor	— charge	3.4.49 friend	— friend
3.4.14 society	— individual	3.4.50 acquaintance	— acquaintance
3.4.15 representative	— elector	3.4.51 stranger	— stranger
3.4.16 instructor/ authority	— learner	3.4.52 outsider	— outsider
3.4.17 adviser	— advisee	3.4.53 adult	— adult
3.4.18 therapist	— patient	3.4.54 child	— child
3.4.19 media	— public	3.4.55 own generation	— own generation
3.4.20 consultant	— client	3.4.56 own class	— own class
3.4.21 consumer	— producer	3.4.57 spouse	— spouse
3.4.22 buyer	— seller	3.4.58 parent	— parent
3.4.23 customer	— server	3.4.59 offspring	— offspring
3.4.24 insider	— outsider	3.4.60 relative	— relative
3.4.25 professional	— non-professional	3.4.61 own sex	— own sex
3.4.26 native	— non-native		
3.4.27 host	— guest		
3.4.28 benefactor	— beneficiary		
3.4.29 leader	— follower/ supporter		
3.4.30 artiste	— public		
3.4.31 star	— fan		
3.4.32 adult	— child/ adolescent		
3.4.33 older generation	— younger generation		
3.4.34 higher class	— lower class		
3.4.35 man/male	— woman/female		
3.4.36 senior relative	— junior relative		
3.4.37 parent	— offspring		

Social relationships are either symmetrical or asymmetrical. The common denominator of symmetrical relations is *cohesiveness*, in terms of the degree of solidarity or familiarity between the participants. The underlying characteristic of asymmetrical relations, on the other hand, is mainly *power*, in the sense of one participant being able to exercise some degree of control over the other. From this it will be seen that Brown and Gilman (1960) are being followed in their use of the terms 'power' and 'solidarity' for asymmetrical and symmetrical relations respectively, while preference is given to Robinson's (1972) suggestion of 'cohesiveness' for the symmetrical dimension. This is because it subsumes familiarity (which he refers to as intimacy) as well as solidarity, and both need to be covered.

Social relationships may or may not derive their power or cohesiveness from the status obtaining between the participants. This status is based on age, class (social or socio-economic), kinship, occupation, or sex. Additionally, some relationships of power are grounded in the 'educational' or legal standing between the participants. Relationships whose status basis is clear can be marked accordingly. For example, P^a would indicate a relationship where the power of one participant over the other derived from his age status, while C^c would indicate a relationship where the cohesiveness between the participants derived from their same class status. The unmarked forms, P and C, could then be used where the status basis is not clear or for relationships which are not status based. For the purposes of the model it is not necessary to give each social relationship in the inventory a notational marking of this kind, but it is useful in exemplifying the classification of social relationships in Figure 10.

Each of these categories of social relationship is exemplified as follows.

P	:	subordinate	—	superior
P^l	:	authority	—	offender
P^e	:	learner	—	instructor
P^o	:	server	—	customer
P^a	:	adult	—	child
P^c	:	lower class	—	higher class
P^s	:	male	—	female
P^k	:	parent	—	offspring
C	:	equal	—	equal
C^o	:	professional	—	professional

C^a : adult — adult
C^c : own class — own class
C^s : man — man
C^k : spouse — spouse

This process could be carried out for all the relationships on page 72. If this were done, it would be seen that much the largest category on each dimension of social relationships is the unmarked. P accounts for just under half of the asymmetrical relations, while C covers just over half of the symmetrical. The largest of the status marked categories is P^o with seven exponents, the smallest are P^c, P^s, C^c, and C^s with one each. Of the relationships of power, about sixteen have a hierarchic characteristic, e.g. management — worker, senior — junior. Of the relationships of cohesiveness, the majority are of the solidarity type, e.g. insider — insider, professional — professional, rather than the familiarity type, e.g. acquaintance — acquaintance.

The degree of cohesiveness varies from the strong solidarity of group member — group member to the total lack of it in enemy — enemy, and from the extreme familiarity of intimate — intimate to

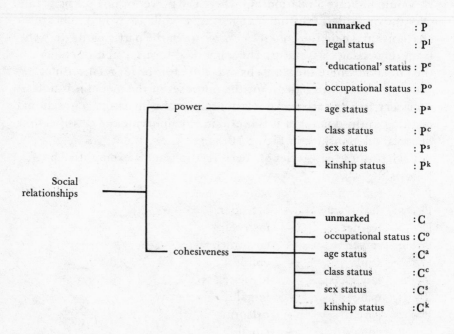

Figure 10 Classification of social relationships

the total lack of it in stranger — stranger. It is perhaps worth pointing out that, although three or four of the asymmetrical relations could be characterised partly by cohesiveness, e.g. leader — follower, the *underlying* characteristic is the control of an area of behaviour by one participant over another, even if such control is exercised obliquely through imposing a sense of obligation, e.g. host — guest. Only, perhaps, in the case of the star — fan relationship is the defining characteristic ambiguous.

In conclusion, it should be repeated that the purpose of specifying the social relationships, that are implied by the interaction of the participant with the members of his target language role-set, is to help predict, later on in the CNP, the attitudinal constraints on the communicative activities in which the participant has to engage. The profile of needs, enlarged after the processing in this parameter, is now passed to the last of the a priori variables.

4. INSTRUMENTALITY

In this parameter, information is obtained on the medium, mode, and channel of communication that the particular participant requires.

Medium (verbal)
This refers to the basic distinction between speaking and writing. The participant's communication in the target language has to take place in either the *spoken* or the *written* medium, or in both of them. Further, given either medium it is necessary to know whether the participant has to be able to produce the target language as well as understand it. This constraint on the medium concerns the type of command required, which will be referred to as *productive* and *receptive*. The terms 'active' and 'passive' are to be found referring to the use of a language, but 'passive' implies by definition a lack of anything active in understanding, a view which fails to take account of the interpretative element in the decoding process. 'Receptive-interpretative' would perhaps be the most apt label, but it is too cumbersome for a high frequency term. Marking the medium for the type of command required of the participant will yield four sub-categories, e.g. spoken: receptive, from which to select one or more for a particular participant. On entry to this parameter, the input is first processed for medium as follows.

4.1 Medium
State the required medium and type of command by selecting from
the following:
   4.1.1 spoken : receptive
   4.1.2 spoken : productive
   4.1.3 written : receptive
   4.1.4 written : productive
This information is fundamental in determining the language skills
that will be required by the participant. However, it will be more useful if it is refined to spell out the distinctions within a medium so
that one can specify what may be termed the mode of communication.

Mode
Gregory (1967) goes into a detailed consideration of the distinctions
which may be made in the relationship of a language user to his
medium in order to help towards a subcategorisation of modes of
discourse. Thus he distinguishes speaking into speaking spontaneously
and speaking non-spontaneously, and then subdivides the former into
conversing and monologuing, from which he postulates conversation
and monologue as modes of discourse. Among the subdivisions of
writing he distinguishes 'writing to be spoken' from 'writing to be
read'. Crystal and Davy (1969) treat medium in much the same way
but handle the distinction between monologue and dialogue, 'which
results from the nature of the participation in the language event', as
part of a separate though related variable which they call participation. They point out that 'there are clear and central co-occurrences
between the categories of medium and those of participation, irres-
pective of the other dimensions: spoken and written monologue and
spoken dialogue are common, as is — perhaps less obviously — written
dialogue'.[5]

   If one takes the two categories of participation and marks them,
with progressively more delicate distinctions of medium, one arrives
at a classification of what is called here *communicative mode* (see
Figure 11). The terminal points of the branches represent the subcategories for which the following examples of exponents can be
found. The most common subcategories are *monologue, spoken to
be heard*, the mode for a lecture and the expository part of most
class-teaching; *monologue, written to be read* (as if written),[6] as
exemplified by the texts of books of non-fiction or journals; and

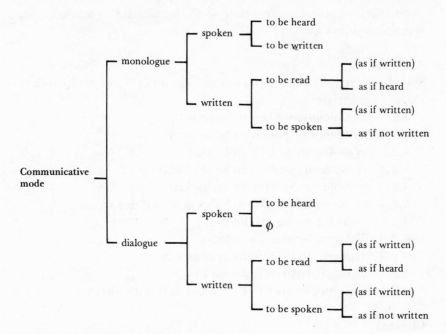

Figure 11 Classification of communicative mode

dialogue, spoken to be heard, as exemplified by conversation and discussion. Less common but still applicable to some likely inputs are *monologue, spoken to be written*, the mode in which dictation would be given to secretaries; *monologue, written to be spoken* (as if written), the mode for news bulletins and airport announcements; *dialogue, written to be read* (as if written), the mode for correspondence; and *dialogue/monologue, written to be spoken as if not written*, the modes used for the scripts for plays, films, and television interviews (dialogue), and certain kinds of public speeches (monologue). The remaining three modes are unlikely to be in much demand: *dialogue, written to be spoken* (as if written), as exemplified by the written reporting of a conversation which is to be read aloud as documentary evidence in court; and *dialogue/monologue, written to be read as if heard*, as exemplified by passages of direct speech in novels where items such as 'he said gently' or 'he screamed', placed before or after the piece of direct speech, are 'invitations to an auditory experience' (Gregory, op. cit.).

These eleven subcategories of communicative mode provide the set from which selection, appropriate to the participant's requirements, is made as follows.

4.2 Mode
Specify the required mode of communication in terms of the following, as appropriate:

4.2.1   monologue, spoken to be heard
4.2.2   monologue, spoken to be written
4.2.3   monologue, written to be read
4.2.4   monologue, written to be read as if heard
4.2.5   monologue, written to be spoken
4.2.6   monologue, written to be spoken as if not written
4.2.7   dialogue, spoken to be heard
4.2.8   dialogue, written to be read
4.2.9   dialogue, written to be read as if heard
4.2.10 dialogue, written to be spoken
4.2.11 dialogue, written to be spoken as if not written

Channel
The third category of the Instrumentality parameter is the *channel* through which the communication in the target language will take place, e.g. television, print. This use of the term is not the same as that of Hymes (1972) who uses it to mean medium (both verbal and non-verbal) of transmission of speech but does not say anything about the feature here described as channel. As a term for this feature is needed, and channel is most apt for it, instrumentality has been selected as the cover term for communicative medium (verbal and non-verbal), mode, and channel.

The channel of communication may be *bilateral*, in the sense that it is open on both sides and available to the participants for responding communicatively to each other, or it may be *unilateral*, in the sense that the recipient of the communication either cannot or is not expected to respond communicatively through the same channel. The bilateral channel subdivides into the subcategories where the participants may communicate *simultaneously* and those where only *one* of the participants can speak or write *at a time*. The unilateral channel subdivides into the subcategories where the communication comes *live* from the speaker and those where it is *recorded*. This classification of communicative channel is set out at Figure 12.

The twelve subcategories of channel may be illustrated with the following examples:

Channel	Likely user
face-to-face (bilateral)	anyone engaging in spoken dialogue
telephone	switchboard operator
radio contact	navigator; police
print (bilateral)	company secretary; hotel reception
face-to-face (unilateral)	lecturer; student
public address system	airport announcer; air hostess
radio (live)	commentator
television (live)	newsreader
disc	opera singer
tape	student (especially of language)
film	actor; teacher
print (unilateral)	anyone needing to read books and journals

Of these channels the most commonly required are the two face-to-face and the two print channels.

From these subcategories of communicative channel, whichever is appropriate for the particular participant is specified as follows:

4.3 Channel
Select the channel of communication, as appropriate, from the following:

4.3.1 face-to-face [bilateral]
4.3.2 telephone
4.3.3 radio contact
4.3.4 print [bilateral]
4.3.5 face-to-face [unilateral]
4.3.6 public address system
4.3.7 radio [live relay]
4.3.8 television [live relay]
4.3.9 disc
4.3.10 tape [audio/video]
4.3.11 film
4.3.12 print [unilateral]

Non-verbal medium
It was pointed out in Chapter 2 that the non-verbal code would not

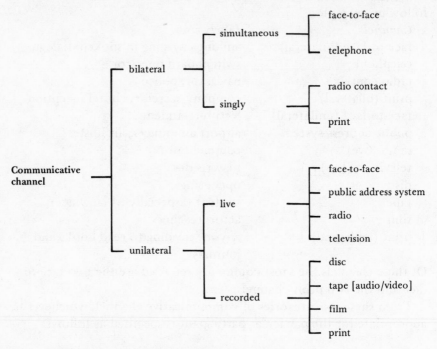

Figure 12 Classification of communicative channel

be dealt with, except in passing. If it were, the *non-verbal medium* is the parameter where it would receive its first attention. At this stage it is possible to consider the different types of non-verbal medium of communication, without having to be concerned with the constituent elements of each type or the business of subsequent extra-linguistic encoding.

In order to find out if the participant needed to be able to handle productively or receptively any extra-linguistic form of communication, and if so the non-verbal medium involved, a question could be set up as follows:

4.4 Non-verbal medium
If applicable, state the required non-verbal medium of communication by selecting from the following as appropriate:
    4.4.1 pictorial   [unlabelled illustrations, charts, and plans]
    4.4.2 symbolic (non-linguistic)   [signs, mime]

4.4.3 mathematical and other scientific   [arithmetical, algebraic, geometrical, chemical symbols]

4.4.4 personal   [sartorial features, interactional proximity]

4.4.5 kinesic   [facial and body movements or gestures]

4.4.6 paralinguistic   [vocal effects, e.g. whisper, giggle]

and state whether the type of command required is:

receptive/productive/both.

These media are non-verbal in the sense that the message is not communicated verbally. For this reason, 'diagrammatic' is not a non-verbal medium, since histograms, branching and pie diagrams, graphs and grids always require some *verbal labelling* or language before they can be understood or interpreted. *Labelled* illustrations, charts and plans, therefore, are also types of diagrammatic display, which may be regarded as a semi-verbal medium from which certain language skills derive (see below). Of the non-verbal media listed here, the kinesic would seem to have wide applicability when the interaction is visual.

Finally, a contrast should be made between the procedure here, where the information on medium, mode and channel is obtained *separately*, with the kind of questions that result from a conflation of these and other categories, as with Richterich's on 'means' (1972: 41–2); it may also be worth noting that the information from this parameter will be a major determinant in the *subsequent* selection of language skills.

NOTES

1 This objection reflects the ethnomethodological concern with the creative aspect of behaviour by an individual in everyday social interaction.

2 The sociologist is interested in examining how particular roles are related to the structure of society.

3 'in terms of role theory different members of the role-set are making incompatible demands' (Worsley et al., 1970).

4 Private sector institutions of English teaching.

5 Crystal and Davy define monologue as 'utterance with no expectation of a response', and dialogue as 'utterance with alternating participants, usually, though not necessarily, two in number'.

6 The brackets around a subcategory indicate that it is the full form of the subcategory at the node above it (i.e. to its left). This full form only needs to be used when differentiating within the subcategory of which it is a part.

5

COMMUNICATION NEEDS:
DIALECT AND TARGET LEVEL

The construction of a profile of communication needs now continues, in this chapter and the next, with the processing of the participant through the lower band of parameters of the CNP. These are dependent upon the a priori variables for input information which will enable them to become operational. These a posteriori variables are dialect, target level, communicative event, and communicative key, whose operational order and derivational sources are shown in Figure 5. The particular category of each source parameter, from which the relevant input derives, will be indicated below.

5.0 DIALECT

It is necessary to identify, as part of the communication requirements of a participant, the dialects of the target language which he will have to command receptively and productively. The information that is needed in order to do this has been obtained from the processing to date; the resultant information will be required at the linguistic encoding stage when account is taken, where possible, of the features of grammar, vocabulary, and pronunciation, which characterise a particular dialectal variety of English. Dialectal varieties are concerned with 'The linguistic reflections of reasonably permanent characteristics of the USER in language situations' (Gregory, 1967). Dialects, such as Scottish English, are instances of dimensions of dialectal language variety. Gregory posits five contextual categories:[1] idiolect, temporal dialect, geographical dialect, social dialect, and standard/non-standard dialect.

One is not concerned with the idiosyncratic aspects of a person's *idiolect*. Trudgill (1974) has pointed out, in connection with social-class dialects, that 'the speech of a single speaker (his idiolect) may differ considerably from those of others like him. Moreover, it may also be internally very inconsistent.' Apart from this, one has to deal in terms of the stereotypes of the members of the role-set with whom the participant has to interact.

Temporal dialect is unlikely to be significant for any of our participants except those needing English in order to study English literature or historical texts, or to act in plays. For most participants the required dialects from this dimension will be contemporary English. Other possibilities, for our purposes, are shown in Figure 13. Input information relevant to the specification of a temporal dialect of English comes from purposive domain and interaction; the derivational source for the specification of sixteenth- and seventeenth-century English would be the educational or occupational purpose category of domain and the role-set category of interaction. The influence of setting on temporal dialect occurs in the diglossia situation, e.g. in the choice of classical Arabic for the public setting of a university lecture but colloquial Arabic for the private setting of the home (Ferguson, 1959). In present day English society the nearest approach to a situation of diglossia is in the use of standard and regional dialects side by side by all members of the community, but this is not a matter of temporal dialect.

The largest dimension of dialectal language variety, and one which affects all participants is geographical or *regional* dialect. Language variation according to region is most marked in the speaker's pronunciation, least marked in his grammar. This is reflected in the variation between British and American varieties of Standard English, as summed up by Strevens (1972): 'Compared with the small number of grammatical differences between American and British English, differences of pronunciation are many indeed, and compared with the

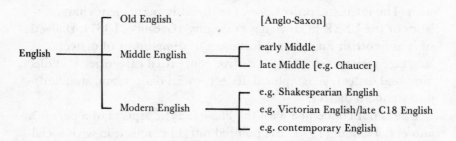

Figure 13 Basic classification of temporal dialect

somewhat random and individual nature of vocabulary differences, differences of pronunciation are rather systematic.' Participants, therefore, who need English in order to work in a Yorkshire wool factory will need to understand the dialect for that region, especially its pronunciation.

Quirk, Greenbaum, Leech and Svartvik (1972) point out that the dialects of English are 'indefinitely many, depending solely on how detailed we wish to be in our observations', and 'the degree of generality in our observation depends crucially upon our standpoint as well as upon our experience'.[2] As Trudgill (1974) says 'it is possible to speak of "the Norfolk dialect" or "the Suffolk dialect". On the other hand, one can also talk of more than one "Norfolk dialect" — "East Norfolk" or "South Norfolk", for instance.' East Anglian would probably suffice for our purposes, though the division into Norfolk or Suffolk could be made in any case where not to do so would hinder communication. Similarly, in America one would want Southern American as a major subcategory, within which Texas dialect and Virginian dialect may be specified where necessary. A classification of regional dialect that is suitable for the CNP is drawn up at Figure 14. In doing this one should recall Trudgill's caveat about the danger of talking about different dialectal varieties as if they were clearly distinct entities, recognising that different English dialects have so much in common that they are perhaps more realistically regarded in terms of a continuum rather than as discrete categories. This kind of classification, which partly follows the suggestion of Quirk et al. of 'some broad dialectal divisions which are rather generally recognised', is based on the position of phonology as the prime indicator of regional variation and facilitates correlation with spatial setting and role-set identity from which is derived the specification of required regional dialect.

Whether or not they require to use, or just understand, a regional dialect, many participants will need Standard English. This is a *non-regional* dialect, a superposed and supra-national variety reflecting the general consensus of educated and influentially placed users of English concerning its orthography, vocabulary and grammar, but not its pronunciation. There is no standard accent for English, so regional accents can be used with Standard English. However, in England, there is one non-regional accent, which can only be used with Standard English, and this is known as 'Received Pronunciation' (RP), the

85

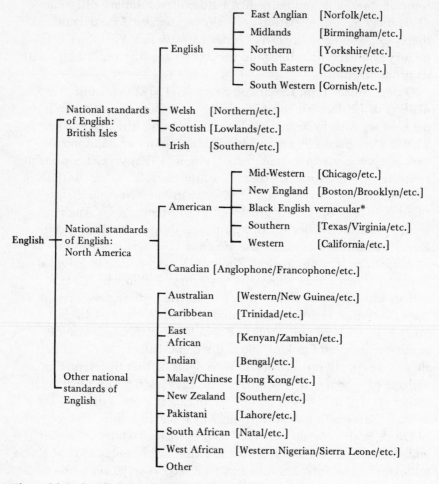

Figure 14 A classification of regional dialect

American equivalent of which is 'General American' or 'network English'. RP has prestige and wide intelligibility in the English-speaking world, as has Standard English, factors which will influence the specification of the dialect and accent required by the participant. Such factors derive from information previously obtained on the participant's role-set, location and scale of use required. For example, if we have a participant who needs English for international use with

*Trudgill's view (1974) that 'black English vernacular' functions as a separate ethnic group variety would not seem to debar its inclusion here.

senior American and British officials, the dialect required is Standard English with either a General American or RP accent. If, on the other hand, we have an Indian participant who needs English for *intra-national* use with other Indians from all over the sub-continent, the appropriate dialect is Standard Indian English, which is a national standard* of English, to be used with a General Indian pronunciation. Further, if the participant is an immigrant who needs English mainly for local use as a factory worker in the wool industry in Yorkshire, he will need the Yorkshire dialect with its local accent.

Non-standard dialect (which is not to be interpreted as sub-standard) refers to varieties other than the standard dialect. As Standard English is a non-regional dialect, non-standard varieties of English may be regarded as regional dialects. For this reason the Standard/Non-standard aspect will not be treated as a separate dimension of dialect but as the initial question to be answered in this parameter.

The remaining dimension of dialectal variation is that according to social class. In some parts of the English-speaking world there is a form of social stratification which results in *social-class dialects* (not to be confused with caste dialects, as found in India, for example). Trudgill defines social classes as 'simply aggregates of people with similar social and economic characteristics', and this definition will be followed here. In England social-class variation is directly related to the use of standard or non-standard English and to RP or a regional accent. Trudgill (1974) shows this correlation as a pyramid with the lowest class at the bottom, where the regional variation is greatest, and the highest class at the top, where standard English is used with little variation according to region, and the accent is RP.[3] Strevens (1977a) points out that there are two types of RP, the first being an upper-class social marker while the second, which is the descendant of the former, indicates middle class and usually tertiary education. He makes the further point that this second version of RP 'often retains a small amount of information about regional origins — not a broad regional or local accent, but an identifiable trace'. It is the first type, therefore, which is at the apex of Trudgill's pyramid. The second, and more widely spoken type of RP would presumably occur immediately below this, but we do not yet know 'how far RP extends

*Term given by Quirk et al. (1972) to L1 national variants having the status of a standard. We extend it to L2 national variants with similar status — see Figure 14, cf. Kachru (1976).

down the social scale in different places; what kind of speaker uses the regional standard pronunciation; and exactly what the intermediate and localised accents are like' (Trudgill).

In his survey of Norwich dialects, Trudgill found that the biggest gap between any two scores was between 'lower middle class' and 'upper working class'. This suggested that 'the division of society into two main class groups, "middle class" and "working class", a division made largely but not entirely on the basis of the difference between manual and non-manual occupations, is of some validity and importance, since the social barrier is clearly reflected in language.'[4]

The main points about dialectal variation according to social-class are: that not much is known as yet about the detailed realisations of social-class dialects and accents other than Standard English and RP, that such dialects (which are part of a continuum) can at least be grouped into 'middle class' and 'working class', that the main indicator of class would seem to be accent, and that dialect and accent co-vary with regional difference, ranging from Standard English and the older form of RP for the top end of the social scale to the most localised dialect and accent at the bottom end. As the question of standard/non-standard dialect and general/regional accent is already dealt with in this parameter, it may be thought unnecessary to consider the question of social-class dialect at all. However, the specification of dialect and accent could depend on information on the participant's role-set and occupational purpose which suggest social-class rather than regional variation. This aspect of dialect will therefore be treated, albeit briefly, by seeking to establish in the broadest hierarchical terms what social-class dialect/accent of English the

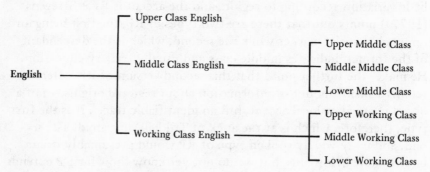

Figure 15 A classification of social-class dialect

participant needs to be able to handle. If it is thought to be relevant, a more delicate level of specification can be made in Trudgill's terms, which has been slightly expanded in Figure 15.

In this parameter, then, one is mainly concerned with matters of regional and non-regional dialect, including accent, though any needs that the participant may have with regard to social-class and temporal dialect should not go by default.

The information required from this parameter is obtained as follows:

5.0 DIALECT

Taking account of the relevant variables, what dialects of English are required by the participant?

5.1 Regional
Input
State the relevant input information from the following derivational sources:
Setting
    Location   : [e.g. England; Bradford]
    Place   : [e.g. factory; and neighbourhood]
    Scale of use: [e.g. mainly local]
Interaction
    Role-set identity (nationality): [e.g. mostly English]
Dialect and accent
5.1.1 Which of the following (one or more) does the participant need to be able to understand/produce?
    Standard English/a national standard/a local dialect
        [e.g. understand and produce local dialect; understand Standard English]
    5.1.1.1 Where applicable, specify the national standard/local dialect, using the classification of regional dialect
        [e.g. Yorkshire dialect]
5.1.2 Does the participant need to be able to understand/produce a general or a regional accent of English, or both?
    5.1.2.1 If general, specify RP/General American/General Indian/ etc.
        [e.g. understand RP]

5.1.2.2 If regional, state the localised accent for the specification at 5.1.1.1.

[e.g. understand and produce Yorkshire accent]

5.2 Social class
Input

State the relevant input information from the following derivational sources:

Purposive domain

Occupational classification: [e.g. semi-skilled manual worker in industry]

Interaction

Role-set: [e.g. other workers; foreman; local community]

Dialect and accent

5.2.1 Which of the following (one or more) does the participant need to be able to understand/produce?

Upper Class English/Middle Class English/Working Class English [e.g. understand and produce Working Class English; understand Middle Class English]

5.2.2 If relevant, specify the sub-class, e.g. Lower Working Class English.

[e.g. N/A]

5.3 Temporal
Input

State the relevant input information from the following derivational sources:

Purposive domain

Educational purpose: [e.g. English Literature]

Occupational purpose: [e.g. curator of museum/actor]

Interaction

Role-set: [e.g. other Shakesperian actors]

Role-set identity (age): [e.g. elderly]

Dialect

Select, as appropriate from the following:[5]

5.3.1 contemporary

5.3.2 early twentieth century

5.3.3 nineteenth century

5.3.4 eighteenth century

5.3.5 sixteenth—seventeenth century

5.3.6 late Middle English

5.3.7 early Middle English

5.3.8 Anglo-Saxon

    [e.g. contemporary; and sixteenth—seventeenth century English]

6.0 TARGET LEVEL

In Chapter 2 it was pointed out that the identification of the target level of command should not be confused with the specification of the particular language behaviours for which English is required. This point is often missed, though not by Wilkins (1977) who says that his behavioural statements, which constitute his proposed levels, 'are *not* intended to be interpreted as non-specific language learning objectives . . . their real function is to act as reference points in the development of learning programmes for specific categories of learners'. It may well be that the system he proposes will serve the aims of the Council of Europe's unit/credit programme, for which it is intended, but it is not entirely suitable for our purposes. The way his levels are written out as a set of generalised language behavioural descriptions with fixed features for each level makes it inevitably less flexible than we would want for handling participants from the same category but whose needs are different, at least in some respects.* There is also an inescapable arbitrariness (because made 'in vacuo') about Wilkins' assignation of a certain feature to a particular level. On the whole his is an admirable exercise of its kind, but here a less pre-determined and more context-sensitive system is required.

    In this system, broad values are assigned — on the basis of relevant input information for the participant — to the defining characteristics of level. These values, which derive from a separate interpretation of the a priori variables for each participant will then guide the subsequent processing of that particular profile of needs into the required communicative competence specification. The process of arriving at the target level guide is shown at Figure 16.

    The defining characteristics of level are its dimensions, and the conditions on those dimensions, all as related to verbal medium. Six

---

*It is worth repeating here the caveat (expressed at note 1 of chapter 3) about setting up broad types as if they applied in all contexts. The variables should be checked out each time, even for a broad type or participant category.

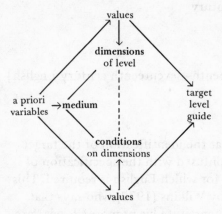

Figure 16 Target level specification

dimensions of level may be postulated: *size, complexity, range, delicacy, speed,* and *flexibility*. One wants to know the size and complexity of the utterance or text, the range and delicacy of the forms, micro-functions and micro-skills, and the speed and flexibility of communication, which the participant needs to be able to handle receptively or productively. A few points need to be made with regard to the use of these terms. Size, here, is a matter of length; range, a matter of quantitative extent. Complexity (grammatical,[6] etc.) includes discourse coherence and the capacity to handle redundancy, while delicacy refers to the level of specificity and detail. Speed is concerned with rapidity of flow, but can be extended to include deliberateness of speech; and flexibility covers the capacity to handle novelty or communication unrelated to the participant's own purposive domain, and adaptability to switching of subject, style, or interlocutor. Each of these dimensions is marked on a seven-point scale of broad values from very low/very small to very high/very large (see below). The decision to assign a particular value is made after referring to relevant input information. The derivational sources for this input information are the occupational or educational purpose, the role-set, role-set identity (age-group, and nationality), scale of use, the psychosocial environment, communicative mode and channel. Of these, purpose and role-set seem to be relevant to all dimensions, with psychosocial environment the most pervasive influence of the remainder.

Although a participant may need to handle a fairly high level of complexity, his communicative situation (as determined by the a priori variables) may allow a fairly high tolerance level of error. Or, a participant may need to understand utterances spoken at high speed where the tolerance level of asking for repetition is low. Such tolerance factors, which operate as conditions or constraints on the dimensions of level, need to be taken into consideration in the specification of target level. There appear to be five such conditions, viz. tolerance of: *error, stylistic failure, reference, repetition,* and *hesitancy*. Error is concerned with linguistic accuracy, stylistic failure with not seeing and understanding stylistic features or not using appropriate language. Reference means looking things up in a dictionary, or referring to the addressee, etc.; while repetition covers re-reading as well as asking the speaker to repeat. Hesitation is concerned with lack of fluency (ease of flow). To mark these conditions use is made of a five-point scale of broad values from very low to very high tolerance (see below). Of the variables which provide the input information which influences the selection of tolerance levels, psychosocial environment and channel apply to all the conditions.

Dimensions and conditions relate to medium, viz. the receptive or productive command of spoken and written English. This is expressed as two grids, with medium along one axis and either dimensions or conditions along the other. The values are placed in the empty cells at the intersections of the two axes. The grids, completed as applicable to the particular participant, represent the target level guide. This parameter will now be set out operationally, and its working with two different kinds of participant will be illustrated.

6.0 TARGET LEVEL

Specify the target levels for the participant's command of English by completing each grid, where applicable, with values from its own scale. In assigning values, refer to relevant input information.

[Example 1]
Input
Purposive domain
    Occupational purpose: hotel employee; head waiter; receptionist
    (routine)

Educational purpose: N/A
Setting
    Place of study: N/A
    Scale of use: international
    Psychosocial environment: non-intellectual; occasionally aesthetic;
    public; familiar physical; unfamiliar and familiar human; often
    noisy; hurried; generally formal; often entertaining.
Interaction
    Role-set: (a) customers in restaurant; (b) hotel residents; (c) reser-
    vation seekers.
    Role-set age-group: (a) and (b) mainly adult, some adolescent;
    (c) adult.
    Role-set nationality: (a), (b) and (c) mainly British, some Americans.
Instrumentality
    Medium: spoken, receptive and productive; written, receptive and
    productive.
    Mode: dialogue, spoken to be heard; dialogue, written to be read.
    Channel: face-to-face (bilateral); telephone; print (bilateral).

Target level guide

		Medium		
		Spoken		Written
6.1 Dimensions	Rec.	Prod.	Rec.	Prod.
6.1.1 *Size* of utterance/text	2	2	3	2
6.1.2 *Complexity* of utterance/text	3	3	4	3
6.1.3 *Range* of forms/micro- functions/micro-skills	3	2	2	2
6.1.4 *Delicacy* of forms/micro- functions/micro-skills	5	4	4	3
6.1.5 *Speed* of communication	5	4	2/1	2/1
6.1.6 *Flexibility* of communication	4	3	2/1	2/1

Scale: *Value*
        1 = very low/very small
        2 = low/small
        3 = fairly low/fairly small
        4 = middling
        5 = fairly high/fairly large
        6 = high/large
        7 = very high/very large

6.2 Conditions

	Medium			
	Spoken		Written	
Tolerance of:	Rec.	Prod.	Rec.	Prod.
6.2.1 error (linguistic)	3	4	2/1	3
6.2.2 stylistic failure	3	2	4	2
6.2.3 reference (to dictionary/ addressee, etc.)	3	3	5	5
6.2.4 repetition (re-read/ask for repeat)	2	–	5	–
6.2.5 hesitation (lack of fluency)	–	2	–	5

Scale: *Value*
1 = very low (tolerance of)
2 = fairly low "
3 = middling "
· 4 = fairly high "
5 = very high "

Later, these values will serve as a guide when processing the participant's activities and keys into micro-skills and micro-functions, when marking them for attitudinal tone, and subsequently when coming to their linguistic realisations. For example, for this participant's productive command of spoken English, the range of micro-functions will be small but their specification will be at the middling level of delicacy. The complexity of the linguistic realisations, however, will be fairly low. On the receptive side of the spoken medium, by slight contrast, the participant is expected to cope with a fairly high level of delicacy and a middling degree of complexity. The first grid of the target level guide contains a lot of information of this kind. In the second grid one can see, for example, that the tolerance of error is fairly high for the participant's production of spoken English but low for his reception of written English (e.g. when he has to read and understand correspondence as a receptionist). When considering the two grids in combination, one notes, for example, that the participant may have to read texts of middling complexity, but the tolerance level of reference and repetition is very high, i.e. the fact that there is apparently no problem in looking things up, and plenty of opportunity for re-reading, probably offsets the complexity factor. In listening, on the other hand, he has to understand English spoken at a fairly high speed with a fairly low tolerance of his asking for repetition.

[Example 2]
Input
Purposive domain
    Occupational purpose: N/A
    Educational purpose: veterinary medicine; animal pathology; anat-
    omy, animal physiology.
Setting
    Place of study: university; library/private study
    Scale of use: international
    Psychosocial environment: intellectual; quasi-professional; private;
    quiet; demanding; unhurried.
Interaction
    Role-set: writers on areas of academic study
    Role-set age-group: N/A
Instrumentality
    Medium: written, receptive
    Mode: monologue, written to be read
    Channel: print (unilateral)

Target level guide

	Medium			
	Spoken		Written	
6.1 Dimensions	Rec.	Prod.	Rec.	Prod.
6.1.1 *Size* of utterance/text	—	—	7	—
6.1.2 *Complexity* of utterance/text	—	—	6	—
6.1.3 *Range* of forms/micro-functions/micro-skills	—	—	4	—
6.1.4 *Delicacy* of forms/micro-functions/micro-skills	—	—	6/5	—
6.1.5 *Speed* of communication	—	—	4/3	—
6.1.6 *Flexibility* of communication	—	—	1	—

[The scale would be set out here as in Example 1]

This target level guide is completed for only the third column since
the input information indicates that this participant needs only a
receptive command of the written medium. In contrast to the first
example, one immediately notices the much higher values given to all
the dimensions except flexibility. The very low flexibility of communication required by this participant arises from the very small

6.2 Conditions	*Medium*			
	Spoken		Written	
Tolerance of:	Rec.	Prod.	Rec.	Prod.
6.2.1 error (linguistic)	–	–	2	–
6.2.2 stylistic failure	–	–	3/4	–
6.2.3 reference (to dictionary/ addressee, etc.)	–	–	3	–
6.2.4 repetition (re-read/ask for repeat)	–	–	5	–
6.2.5 hesitation (lack of fluency)	–	–	–	–

[The scale would be set out here as in Example 1]

demands that will be made of him in subject matter switching, style shift and variation within the role-set, and the fact that his reading is all related to his specialist field. The high values for size, complexity and delicacy reflect the need for very specific micro-skills to handle demanding tasks intellectually presented over long spans of print. The very high value for repetition reflects the almost total lack of constraint on re-reading in the unhurried, private study environment indicated by the input information. Finally, it appears that there is an almost middling tolerance level of stylistic failure (i.e. missing or not understanding the significance of stylistic features), which might be compared with the fairly low tolerance of it in the hotel employee's spoken English, where his use of appropriate language is rated highly.

NOTES

1 The last only 'rather tentatively'. It seems preferable to regard these categories as dimensions.
2 This is the reason for the 'etc'. in Figure 14.
3 cf. Ida C. Ward, in *The phonetics of English* (1929), who attributes a similar diagram to Daniel Jones.
4 Strevens suggests that the true basis of social-class distinction lies in the number of years of formal education – which in turn determines whether the occupation is manual or non-manual (personal communication).
5 It is realised that, of the choices listed, only 'contemporary' is likely to be relevant for the vast majority of participants.
6 e.g. amount and type of embedding.

6

COMMUNICATION NEEDS:
COMMUNICATIVE EVENT AND COMMUNICATIVE
KEY

7.0 COMMUNICATIVE EVENT[1]

In this parameter of the CNP it is specified what the participant has
to be able to do, receptively or productively. This specification is
based on relevant input information from the a priori variables and is
made in terms of the activities and subject matter which comprise
each communicative event. It has already been explained what is
meant by activity as distinguished from the terms act, skill and function (see Chapter 2: sections 3.7, 4 and 5). Therefore only a few
salient points will be briefly recapitulated before an illustration is
given of the working of this parameter.

Events derive basically from the nature of the participant's work
(information obtained from purposive domain) and the interaction
of relevant inputs from the following variables: occupational/edu-
cational purpose, physical setting, role-set, medium, mode and channel. In the occupational context an event such as 'interchange
between air traffic controller and pilot/navigator on approach to airport' is then broken down into its componential activities and subject
matter. An example of an activity in this event would be 'providing
information on landing conditions'. These activities, from which
grammatical features eventually derive, are later processed into micro-
functions and then linguistically realised. The subject matter of an
event, which is the main generator of lexis, consists of referential
vocabulary categories for narrowly defined or highly specific activities such as in this example. Where the event is more broadly defined
or the activities are of the discoursal type (see next example), the
subject matter consists of topics. Examples of referential vocabulary
categories for the above activity would be visibility and altitude. In
the academic study context, an event such as 'agriculture student
attending lectures' consists of activities such as 'listening and taking

notes' on topics such as soil conservation and crop protection. Activities, especially of the discoursal type, are later interpreted for the specific language skills required for their realisation.

The specification of information in this parameter is made as follows.

7.0 COMMUNICATIVE EVENT

Input
State the relevant input information from the following derivational sources:
[For example]
Purposive domain
    Occupational purpose: civil aviation authority official; air traffic controller
    Educational purpose: N/A
Setting
    Location: Italy, Rome
    Place of work/study: airport, control tower
    Study setting: N/A
    Other places: N/A
    Size of institution: large
Interaction
    Role-set: pilots and navigators
Instrumentality
    Medium: spoken, receptive and productive
    Mode: dialogue, spoken to be heard
    Channel: radio contact
Communicative events
State the main and other communicative events that the participant is required to handle in English, and then specify for each event its activities and subject matter.
[For example]
Main: 7.1 Interchange between air traffic controller and pilot/navigator on approach to airport.
        7.2 Interchange between air traffic controller and pilot/navigator on departure from airport.
Other: 7.3 Air traffic controller providing information to navigator en route.

7.4 Air traffic controller handling exceptional circumstances.
⋮

Event 7.1

Communicative activities
[For example]
7.1.1 Establishing contact
7.1.2 Response to request for permission to land
7.1.3 Instructions concerning approach route
7.1.4 Providing information on landing conditions
7.1.5 Guiding descent in adverse conditions
7.1.6 Confirmation/postponement of clearance to land.
⋮

Subject matter
Referential vocabulary categories/Topics for above activities:
[For example]
[a] identification terminology
[b] traffic flow
[c] time
[d] direction
[e] altitude/distance
[f] weather conditions
[g] runway conditions
[h] speed
⋮

Each event is specified in this way. In the case of this particular participant, there happen to be two main events where the subject matter is virtually identical, but there would be differences for event 7.3.

The derivational sources listed here under 'input' are those considered to have a potential for affecting the specification of communicative events in some way. Therefore, although educational purpose is not applicable to this participant, it is included since it is relevant when the participant is a student. On the other hand, variables such as psychosocial setting and social relationships, from which events do not derive whoever the participant may be, are excluded as sources for this parameter. Of those listed here, occupational/educational purpose, study setting, and role-set are the most influential in the specification of activities and subject matter. The location has a delimiting effect on the nature and range of events that the participant needs to be able to handle in English. The fact that the location

is Rome (or Bahrain, etc.) and not England means that he is unlikely
to need to use English away from his place of work. One can appreci-
ate this more forcibly in the case of a waiter in Istanbul who would
not even need to use English for passing on the customer's order to
the kitchen; whereas he might well have to do so in London, where
he would need English in a wider setting with a larger role-set, resulting in more events for which English is required. The place of work
will determine large areas of subject matter. 'Other places' is included,
not to provide a catch-all subcategory more suited to general English,
but because there may be cases where English is required for a specific
purpose in a place other than the place of work or study. The input
for size of institution is unlikely to be significant here; but (as we
noted earlier) the information that a head waiter is working in a *small*
tourist hotel may well affect the range of his duties and the events
that derive from them, e.g. as receptionist. The input from medium,
especially the receptive/productive command required, and that from
mode and channel, combine with the input from other sources (e.g.
study setting) in the specification of activities, e.g. discussion with
other medical students in seminar. In the example above it delimits
the range of events, confining them to the spoken medium, and the
input from channel severely constrains the nature of the communication. Occupational-type activities, such as those listed at 7.1, will
also be overtly affected by the input information on medium in the
meaning processor, when each activity is divided into its micro-
functions that have to be handled receptively and those that have to
be controlled productively.

It may be worth repeating here that in the specification of event,
activities should not be confused with the language skills[2] required
for the realisation of the activities; nor should they be confused with
the micro-functions into which the activities are converted or processed before being realised as linguistic forms.[3] Therefore, in this
parameter 'contradicting' and 'exemplifying' should not appear as
activities along with 'discussion with other students in seminar' since
they are constituents of that activity, to be handled later in the meaning processor. In the example above, 'permission' is not listed as an
activity since it is a micro-function which figures as a semantic element
in the activity 'response to request for permission to land'. For procedural as well as theoretical reasons, it is desirable not to blur the distinction between an activity and a language skill or micro-function.

In his 'model for the definition of adult language needs' Richterich (1972) postulates a language operations component consisting of three categories: the functions (which the act of communication has to fulfil); the objects (to which that act will relate); and the means (used to produce that act). His functions consist of eight pairs of elements such as expression/exchange and argumentation/persuasion; and his objects comprise seven pairs of elements such as idea/opinion and action/fact. These sets of functions and objects are too small, and most of their exponents consequently too general, to capture the full range in the kind of detail that would be useful, i.e. where selection is meaningful. A look at his analytical sheets which exemplify the results of defining language needs by working through his model reveals the inadequacy of this sector of his model. For example, the definition of needs for an Italian speaking waiter requiring French in a French-speaking country includes the following: 'to be able to use lexical and syntactic groups appropriate to these functions and objects, [specified as] expression/exchange, request/order; and information/notification, contact/relation, and animate/inanimate, in a manner befitting a waiter'. (The needs here also include 'have a very good comprehension'.) Richterich has here fallen between two stools: on the one hand, his functions and objects are really part of what Wilkins calls categories of communicative function, and therefore, it seems to me, prematurely pressed into service in a model aiming to define needs; and on the other hand, as part of his operations component (re-titled 'the objectives' in a subsequent paper given at Lancaster in 1973) they fail to handle the analysis and specification of communicative events that should be prior to the selection of functional subcategories or micro-functions.

8.0 COMMUNICATIVE KEY

This is the final variable in the processing of a profile of communication needs. The term 'key' is taken from Hymes (1972) for whom it was 'the tone, manner, and spirit in which an act is done'. In the communicative event parameter, the activities that the participant needs to handle are worked out; here, a specification is given of the keys that need to be understood or produced for each of those activities. This specification is based on input information from relevant derivational sources, viz. the participant's identity, role-set identity, social relationships, and psychosocial setting. It is worth noting that these sources of input information are different from the derivational sources for communicative events. The keys are selected from a taxonomy of such features, which has been devised for this purpose and for the subsequent marking of micro-functions for attitudinal-tone.

In order to select keys it was necessary to have a set of such features from which to make a selection. As no such set existed, a formidable problem had to be faced: this was the task of categorising, in effect, a major part of the universe. One such categorisation, although for different purposes, already exists in Roget's Thesaurus (1966 edition by R.A. Dutch). This difference of purpose is reflected in the way it is organised and set out, which is unsuitable for present needs. However, it has proved invaluable as the primary source for investigations. In devising the system, a thorough examination was made of Roget, with regular recourse to other sources of lexical reference, in the search for those affective, volitive and other features which affect the choice of linguistic realisations for communicative activities. Then, using Lyons' (1968) tests for determining antonymy and hyponymy, I have organised the results of that extensive search into an *attitudinal-tone index*. This consists of a potentially finite set of continua, each one labelled with a pair of antonymous keys which are superordinate to the other terms on that continuum (see below). These other terms, each of which is therefore in a relationship of hyponymy to its own superordinate term, are defined as the more likely attitudinal-tones for each continuum. In a few cases, where a superordinate does not call up its more familiar hyponyms except with difficulty, or where no superordinate appears to exist, the continuum is labelled with the most representative co-hyponyms. The relationship between individual co-hyponyms is deliberately not made explicit since such differences do not in any way affect the selection process, and the only semantic relationships that are material to this framework are antonymy (horizontal axis) and hyponymy (vertical axis), not synonymy, etc. It should be stressed that the horizontal axis is a continuum, not a cline. As the hyponyms are not intended to be exhaustive, a new attitudinal-tone can be added to an existing continuum wherever experience, and a thorough search of the index (since the apparently missing term may be located on a different continuum), reveals an undesirable omission. On the

Attitudinal-tone index

happy—unhappy

happy
delighted, ecstatic, joyful

unhappy
wretched, sad, heartbroken, sorrowful, suffering, harrowed

content – discontented

content
contented, satisfied, complacent

discontented
dissatisfied, disgruntled, grumbling, complaining, petulant

pleasant – unpleasant

pleasant
agreeable, genial, amiable, appealing

unpleasant
disagreeable, annoying, distressing, frightening, abrasive, spooky

cheerful – dejected

cheerful
hearty, laughing, light-hearted, jaunty, gay, merry, jolly, festive, convivial

dejected
gloomy, despondent, depressed, disappointed, melancholic, cheerless, depressing, sombre, disconsolate

frivolous — serious

frivolous
flippant, levitous, joking, trivial, playful

serious
earnest, grave, solemn, weighty

rejoicing — lamenting

rejoicing
jubilant, gleeful, exultant, triumphant

lamenting
tearful, mournful, plaintive, doleful, pathetic

entertaining – tedious

entertaining
amusing, diverting, interesting

tedious
dreary, dull, soporific, boring, monotonous

exciting – unexciting

exciting
stirring, stimulating, dramatic, sensational

unexciting
uneventful, dull, bored

humorous – humourless

humorous
funny, amusing, comical, farcical, witty, droll, ridiculous

humourless
unamusing, unfunny, uncomical, straight, serious

sensitive/discriminating — insensitive/indiscriminating

sensitive/discriminating
delicate, aesthetic, discerning, subtle, sophisticated, fastidious, tactful

insensitive/indiscriminating
vulgar, coarse, Philistine, undiscerning, naive, unsophisticated, raucous, tactless

hoping — hopeless

hoping
expectant, sanguine, optimistic, encouraging, wishful, hopeful

hopeless
despairing, desperate, pessimistic, unhopeful

courageous — fearing

courageous
heroic, brave, bold, audacious, plucky, spirited, intrepid, fearless, undismayed

fearing
afraid, panicky, dismayed, petrified, nervous, timid, apprehensive, cowardly, funky, diffident

cautious — incautious

cautious
wary, guarded, circumspect, tentative, careful, discreet

incautious
reckless, heedless, unguarded, rash, wild, careless, indiscreet

caring — indifferent

caring
concerned, interested, enthusiastic, eager, keen, personal, anxious, worried, curious, fascinated

indifferent
uncaring, unconcerned, uninterested, lukewarm, impersonal, unenthusiastic, incurious, nonchalant, apathetic, perfunctory

wondering — unastonished

wondering
marvelling, amazed, aghast, surprised, bewildered

unastonished
bewildered, unsurprised, unimpressed, expectant, matter-of-fact

modest — prideful

modest
self-effacing, unassuming, humble, meek, bashful, retiring, demure, unboastful

prideful
conceited, boastful, proud, snobbish, supercilious, patronising, condescending, pompous, ostentatious, arrogant

formal — informal

formal
ceremonious, punctilious, correct, detached, stiff, conventional

informal
unceremonious, casual, familiar, intimate, chatty, relaxed, irregular

friendly — inimical	**friendly** . . . . sympathetic, cordial, amiable, intimate, warm	**inimical** unfriendly, unsympathetic, hostile, cold, disliking
courteous — discourteous	**courteous** . . . . chivalrous, polite, civil, urbane, dignified, gracious, gallant	**discourteous** ungallant, impolite, rude, off-handed, boorish, ungracious, brusque, abrupt, offensive
sociable — unsociable	**sociable** . . . . hospitable, welcoming, affable, approachable, loquacious, effusive, unreserved	**unsociable** inhospitable, unwelcoming, stand-offish, taciturn, sullen, sulky, aloof, reserved, preoccupied, ignoring
loving — hating	**loving** . . . . affectionate, tender, caressing, amorous, desiring, infatuated, adoring, erotic	**hating** antipathetic, loathing, rancorous, abhorring
unresentful — resentful	**unresentful** . . . . ungrudging, mild, unenvious, unjealous	**resentful** piqued, hurt, indignant, affronted, bitter, acrimonious, envious, jealous
pleased — displeased	**pleased** . . . . glad	**displeased** angry, cross, annoyed, infuriated, apoplectic, exasperated
benevolent — malevolent	**benevolent** . . . . benign, kind, obliging, altruistic, generous, charitable, pitying, compassionate	**malevolent** spiteful, vicious, malicious, unkind, uncharitable, cruel, sadistic, brutal, pitiless
forgiving — unforgiving	**forgiving** . . . . pardoning, merciful, condoning, placable	**unforgiving** retaliatory, revengeful, vindictive, implacable, merciless

patient — impatient	**patient** uncomplaining, forbearing, long-suffering, persevering, stoical, painstaking	**impatient** restless, over-eager, hasty, fretful, impetuous, unforbearing, unpersevering
grateful — ungrateful	**grateful** thankful, appreciative, obliged, acknowledging	**ungrateful** unthankful, unmindful, unappreciative, taking for granted
honest — dishonest	**honest** candid, frank, ingenuous, straightforward, sincere, genuine, truthful, upright, fair, just	**dishonest** disingenuous, insincere, hypocritical, sanctimonious, cunning, devious, corrupt, perfidious, unfair, unjust
disinterested — biased/selfish	**disinterested** impartial, unbiased, unprejudiced, dispassionate, unselfish, considerate, altruistic, generous, magnanimous	**biased/selfish** prejudiced, nationalistic, chauvinistic, bigoted, egotistical, ungenerous, mercenary, avaricious, self-seeking, inconsiderate
respectful — disrespectful	**respectful** deferential, reverential, obsequious, dutiful	**disrespectful** lacking in deference, familiar, cheeky, impertinent, brash, presumptuous, irreverent
admiring — contemptuous	**admiring** regarding highly, appreciative, impressed	**contemptuous** despising, disdainful, scornful, snobbish, cynical, derisive, mocking, sardonic, insulting, insolent
praising — detracting	**praising** complimentary, commendatory, laudatory, eulogistic, flattering, sycophantic	**detracting** derogatory, pejorative, disparaging, defamatory, denigratory, sarcastic, satirical, uncomplimentary

approving — disapproving

approving . . . .
favourable, supporting, assenting, well-inclined

disapproving
unfavourable, critical, censorious, reproachful, intolerant, shocked, deprecating, admonitory

regretting — unregretting

regretting . . . .
regretful, sorry, apologetic, contrite, remorseful, penitent, repentant

unregretting
unapologetic, unrepentant, uncontrite, unpenitent, unashamed, brazen

temperate — intemperate

temperate . . . .
moderate, sober, restrained, ascetic, austere

intemperate
immoderate, drunken, unrestrained, sensual, hedonistic

pure — impure

pure . . . .
clean, innocent, chaste, honourable, platonic, decent, edifying, printable, prudish, puritanical

impure
dirty, immoral, risqué, obscene, pornographic, whorish, lecherous, lewd, licentious, depraved

pious — irreligious

pious . . . .
religious, spiritual, worshipping, prayerful, devotional, invocatory, mystical

irreligious
impious, secular, unbelieving, profane, blasphemous, idolatrous, diabolical

excitable — inexcitable

excitable . . . .
impassioned, excited, agitated, tense, irascible, embarrassed, frantic, hysterical, disconcerted, hot-tempered

inexcitable
impassive, phlegmatic, cool, imperturbable, composed, calm, unruffled, placid, equable

willing — unwilling

willing . . . .
desirous, ready, enthusiastic, helpful, cooperative

unwilling
reluctant, unhelpful, uncooperative, disinclined, unenthusiastic

resolute — irresolute

resolute . . . .
determined, firm, persistent, stubborn, obstinate, constant, adamant, militant

irresolute
hesitating, vacillating, indecisive, capricious, half-hearted, wavering

inducive ....
persuasive, encouraging, provocative, inciting, urging, seductive, recommendatory

dissuasive
discouraging, damping, intimidating, cautionary, deprecatory, threatening, ominous

active ....
energetic, lively, businesslike, busy, industrious, studious, officious, efficient

inactive
lazy, languid, listless, leisurely, sleepy, soporific, fatigued, tranquil, sloppy, dilatory

concordant ....
harmonious, amicable, congenial, peaceful, soothing, pacificatory, conciliatory, placatory, mediatory, diplomatic

discordant
dissentient, quarrelling, argumentative, irascible, aggravating, bellicose, aggressive, contentious, polemical, undiplomatic

lenient ....
gentle, mild, indulgent, tolerant, easy-going, permissive, accommodating

severe
harsh, stern, strict, intolerant, violent, forbidding, uncompromising

authoritative ....
official, commanding, dignified, majestic, imperious, dominant, self-assured, imposing, didactic, permitting

lacking in authority
unofficial, insignificant, undignified, anarchic, diffident, servile, unimposing

compelling ....
urgent, forceful, coercive, peremptory, bossy, insistent, authoritarian, demanding

uncompelling
unimportant, weak, feeble, unassertive, laissez-faire, innocuous

obedient ....
compliant, submissive, docile, meek, dutiful, loyal

disobedient
insubordinate, rebellious, recalcitrant, naughty, contumacious, subversive, seditious, disloyal

inducive — dissuasive

active — inactive

concordant — discordant

lenient — severe

authoritative — lacking in authority

compelling — uncompelling

obedient — disobedient

109

certain — uncertain

certain . . . .
sure, unequivocal, unambiguous, confident, believing, opinionated, dogmatic, trustful, convincing

uncertain
unsure, ambiguous, puzzled, vague, doubting, sceptical, incredulous, suppositional, distrustful, suspicious, unconvincing

open — secret

open . . . .
plain, clear, public, revelatory, undisguised, unreserved, blatant

secret
secretive, abstruse, cryptic, mysterious, reticent, cabalistic, conspiratorial, confidential, private

intelligent/thinking —
unthinking/unintelligent

intelligent/thinking . . . .
clever, wise, intellectual, shrewd, rational, erudite, knowing, thoughtful, discreet

unthinking/unintelligent
stupid, unwise, foolish, unintellectual, silly, irrational, fatuous, ignorant, indiscreet

assenting — dissenting

assenting . . . .
agreeing, consenting, acquiescent, concurring, admitting, confirmatory, affirmative

dissenting
disagreeing, refusing, protesting, querying, arguing, denying, retorting, negative, qualifying

110

other hand, it should not be easy to increase the number of continua, nor is it desirable for procedural reasons to have it any larger than necessary.

It will be recalled that the use of the continuum avoids polarising the terms on each side of the continuum as independent qualities, since such features are in a 'more than' and 'less than' relationship to some relevant implicit norm. Furthermore, co-hyponyms vary in the comparative degree to which they imply their superordinate key. For example, 'apprehensive' and 'afraid' are at different points on the 'fearing' half of their continuum. A continuum also allows for the specification of those attitudinal-tones which are 'mid-way' with respect to the extremes of their continua, e.g. 'half-satisfied', 'half-serious', 'semi-sophisticated', 'semi-optimistic', 'half-caring', 'semi-formal', 'half-willing', 'semi-official', 'half-certain'.

In this parameter of the CNP it is sufficient to work from the superordinate terms which are listed as pairs on the left-hand side of the index. Of course it is possible, and may be necessary (especially when inexperienced in the use of the index), to refer across to the hyponyms for clarification before selecting or rejecting a key, but at this stage in the processing one is not yet concerned with micro-level specification. It is when the activities are broken down into their functional subcategories, in the meaning processor, that the actual marking of each micro-function for attitudinal-tone takes place. Here, one starts the process by specifying the keys that may reasonably be expected in connection with an activity, given the particular input information on the social relationships, etc., that has previously been identified. On the receptive side, this specification is more a prediction of the keys that are likely to be met, given the same input information. The keys that are specified are only those that the participant *needs* to be able to understand or produce.

Here is an illustration of the working of this parameter for a particular participant (a customs officer).

8.0 COMMUNICATIVE KEY

Input
State the relevant input information from the following derivational sources:
[For example]

Participant
  Identity: mid-thirties; male; Fantasian.
Interaction
  Role-set identity: individuals; adult; mixed sex; Fantasian and UK
  speakers of British English, and some American.
  Social relationships: official to public; investigator to subject;
  authority to offender; male to female; stranger to stranger; adult
  to adult.
Setting
  Psychosocial environments: non-intellectual; ethical; mainly
  public; familiar physical; unfamiliar human; basically unhurried;
  formal; possibly authoritarian; argumentative; reserved;
  unsympathetic.
Instrumentality
  Command of medium: receptive and productive
Event
  Activities: all.

Communicative key

For each event, list the activities previously identified (in section 7),
and opposite each activity specify those keys which the participant
needs to be able to [i] produce (P), and [ii] recognise and understand (R), as applicable, in connection with that activity. The keys
should be selected from the *left-hand* column of the attitudinal-tone
index, and the specification should be based on the input information
above.
[For example]
7.1 Event: Customs officer checking for illegal export of goods.

Activities	Key (P)	Key (R)
7.1.1 Ensuring passenger understands regulations on illegal exports	courteous formal dissuasive	caring — indifferent certain — uncertain
7.1.2 Persisting with questioning/ interrogating suspect	discriminating cautious courteous patient resolute inducive	fearing cautious — incautious honest — dishonest resolute — irresolute unwilling certain — uncertain frivolous

Activities	*Key (P)*	*Key (R)*
7.1.3 Arguing over a	patient	hoping
discovered item	disinterested	displeased
	inexcitable	certain — uncertain
	formal	excitable — inexcitable
	authoritative	resolute — irresolute
	certain	inducive
	uncertain	dissenting
7.1.4 Impounding an	serious	discontented
item	formal	resentful
	authoritative	assenting — dissenting
7.1.5 Deciding in favour	content	grateful
of passenger	assenting	

n.b. *Each* event is processed for communicative key in this way.

The keys opposite an activity are all expected to be present in connection with that activity, either singly or in combination, i.e. one attitudinal-tone or more will be used to mark each micro-function subsequently processed from the activity. The keys in the productive column are those that the participant needs to be able to produce in his own speech or writing. The keys in the receptive column are those that the participant needs to be able to recognise and understand in the speech or writing of others.

Where both the antonymous keys of a continuum are specified together, e.g. caring — indifferent, it indicates that the participant must be able to handle one or both of them, or perhaps a 'mid-way' key, in connection with that activity. As one would expect, this kind of specification happens mostly in the receptive medium, since which of the possibilities actually occurs will depend on the particular interlocutor. On the productive side, an unseparated specification is more likely to indicate a mid-way key.

Of the derivational sources the most influential in the specification of key are social relationships and psychosocial environments. For example, in the illustration above, the lack of anything more favourable to the interlocutor than 'courteous' is mainly a result of finding 'reserved' and 'unsympathetic' among the input information for psychosocial environments. Also from this source, 'basically unhurried' is reflected in the specification of 'patient' for the activities at 7.1.2 and 7.1.3. The 'argumentative' environment and the 'investigator to subject' social relationship are reflected in the proliferation of keys such as 'excitable', 'inexcitable', 'inducive', 'dissuasive', 'resolute', 'irresolute', 'certain', 'uncertain', and 'dissenting'; while the specification of 'authoritative' and 'disinterested' are influenced by the social relationship 'official to public'. The 'ethical' aspect of the psychosocial environment and the potential or actual 'authority to offender' relationship with the interlocutor makes it necessary for the participant to interrogate a suspect tactfully ('discriminating') and cautiously, and it would clearly be a considerable advantage to him to be able to detect honesty or dishonesty, or at least vacillation ('irresolute'), in the way the interlocutor responds in English.

From the foregoing it will be clear that the variable being handled in this parameter of the CNP includes Gregory's (1967) tenor of discourse, Crystal and Davy's (1969) status, and what Joos (1961) calls style; but this variable goes well beyond the usual concern with social standing and degrees of formality. Joos uses the term 'style' for a usage-scale of five levels of formality.[4] Gregory raises the question of types of tenor other than personal tenor (of which Formal/Informal English are examples) and suggests a second category which he calls functional tenor, of which Didactic and Non-Didactic English are given as examples. Crystal and Davy agree that there are other categories of status (which they describe as the relative social standing between the participants) covering, for example, respect and politeness, but they deal mainly with the formal and informal categories. Leech and Svartvik (1975) add 'polite — familiar' as a third major pair of contrasting 'levels of usage', the others being 'formal — informal' and 'written — spoken'. All these authorities are concerned with analysing or describing varieties of English, or indicating the varieties to which particular forms of English belong, and their concentration on features such as formality may have much to do with the fact that such variation is 'perhaps the most noticeable' (Crystal and Davy, op. cit.). However, here one is not analysing or describing varieties but constructing a profile of communication needs for specific participants. Perhaps it is not surprising, therefore, that it is Richterich (1972) who is more illuminating in matters related to this variable. Although he gives only limited examples of 'social roles' (comparable to what are described here as social relationships) and what he calls 'psychological roles' (a perplexing use of 'role' for 'respect', 'affection', etc.), they are enough to show that a common concern is shared here. Finally, to emphasise the importance of Key as an independent variable in communication let us return to Hymes (1972): 'The significance of key is underlined by the fact that, when it is in conflict with the overt content of an act, it often overrides the latter (as in sarcasm).'

A simple way of characterising the variables in any act of communication is to ask the question: Who is communicating with whom, why, where, when, how, at what level, about what, and in what way? By using the model, one can now construct a profile of the communication needs of a particular participant or category of participant, in which account has *systematically* been taken of all these variables that determine or constrain the communication requirements of that participant.

NOTES

1 The use of this term derives from Hymes' (1972) notion of the speech event, although it is not being used in an identical sense.
2 In the micro-concept sense in which the term is being used — see Chapter 2, section 4.
3 See Chapter 2, section 5 for a full discussion of the important point that an activity is not ready for verbal realisation whereas a micro-function (suitably contextualised) is.
4 cf. Kirkwood (1973b) who uses Tarasov's five types of tonality (from Russian stylistics).

7

LANGUAGE SKILLS SELECTION

In this sector of the model, the profile of communication needs for a participant is interpreted in terms of the language skills required for its realisation. The customary division of language skill into listening, speaking, reading, and writing (the 'four skills', as they are often described), and their treatment as macro-concepts, will not serve here. In fact it is often inadequate for other purposes,[1] but there have been few major attempts to elaborate in detail on a comprehensive scale.

The term 'skill' is used here as a micro-concept, to be distinguished from the macro-concept of an activity, to which its relation is that of enabling factor to resultant activity. Thus, reading and understanding this piece of text (about skill as a micro-concept) is an activity which the reader is able to perform because he can, inter alia, follow relationships of thought between this sentence and the preceding and following ones. Moreover, he is enabled to do this through his understanding of the cohesive function of 'thus', indicating that what follows is an explanatory apposition to the previous statement, and 'moreover', which indicates that what follows reinforces the previous statement. One may say that the reader needs to be able to 'understand relations between parts of a text through the grammatical cohesion device of logical connecters' (a language skill) in order to be able to read and understand the passage (a communicative activity). It might also be noted that realising that the previous sentence is fulfilling the function of summarising the distinction under consideration is an example of another skill, viz. understanding the communicative value of sentences without explicit indicators. Here, there is no overt indication that the sentence is in a relation of summation to what has gone before. Activities, then, such as listening and taking notes[2] (on, for example, crop protection), are specified in the Communication Needs Processor; here, the skills required for the realisation of these activities are selected.

116

It was necessary, then, to identify these enabling factors and to organise them as a reference source from which systematic selection could be made. This resulted in the setting up of a taxonomy of language skills (see below). The organisation reflects the distinction between receptive (short for receptive-interpretive) and productive performance.

The formulation of the categories reflects a view of a language skill [S] as consisting of an operational element[3] [O] dominating a communicative feature [F] which in turn dominates any extension of the feature [E]. For example, in skill number 32.6 of our taxonomy, 'understanding' is the [O], 'relations between different parts of a text' is the [F], and 'through the grammatical cohesion device of logical connecters' is [E]. Taking skill number 4.3 as another example, we have:— articulating [O] sounds in connected speech [F]: reduction of unstressed vowels [E]. Other examples of [O] are 'discriminating', 'recognising', 'interpreting', 'expressing', 'expanding', 'reducing', 'skimming', 'initiating'; and other examples of [F] are 'attitudinal meaning' and 'indicators in discourse'. This view of a language skill may be characterised as the following rewrite rule: $S \rightarrow O + F + (E)$, where E is optional.

Sometimes the extension of the feature consists of the operational element and communicative feature rewritten at a finer level of delicacy $[o + f]$. Mostly, however, the extension takes the form of either a subcategorisation of the communicative feature $[f^s]$, or an instrumental subclassification of the communicative feature $[f^i]$, or both $[f^s + f^i]$. Examples of $[f^s]$ are 'reduction of unstressed vowels' (skill 4.3), and 'transition to another idea' (36.3); while examples of $[f^i]$ are 'through the grammatical cohesion device of logical connecters' (32.6), and 'through making inferences' (22.1). This provides another rewrite rule: $E \rightarrow f^s$ *or* f^i *or* $f^s + f^i$ *or* $o + f$. On occasion, it may be necessary to subcategorise further or to exemplify with functional or linguistic exponents.

This taxonomy consists of some two hundred and sixty skills subcategorised in fifty-four groups. It is hoped that this organisation will facilitate the process of selecting skills appropriate to previously specified activities.[4] The list is not exhaustive although it is hoped that no significant category has been omitted. The selection of such skills is affected by and weighted according to the values assigned in the target level guide (of the profile of needs) for the required size

117

and complexity of utterance or text, delicacy and range of skills, and speed and flexibility of communication, such values being constrained by the tolerance factor values for accuracy, repetition, etc. (see Chapter 5 above). For example, the specification of a low value for complexity in a particular context might mean that one would modify the selection of skill 27.1 to read ' . . . *common* explicit indicators', and that one would not select a skill such as 13.6 at all. On the other hand, a high value for complexity might mean that one would specify 'long noun phrases' for 28.1, and modify the selection of 32.4 to read ' . . . *heavy* ellipsis'.

Here follow some clarificatory or explanatory comments on the skills themselves. These comments are necessarily brief, as it would be outside the precise scope of this book to elaborate further on the items in the taxonomy. This is a major area for further research. Some selected reference sources have been included, where appropriate, and the user of this taxonomy may turn to them for further explanation or detail.

Groups 1–10, and 17–18

These are mostly motor-perceptual skills, receptive and productive, for both the spoken and written medium. The target level values for delicacy and speed, and for tolerance of error, repetition, and hesitation, will be reflected in the selection of these skills: either in the fact of a skill being selected or not, or in the modification of the wording of the skill, or in the eventual pedagogic treatment by the materials writer. A standard reference source for these spoken medium skills is Gimson (1970).

Groups 11–16

These are skills concerned with understanding and conveying meaning, especially attitudinal meaning, mainly through intonation. The approach to intonation followed here derives from Halliday (1963 especially, 1967 and 1970b; cf. also W.S. Allen, 1954), although the more widely used term 'nucleus' is preferred here to his 'tonic'. Since the meaning of intonation resides in the nucleus (i.e. choice of primary tone or position of nucleus), the distinctive communicative feature in each of the skills from 11.1 to 14.7 is expressed in terms of the nuclear syllable, and mention is not made of the non-significant behaviour of pre-heads, tails, etc. The relation between categories 11 and 13, and between 12 and 14, might be described as neutral to non-neutral group. For example, the utterance 'Where do you live?' heard as an exponent of 11.2 (nucleus on 'live') indicates a formal, neutral attitude on the part of the speaker to the addressee; whereas the same words, with the same pattern except for the rising nucleus, heard as an exponent of 13.2.1 indicates personal interest or sympathy; while the nuclear shift involved at 13.2.2 indicates surprise or uncertainty and also asks for the information to be repeated. A further significant variation, with the same words, would be the non-neutral position of the nucleus at 13.3, indicating that the speaker is insisting on the information which has not yet been forthcoming. Target level values for complexity and delicacy, as well as the tolerance factors for repetition, etc., will help determine the selection (and modification) here.

Group 19
The ability to handle these skills will save the non-native participant a lot of time spent in unnecessary recourse to a dictionary. 19.1.2 subdivides into prefixes and suffixes. A low value for reference (i.e. low tolerance of looking up words in dictionaries) in the target level guide would indicate the need to give these skills much more attention than they usually receive in a teaching programme. (Reference sources for 19.1 include Appendix 1 to Quirk et al. (1972) and Yorkey (1970), who also discusses 19.2.)

Groups 20–23
The ability to perform skills 20, 21, 22.1 and 23.1 appears to involve operating at a lower (or grosser) level of delicacy than that for related skills such as those at 32. Although they have, therefore, potentially very wide applicability, this does not mean that their effective pedagogic treatment may be taken for granted. This happens all too often in comprehension textbooks where the lack of an explicit method and systematic techniques for developing such skills results in questions that are in fact tests.

Groups 24–25
This is an illustrative set: more items can be added when necessary (see Leech and Svartvik (1975) as a reference source). The important areas of conceptual meaning listed here can, of course, be handled at

119

different levels of delicacy. For example, 24.1 will be required by both travel agents and engineers, but at a much higher level of delicacy for the latter.

Groups 26—27
These skills, in particular, relate psycholinguistic process to micro-function. 26.1 and 27.1 would be selected where the target level guide specified a lower level of complexity than would be needed to handle utterances where the communicative value is not explicitly stated. For example, if on entering the sitting room I say to my children 'the newspaper is all over the floor', they will collect it up and put it on a table. In other words they have understood that the utterance is an order (has the communicative value of ordering) even though the micro-function is not explicitly indicated. They understand the illocutionary force of the utterance, which overrides the propositional content contained in the (explicit) reference and predicate. Similarly, my unsolicited statement 'It's nearly midnight' is understood as a suggestion that they should go to bed, rather than as gratuitous information about the time. 26.2 and 27.2 are also important discourse level skills: for example, understanding that one part of a text has the communicative value of result in relation to another part of the text although there is no explicit indicator such as 'therefore'. A leading advocate of the importance of these skills has been Widdowson (e.g. 1971 and 1977a).[5]

Groups 28—33
The relations covered by the subcategories at 28 and 29 are intra-sentential and structural; those at 30—33 are inter-sentential and semantic. The former is a select list, whereas the latter is an attempt at indicating all the relations of that type which might be required. Quirk et al. (1972) is recommended as the major reference source for the former, and to it should be added Halliday and Hasan (1976) for the latter. Examples of subclasses of 'logical connecters'[6] (32.6 and 33.6) are reinforcement, reformulation, contrast, and cause. A few of the discourse cohesion skills involving understanding relations across sentence boundaries can be illustrated through the following piece of text (taken from Mackay and Klassen, 1975): 'Aberdeen Angus mature into good beef animals. So do Shorthorns and Friesians but the process is slower'. The following inter-sentential skills are needed to

understand this piece of text: 30.2 ('Shorthorns and Friesians' are in a hyponymous relation to 'animals'); 30.7 ('process' is a pro-form or general word for 'mature into good beef animals'); 32.2 ('slower', compared with that for Aberdeen Angus); (32.3 ('do' substitutes for 'mature into good beef animals'); 32.4 (there is ellipsis of 'than that for Aberdeen Angus' after 'slower'); 32.6 ('so' connects the two sentences in a relation of addition). Two textbooks containing exercise material and *explicit* problem-solving methods and techniques for *developing* some of these skills, as well as others (e.g. numbers 20 and 22), are Allen and Widdowson (1974)[7] and Munby (1968). See also Brumfit (1977).

Group 34
The skills in this set involve relating information in the text to information not contained in the text. Reference is exophoric (Halliday and Hasan, op. cit., p. 18) when the referent lies outside the text, in the situation, for example: 'This won't do', where 'this' refers to the unverbalised result of a piece of work.

Groups 35–39
These skills operate at the level of discourse coherence, and are especially pertinent for activities involving the reception or production of long spans of text, e.g. listening to lectures, presenting a paper, reading an article. The discourse 'indicators' referred to in 35 and 36 are called 'cues' by Yorkey (1970), 'linking signals' by Leech and Svartvik (1975), and 'signalling devices' by Heaton (1975), who is the only one to deal with the seventh of these skills. Between them these references also cover the skills in groups 37 and 38.[8] Whereas the skills in groups 35 and 36 can apply to both the spoken and the written medium, the first two of 37 and 38 apply only to the spoken, and the fourth is more suited to the written. The skills in group 39, which are not medium-specific, represent a different approach (suitable for different activities) from that in 37 and 38 to the problem of sorting out the main point or idea.

Groups 40–43
Whereas all the skills here are concerned with different aspects of summarising for different purposes, those in group 43 may be regarded as the basic equipment (to be added to a central skill such

as 39.1) for activities requiring the taking of full notes. For a single reference source for all the skills in 43, see Heaton (1975: especially his detailed treatment of 43.6). On 40—42 it should be pointed out that one is here concerned with skills that enable a participant to respond to real communication activities, not the often artificial exercise of the traditional précis question.[9]

Groups 44—46
Group 45 does not involve close scrutiny of the text; whereas the skills in 46 require rapid reading followed by intensive study, on a graded scale of complexity from 46.1 to 46.5. These valuable and often neglected skills are discussed and a method for developing them exemplified in Munby (1973). Group 44 consists of basic skills required for reference work.

Groups 47—49
These discourse skills, applicable mainly to the spoken medium, can be realised in different ways and at different levels of operation from the rudimentary to the advanced and sophisticated. In the parentheses following each skill an attempt has been made to exemplify the micro-function or indicate the type of communicative feature involved. Major references here include Sinclair and Coulthard (1975), and Candlin, Leather and Bruton (1974, 1976a and b).[10]

Group 50
It has been pointed out (e.g. Widdowson, 1971; White, 1974; Jones amd Roe, 1975) that the functions selectively listed here are of particular relevance to the production of text in activities of a scientific nature. See, for example, text materials such as Bates and Dudley-Evans (1976), Allen and Widdowson (1974—), and *Communication Skills in English* (1976).

Groups 51—54
Widdowson (1975), and Allen and Widdowson (1974), deal with the skills in groups 51—52 under the heading of 'Information Transfer'.[11] By 'transcoding' I mean using a different code of communication for the same message. Although labelled diagrams and graphs may be considered to be a semi-verbal, rather than a non-verbal means of communication, it seems to be a sufficiently distinct code of com-

munication to warrant the use of a term such as transcode. This has the advantage of being related to encode (turning message into form) and decode (turning form into message); and linking further with the use of the term 'recoding' to mean using different forms for the same message, i.e. the process involved in group 53. Finally, the direct and indirect relaying of information, group 54, seem to involve skills not quite covered anywhere else in the taxonomy.

It was mentioned above that this set of comments on the skills listed in this tentative taxonomy would of necessity be brief, but it is hoped that enough has been said to suggest lines and areas for further research. In Chapter 10 the working of this parameter for a particular input will be illustrated.

A taxonomy of language skills
1. Discriminating sounds in isolate word forms:
   1.1 phonemes, especially phonemic contrasts
   1.2 phoneme sequences
   1.3 allophonic variants
   1.4 assimilated and elided forms (esp. reduction of vowels and consonant clusters)
   1.5 permissible phonemic variation

2. Articulating sounds in isolate word forms:
   2.1 phonemes, esp. phonemic contrasts
   2.2 phoneme sequences
   2.3 allophonic variants
   2.4 assimilated and elided forms (esp. reduction of vowels and consonant clusters)
   2.5 permissible phonemic variation

3. Discriminating sounds in connected speech:
   3.1 strong and weak forms
   3.2 neutralisation of weak forms
   3.3 reduction of unstressed vowels
   3.4 modification of sounds, esp. at word boundaries, through
       3.4.1 assimilation
       3.4.2 elision
       3.4.3 liaison
   3.5 phonemic change at word boundaries
   3.6 allophonic variation at word boundaries

4. Articulating sounds in connected speech:
   4.1 strong and weak forms
   4.2 neutralisation of weak forms

     4.3   reduction of unstressed vowels
     4.4   modification of sounds, esp. at word boundaries, through
          4.4.1 assimilation
          4.4.2 elision
          4.4.3 liaison
     4.5   phonemic change at word boundaries
     4.6   allophonic variation at word boundaries

5. Discriminating stress patterns within words:
     5.1   characteristic accentual patterns
     5.2   meaningful accentual patterns
     5.3   compounds

6. Articulating stress patterns within words:
     6.1   characteristic accentual patterns
     6.2   meaningful accentual patterns
     6.3   compounds

7. Recognising variation in stress in connected speech:
     7.1   variation of word accentual patterns for rhythmic considerations (e.g.
          accent shift in 'level-stress' words)
     7.2   variation of word accentual patterns for meaningful prominence
     7.3   non-stressing of pronouns
     7.4   differentiating phrases from compounds

8. Manipulating variation in stress in connected speech:
     8.1   variation of word accentual patterns for rhythmic considerations (e.g.
          accent shift in 'level-stress' words)
     8.2   variation of word accentual patterns for meaningful prominence
     8.3   non-stressing of pronouns
     8.4   differentiating phrases from compounds

9. Recognising the use of stress in connected speech
     9.1   for indicating information units:
          9.1.1 content words and form words
          9.1.2 rhythmic patterning
     9.2   for emphasis, through location of nuclear accent
     9.3   for contrast, through nuclear shift

10. Manipulating the use of stress in connected speech
     10.1 for indicating information units:
          10.1.1 content words and form fords
          10.1.2 rhythmic patterning
     10.2 for emphasis, through location of nuclear accent
     10.3 for contrast, through nuclear shift

11. Understanding intonation patterns: neutral position of nucleus and use of
     tone, in respect of
     11.1 falling tone with declarative/moodless clauses
     11.2 falling tone with interrogative clauses beginning with a question-word

11.3 falling tone with imperative clauses
11.4 rising tone with 'yes/no' interrogative clauses
11.5 rising tone with non-final clauses
11.6 fall—rise tone with any clause type
11.7 rise—fall tone with any clause type
11.8 multi-nuclear patterns
11.9 tones with question-tags
11.10 others

12. Producing intonation patterns: neutral position of nucleus and use of tone, in respect of
12.1 falling tone with declarative/moodless clauses
12.2 falling tone with interrogative clauses beginning with a question word
12.3 falling tone with imperative clauses
12.4 rising tone with 'yes/no' interrogative clauses
12.5 rising tone with non-final clauses
12.6 fall—rise tone with any clause type
12.7 rise—fall tone with any clause type
12.8 multi-nuclear patterns
12.9 tones with question-tags
12.10 others

13. Understanding intonation patterns: interpreting attitudinal meaning through variation of tone or nuclear shift, viz.
13.1 rising tone with declarative/moodless clauses
13.2 rising tone with interrogatives beginning with a question word, having the nucleus in
13.2.1 end position
13.2.2 front position
13.3 same as 11.2 but nuclear shift to front position
13.4 rising tone with imperative clauses
13.5 falling tone with 'yes/no' interrogative clauses
13.6 same as 11.4 but nuclear shift to front position
13.7 others

14. Producing intonation patterns: expressing attitudinal meaning through variation of tone or nuclear shift, viz.
14.1 rising tone with declarative/moodless clauses
14.2 rising tone with interrogatives beginning with a question word, having the nucleus in
14.2.1 end position
14.2.2 front position
14.3 same as 12.2 but nuclear shift to front position
14.4 rising tone with imperative clauses
14.5 falling tone with 'yes/no' interrogative clauses
14.6 same as 12.4 but nuclear shift to front position
14.7 others

15. Interpreting attitudinal meaning through
    15.1 pitch height
    15.2 pitch range
    15.3 pause
    15.4 tempo

16. Expressing attitudinal meaning through
    16.1 pitch height
    16.2 pitch range
    16.3 pause
    16.4 tempo

17. Recognising the script of a language:
    17.1 discriminating the graphemes
    17.2 following grapheme sequences (spelling system)
    17.3 understanding punctuation

18. Manipulating the script of a language:
    18.1 forming the graphemes
    18.2 catenating grapheme sequences (spelling system)
    18.3 using punctuation

19. Deducing the meaning and use of unfamiliar lexical items, through
    19.1 understanding word formation:
        19.1.1 stems/roots
        19.1.2 affixation
        19.1.3 derivation
        19.1.4 compounding
    19.2 contextual clues

20. Understanding explicitly stated information

21. Expressing information explicitly

22. Understanding information in the text, not explicitly stated, through
    22.1 making inferences
    22.2 understanding figurative language

23. Expressing information implicitly, through
    23.1 inference
    23.2 figurative language

24. Understanding conceptual meaning, especially
    24.1 quantity and amount
    24.2 definiteness and indefiniteness
    24.3 comparison; degree
    24.4 time (esp. tense and aspect)
    24.5 location; direction
    24.6 means; instrument
    24.7 cause; result; purpose; reason; condition; contrast

25. Expressing conceptual meaning, especially
    25.1 quantity and amount
    25.2 definiteness and indefiniteness
    25.3 comparison; degree
    25.4 time (esp. tense and aspect)
    25.5 location; direction
    25.6 means; instrument
    25.7 cause; result; purpose; reason; condition; contrast

26. Understanding the communicative value (function) of sentences and utterances
    26.1 with explicit indicators
    26.2 without explicit indicators
        e.g. an interrogative that is a polite command; a statement that is in fact a suggestion, warning, etc. depending on the context; relationships of result, reformulation, etc., without 'therefore', 'in other words', etc.

27. Expressing the communicative value (function) of sentences and utterances
    27.1 using explicit indicators
    27.2 without explicit indicators

28. Understanding relations within the sentence, especially
    28.1 elements of sentence structure
    28.2 modification structure:
        28.2.1 premodification
        28.2.2 postmodification
        28.2.3 disjuncts
    28.3 negation
    28.4 modal auxiliaries
    28.5 intra-sentential connectors
    28.6 complex embedding
    28.7 focus and theme:
        28.7.1 thematic fronting; and inversion
        28.7.2 postponement

29. Expressing relations within the sentence, using especially
    29.1 elements of sentence structure
    29.2 modification structure:
        29.2.1 premodification
        29.2.2 postmodification
        29.2.3 disjuncts
    29.3 negation
    29.4 modal auxiliaries
    29.5 intra-sentential connectors
    29.6 complex embedding
    29.7 focus and theme:
        29.7.1 thematic fronting; and inversion
        29.7.2 postponement

30. Understanding relations between parts of a text through lexical cohesion devices of
    30.1 repetition
    30.2 synonymy
    30.3 hyponymy
    30.4 antithesis
    30.5 apposition
    30.6 lexical set/collocation
    30.7 pro-forms/general words

31. Expressing relations between parts of a text through lexical cohesion devices of
    31.1 repetition
    31.2 synonymy
    31.3 hyponymy
    31.4 antithesis
    31.5 apposition
    31.6 lexical set/collocation
    31.7 pro-forms/general words

32. Understanding relations between parts of a text through grammatical cohesion devices of
    32.1 reference (anaphoric and cataphoric)
    32.2 comparison
    32.3 substitution
    32.4 ellipsis
    32.5 time and place relaters
    32.6 logical connecters

33. Expressing relations between parts of a text through grammatical cohesion devices of
    33.1 reference (anaphoric and cataphoric)
    33.2 comparison
    33.3 substitution
    33.4 ellipsis
    33.5 time and place relaters
    33.6 logical connecters

34. Interpreting text by going outside it,
    34.1 using exophoric reference
    34.2 'reading between the lines'
    34.3 integrating data in the text with own experience or knowledge of the world

35. Recognising indicators in discourse for
    35.1 introducing an idea
    35.2 developing an idea (e.g. adding points, reinforcing argument)
    35.3 transition to another idea
    35.4 concluding an idea

35.5 emphasising a point

35.6 explanation or clarification of point already made

35.7 anticipating an objection or contrary view

36. Using indicators in discourse for
    36.1 introducing an idea
    36.2 developing an idea (e.g. adding points, reinforcing argument)
    36.3 transition to another idea
    36.4 concluding an idea
    36.5 emphasising a point
    36.6 explanation or clarification of point already made
    36.7 anticipating an objection or contrary view

37. Identifying the main point or important information in a piece of discourse, through
    37.1 vocal underlining (e.g. decreased speed, increased volume)
    37.2 end-focus and end-weight
    37.3 verbal cues (e.g. 'The point I want to make is . . . ')
    37.4 topic sentence, in paragraphs of
        37.4.1 inductive organisation
        37.4.2 deductive organisation

38. Indicating the main point or important information in a piece of discourse, through
    38.1 vocal underlining (e.g. decreased speed, increased volume)
    38.2 end-focus and end-weight
    38.3 verbal cues (e.g. 'The point I want to make is . . . ')
    38.4 topic sentence, in paragraphs of
        38.4.1 inductive organisation
        38.4.2 deductive organisation

39. Distinguishing the main idea from supporting details, by differentiating
    39.1 primary from secondary significance
    39.2 the whole from its parts
    39.3 a process from its stages
    39.4 category from exponent
    39.5 statement from example
    39.6 fact from opinion
    39.7 a proposition from its argument

40. Extracting salient points to summarise
    40.1 the whole text
    40.2 a specific idea/topic in the text
    40.3 the underlying idea or point of the text

41. Selective extraction of relevant points from a text, involving
    41.1 the coordination of related information
    41.2 the ordered rearrangement of contrasting items
    41.3 the tabulation of information for comparison and contrast

42. Expanding salient/relevant points into summary of
    42.1 the whole text
    42.2 a specific idea/topic in the text

43. Reducing the text through rejecting redundant or irrelevant information and items, especially
    43.1 omission of closed-system items (e.g. determiners)
    43.2 omission of repetition, circumlocution, digression, false starts
    43.3 compression of sentences or word groups
    43.4 compression of examples
    43.5 use of abbreviations
    43.6 use of symbols denoting relationships between states, processes, etc.

44. Basic reference skills: understanding and use of
    44.1 graphic presentation, viz. headings, sub-headings, numbering, indentation, bold print, footnotes
    44.2 table of contents and index
    44.3 cross-referencing
    44.4 card catalogue
    44.5 phonetic transcription/diacritics

45. Skimming to obtain
    45.1 the gist of the text
    45.2 a general impression of the text

46. Scanning to locate specifically required information on
    46.1 a single point, involving a simple search
    46.2 a single point, involving a complex search
    46.3 more than one point, involving a simple search
    46.4 more than one point, involving a complex search
    46.5 a whole topic

47. Initiating in discourse:
    47.1 how to initiate the discourse (elicit, inform, direct, etc.)
    47.2 how to introduce a new point (using verbal and vocal cues)
    47.3 how to introduce a topic (using appropriate micro-functions such as explanation, hypothesis, question)

48. Maintaining the discourse:
    48.1 how to respond (acknowledge, reply, loop, agree, disagree, etc.)
    48.2 how to continue (add, exemplify, justify, evaluate, etc.)
    48.3 how to adapt, as result of feedback, esp. in mid-utterance (amplify, omit, reformulate, etc.)
    48.4 how to turn-take (interrupt, challenge, inquire, dove-tail, etc.)
    48.5 how to mark time (stall, 'breathing-space' formulae, etc.)

49. Terminating in discourse
    49.1 how to mark boundaries in discourse (verbal and vocal cues)
    49.2 how to come out of the discourse (excuse, concede, pass, etc.)

49.3 how to conclude a topic (using appropriate micro-functions such as substantiation, and verbal cues for summing up, etc.)

50. Planning and organising information in expository language (esp. presentation of reports, expounding an argument, evaluation of evidence), using rhetorical functions, especially
50.1 definition
50.2 classification
50.3 description of properties
50.4 description of process
50.5 description of change of state

51. Transcoding information presented in diagrammatic display, involving
51.1 straight conversion of diagram/table/graph into speech/writing
51.2 interpretation or comparison of diagrams/tables/graphs in speech/writing

52. Transcoding information in speech/writing to diagrammatic display, through
52.1 completing a diagram/table/graph
52.2 constructing one or more diagrams/tables/graphs

53. Recoding information (expressing/understanding equivalence of meaning)
53.1 within the same style (e.g. paraphrasing to avoid repetition)
53.2 across different styles (e.g. from technical to lay)

54. Relaying information
54.1 directly (commentary/description concurrent with action)
54.2 indirectly (reporting)

NOTES

1 See Corder (1973) for a clear statement on the superficiality of this categorisation.
2 See Wingard (1971) for an account of different types of exercise used to train undergraduates in an L2 context to handle this activity.
3 cf. Corder's 'psycholinguistic process' (1973).
4 Without, of course, attempting to set out the ordered steps in the actual process of comprehension/production, although many of the skills listed are clearly involved.
5 See Allen and Widdowson (1974) for exercises on these skills.
6 The term 'logical connecters' follows Quirk et al. (op. cit.). cf. Halliday and Hasan's 'Conjunctive Relations' (op. cit., pp. 242–3).
7 Also the other books in the *English in Focus* series, edited by these authors. See also Widdowson (1976).
8 Specifically Leech and Svartvik on the second, and Yorkey, from whom we take the term 'vocal underlining' for 37.1, on the fourth.
9 See Bright and McGregor, 1970, pp. 168–73, for a clear discussion of this point.

10 Skills 48.3 and 48.5 come from Rivers (1968).
11 See also the other authors in the *English in focus* series; and cf. Yorkey (op. cit., pp. 142—60) for exercises on 51.

8

SOCIOSEMANTIC PROCESSING AND LINGUISTIC ENCODING

In the Meaning Processor component of the model the profile of communication needs for a participant is interpreted in terms of the micro-functions, marked for attitudinal-tone, which are required for its realisation. Where the course content specification is to focus on language skills, the micro-functions will appear as parts of certain skills, e.g. in groups 26, 27, 47, 48, 49, and 50, selected from the taxonomy of language skills (see Chapter 7). Where, however, the course content is to be specified mainly in terms of functions and forms, parts of the profile of needs are converted into units of meaning before being realised, in the Linguistic Encoder, as utterances or text. In the course of this chapter this sociosemantic processing and linguistic encoding will be illustrated.

Chapter 2 (pp. 42–47) discussed in some detail the kind of semantic unit with which one is here concerned and the argument for, and nature of, the conversion of communicative activities into such units of meaning. In the course of that discussion consideration was given to different and often interchangeable uses of terms like 'function' and 'act'. The conclusion was that we are concerned with function as a micro-concept, whence the term 'micro-function' for the units of meaning; that these units are semantic subcategories of a predominantly pragmatic as well as logical kind (rather than the kind found in conventional semantics), so that the conversion of activities into such micro-functions and their marking for attitudinal-tone can be described as essentially sociosemantic processing; that an activity is not ready for verbal realisation whereas a micro-function is; and that there are theoretical as well as pragmatic reasons for processing an activity into sociosemantic units before attempting its linguistic encoding. Some indication was also given of how a micro-function is marked for attitudinal-tone and subsequently realised as linguistic form.

Figure 17 summarises the relation between what may be called 'communicative' views of meaning as represented by leading protagonists in this field.

For a discussion of these positions, their relation to each other and points of difference (e.g. Wilkins' functional categories include items handled by Leech and Svartvik at their layer 2), see Chapter 2, pp. 42–4. In terms of this diagram, the types of meaning explicitly handled in the Meaning Processor come from Wilkins' categories of communicative function and modal meaning, Leech and Svartvik's layers 3 and 2, and Candlin's layer 3. Layer 4, which is concerned with textual cohesion and discourse coherence, is handled in the Language Skills Selector. It has been said that converting activities into their units of meaning at layer 1 is unlikely to be significant for subsequent encoding. In English, the semantico-grammatical or conceptual categories permeate activities in such a way that little or nothing would be gained (and a lot of effort expended) by their explicit specification among the cluster of micro-functions for each

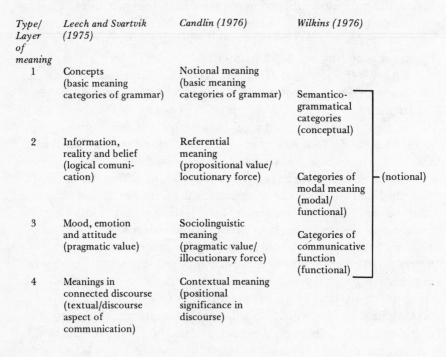

Type/ Layer of meaning	Leech and Svartvik (1975)	Candlin (1976)	Wilkins (1976)	
1	Concepts (basic meaning categories of grammar)	Notional meaning (basic meaning categories of grammar)	Semantico-grammatical categories (conceptual)	
2	Information, reality and belief (logical comunication)	Referential meaning (propositional value/ locutionary force)	Categories of modal meaning (modal/ functional)	(notional)
3	Mood, emotion and attitude (pragmatic value)	Sociolinguistic meaning (pragmatic value/ illocutionary force)	Categories of communicative function (functional)	
4	Meanings in connected discourse (textual/discourse aspect of communication)	Contextual meaning (positional significance in discourse)		

Figure 17 Some communicative views of meaning

activity. For example, 'In many, though not all, languages it is scarcely possible to produce a sentence without being involved in expressing time concepts' (Wilkins, 1976). The fact that conceptual meaning such as time relations, quantity, space, person deixis, agent, cause, etc., are found in the basic semantic categories of English grammar suggests that they do not need separate specification for each activity in order for appropriate linguistic encoding to take place, as is the case with the functional categories. Conceptual categories, then, will not be explicitly specified for each activity. However, specifically required subcategories from layer 1 (e.g. particular time relations, operations, purpose, condition) may be identified in the selection of language skills from groups 24, 25, 28 and 29 of the taxonomy.

What is needed, then, is an inventory of micro-functions from which to select the units required for the processing of the activities that have been specified. It was necessary to set up the item-bank from which to select the attitudinal-tones (see Chapter 6) for marking the functions; this had to be done since no such taxonomy existed. In the case of the functions, however, two reference sources now exist, Wilkins (1976, Ch. 2), and Leech and Svartvik (1975, Part 3), from which to select the items for such an inventory. In fact, a modified version of the Wilkins reference is used below as an inventory of micro-functions. The modifications, which consist essentially of certain omissions, are discussed below. Wilkins' coverage of the kind of items that are needed is more comprehensive than that of Leech and Svartvik, and his arrangement more suitable for our purpose. However, in many instances Leech and Svartvik's generally more detailed treatment of an item, with linguistic illustrations and often some stylistic information, provides clarification and guidance, where required, for both the sociosemantic processing and linguistic encoding. Items in the inventory are therefore cross-referenced to sections in Leech and Svartvik, where possible and appropriate.

Wilkins (1976: Chapter 2) is an updated version of Wilkins (1972). The notional categories which he presented for the first time in the earlier paper have been revised and re-presented in the later book. The alterations include the reorganisation of the earlier 'modality' category into scales of certainty and commitment with their own subdivisions and the moving of the old 'obligation imposed' and 'tolerance' subheads to the category of suasion; sorting out the

135

An inventory of micro-functions
(a modified form of Wilkins, 1976)

Note: the items listed at a subcategory are not intended to be exhaustive.

1. *Scale of certainty*   *Cross-references**
    Impersonalised   § 292—301

    1.1   Affirmation

    1.2   Certainty
          e.g. He is certain to be there.
              He must have known the answer beforehand.
              It has to come out here.

    1.3   Probability
          e.g. It is likely that he will be there
              He should be free in a minute.
              It ought to be a good programme.

    1.4   Possibility
          e.g. He is not certain to be there.
              It is possible that the bus will be late.
              It may be a good programme.

    1.5   Nil certainty
          e.g. He is certain not to be there.
              It is not possible to see him now.
              He can't have known the answer beforehand.

    1.6   Negation
    Personalised   § 302—6

    1.7   Conviction
        be + convinced, positive, sure, certain, confident,
        know, believe
        e.g. I am certain that he will be there.
            I am convinced that he knew the answer beforehand.
        [cf. the examples in 1.2 above for the difference
        between 'impersonalised' and 'personalised']

    1.8   Conjecture
        think, reckon, consider, expect, daresay, be of the
        opinion, presume, suppose, assume, trust, hope,
        surmise, guess, imagine, anticipate, foresee, predict,
        prophesy
        e.g. I think he will be there.
           I expect he will be free in a minute.

    1.9   Doubt
        doubt, wonder, be + sceptical, doubtful, dubious
        e.g. I doubt whether he will be there.
           I am not convinced that he is telling the truth.

    1.10 Disbelief
        above verbs + negative

*The references are to sections in Leech and Svartvik (1975).

e.g. I don't believe he will be there.
I am convinced that he is not telling the truth.

2. *Scale of commitment*
   2.1 Intention   § 334–8; 325; 355
       volition, will, unwilling; wish, want, desire, choice,
       inclination, prefer; mean, intention, contemplate,
       plan, propose; promise, undertake, assure, guarantee
       e.g. I'll pick you up at the station.
       I'd like to see the manager.
   2.2 Obligation   § 341–3
       obligation, necessity (social), onus, liability, duty,
       allegiance, responsibility, conscientiousness
       e.g. They must pay up by the end of the week.
       He ought to stop and help.
       I have to go now.
       You will have to produce the receipt.

3. *Judgement and evaluation*
   3.1 Valuation
       3.1.1 assess, judge, estimate, value; rank, place, grade
       3.1.2 misjudge, prejudge, overestimate
   3.2 Verdiction
       pronounce, rule, find, award
       3.2.1 Committal
             condemn, convict, proscribe, sentence
       3.2.2 Release
             release, exempt, acquit, discharge, let off, excuse;
             pardon, forgive, exculpate, exonerate, absolve,
             reprieve; conciliate, reconcile, extenuate
             e.g. I acquit you of this charge.
                 You are free to go.
                 It wasn't your fault.
   3.3 Approval   § 330
       approve, think well, appreciate, give credit, value;
       commend, praise, applaud; deserve, merit, entitle
   3.4 Disapproval
       disapprove, frown upon, deprecate, deplore; remon-
       strate, complain, allege, impute, accuse, charge;
       blame, reproach, disparage, reprimand, denounce,
       condemn
       e.g. You are to blame.
           It's your fault.
           I take strong exception to your behaviour.

4. *Suasion*   § 350
   4.1 Inducement
       persuade, propose, suggest, advise, recommend;

137

advocate, exhort, beg, urge, incite

e.g. (for suggesting [S] , and advising [A])

(1) I suggest that we go to the zoo. [S]

(1) I advise you to take the job. [A]

(2) Let's go to the zoo. [S]

(2) I think you should take the job. [A]

(3) Perhaps the zoo is open. [S]

(3) Why don't you take the job? [A]

4.2 Compulsion .... § 345–7; 344

command, order, dictate, direct, compel, force,
oblige; prohibit, forbid, disallow

4.3 Prediction .... § 300; 355; 351

predict, warn, caution, menace, threaten,
instruct, direct, invite

4.4 Tolerance (i.e. no hindrance offered to a proposal) .... § 340

allow, tolerate, grant, consent to, agree to, permit,
authorise

5. *Argument*

5.1 Information

5.1.1 stated/asserted .... § 272; 274

state, inform, tell, express, report, publish,
know; proclaim, declare, assert, emphasize,
affirm, maintain; argue, advocate, claim,
contend, protest

e.g. I don't want to appear dogmatic but I
was not responsible

5.1.2 Sought .... § 244–58

question, query; request .... § 348–9; 363

e.g. Would you mind shutting the window?

Could you shut the window?

If you shut the window, we'll soon get warm.

(all three examples are requests)

5.1.3 Denied .... § 273; 275

deny, refute, disclaim, protest; oppose, refuse,
decline, reject; disprove, confute, negate

5.2 Agreement .... *§ 279; 281–2

agree, concur, assent, acquiesce, consent; confirm,
corroborate, endorse, support, ratify, approve

5.3 Disagreement .... § 280

disagree, demur, dissent; dispute, contradict,
repudiate

e.g. That's nonsense.

---

*Leech and Svartvik's § 279 may be handled as agree [+ regretting] or [+ enthusiastic] , and
their § 281 as agree [+ qualifying] . Similarly, one would deal with their § 280 as disagree
[+ tactful] .

> I would disagree with you.
> I see things rather differently.

5.4 Concession   § 212; 361
       concede, grant, admit, yield, defer, allow, submit;
       renounce, withdraw, abjure, abandon, retract,
       resign; confess, apologise

6. *Rational enquiry and exposition*

6.1	proposition, hypothesis; corollary, presupposition	§ 284–7
6.2	substantiation, verification, justification, proof	
6.3	supposition, conjecture, assumption	§ 305–6
6.4	implication, inference, deduction, illation, conclusion, generalisation	§ 372
6.5	interpretation; demonstration, explanation	§ 373
6.6	classification, definition; illustration, exemplification	

       e.g. Thyme is a kind of herb used in cooking.
       The atomicity of an element is the number of
       atoms contained in one molecule of the element.
       (Both examples are definitions.)

7. *Formulaic communication*

7.1	greeting, farewell	§ 358–60
7.2	acknowledgement, thanks; regret, apology	§ 361; 363
7.3	good wishes, congratulations	§ 362
7.4	solicitude, condolence, commiseration	§ 362
7.5	attention signals	§ 254

       e.g. go on, mm.

earlier section on 'judgement' including the transfer of certain items; and the dropping of the 'interpersonal relations' category. All these amendments appear acceptable, though for the purposes of this book further modifications have been made.

Wilkins states that his inventory is 'intended as a tool in the construction of syllabuses' and is 'a simple inventory arranged as far as possible in rational fashion . . . The fact that the categories are presented as an inventory is not meant to suggest that they are mutually exclusive'. In the spirit of these statements, it has been possible to adopt, with certain alterations, his categories and exponential microfunctions of modal meaning and communicative function, with the exception of his categories of 'personal emotions' and 'emotional relations'. For present purposes, the whole of the former group and most of the latter are better treated not as functions but as attitudinal-tones that mark functions. Most of these items, which are handled in our attitudinal-tone index, have therefore been excluded, and those remaining have been included in a new category of formulaic communication. The conceptual subcategories or items (e.g. condition, purpose) have also been omitted from the rational enquiry and exposition category for the reason already given above for excluding his semantico-grammatical categories. Support for this approach is to be found in Leech and Svartvik (1975), who treat all such conceptual subcategories at the first layer of meaning. Minor alterations to the categories adopted concern the rearranging of micro-functions within a subcategory in a more rational way and separating the more homogeneous groups by a semi-colon; the subcategorisation of the micro-functions in the rational enquiry and exposition category; a few additions and omissions of items; and some different examples. It should be emphasised that these modifications are made in order to enable the resultant inventory of micro-functions to be used as an item-bank for the system, into which it therefore has to fit, and not in an attempt to supersede Wilkins' inventory.

An illustration will now be given of the working of the Meaning Processor, and then of the Linguistic Encoder, on the customs officer participant from Chapter 6 (see above for details). The event is 'Customs officer checking for illegal export of goods' (7.1), and our example concerns just one activity from that event, viz. 'Arguing over a discovered item' (7.1.3).

SOCIOSEMANTIC PROCESSING

Input: the profile of needs
Instruction: Interpret the profile in terms of required units of meaning by
    (1) converting each activity into micro-functions selected from the inventory of micro-functions
    (2) marking each micro-function, as far as possible, with one or more attitudinal-tones selected from the attitudinal-tone index.
n.b. (i) tones separated by a comma jointly constrain the function.
    (ii) the productive and receptive command of these units of meaning should be listed separately for each event.
Event 7.1

		Productive
Activity	*Micro-function*	*Attitudinal-tone*
7.1.3	1. obligation	—
	2. assess	[+ certain]

140

3. accuse		[+ formal], [+ dispassionate]
4. warn		[+ disinterested], [+ unruffled]
5. prohibit		[+ official], [+ formal]
6. assert	1.	[+ authoritative], [+ calm], [+ retorting]
	2.	[+ authoritative], [+ forbearing]
7. maintain	1.	[+ patient]
	2.	[+ imperturbable]
8. question		[+ detached], [+ patient]
9. query	1.	[+ sceptical]
	2.	[+ suspicious]
10. reject	1.	[+ correct], [+ unequivocal]
	2.	[+ doubting]
	3.	[+ regretting]
11. agree		[+ official]
12. contradict	1.	[+ dispassionate], [+ calm], [+ formal]
	2.	[+ retorting], [+ unequivocal]
13. defer		[+ doubting], [+ impartial]
14. interpretation		[+ patient], [+ authoritative], [+ unambiguous]
15. classification		[+ authoritative]

Receptive

Activity	Micro-function		Attitudinal-tone
7.1.3	1. wish	1.	[+ hopeful], [+ composed]
		2.	[+ adamant]
	2. exempt	1.	[+ half-hoping], [+ suppositional]
		2.	[+ confident]
	3. beg		[+ apologetic], [+ frantic], [+ urging]
	4. suggest		[+ hoping]
	5. advise		[+ intimidating]
	6. invite		[+ seductive]
	7. state	1.	–
		2.	[+ regretting]
	8. maintain	1.	[+ certain], [+ adamant]
		2.	[+ exasperated]
	9. contend		[+ protesting]

141

10. question	1. [+ annoyed], [+ protesting]
	2. [+ tense], [+ suspicious]
11. deny	1. [+ cool], [+ firm]
	2. [+ retorting], [+ angry]
	3. [+ wavering]
12. dispute	1. [+ annoyed]
	2. [+ incredulous]
13. concede	[+ half-certain], [+ qualifying]
14. verification	[+ convincing]
15. deduction	[+ sanguine]
16. explanation	1. [+ unruffled], [+ retorting]
	2. [+ disconcerted], [+ unsure]
	3. [+ vacillating]
17. conjecture	1. [+ optimistic]
	2. [+ wavering]

Five points of procedure should be noted. Firstly, the possible selection of items from section 1 of the inventory of micro-functions should be left until after the attitudinal-tone marking stage. One is then in a better position to consider whether, for that particular activity, there is any need for a semantic element such as 'certainty' as a function in itself, in addition to any specification that may already have been made of it as a tone marking a function, e.g. assess [+ certain]. In the above example nearly all the instances of certainty or the lack of it appear as attitudinal-tones. Secondly, some additional tones, belonging to keys other than those originally predicted in the profile of needs, may need to be used. These extra markings will suggest themselves once the particular functions are specified and especially when the interaction of one function with another is considered. In the example 'retorting' (productive) and 'regretting' (productive and receptive) have been added.[1] Thirdly, when in doubt about what tone or tones to assign to a particular function, the kind of language realisation that may be expected for that function should be considered. Later, at the linguistic encoding stage, the actual choice of language will depend, in addition to the attitudinal-tone marking and factors such as the target level specification, on the influence of other language forms required for adjacent functions as well as the language specified for the interlocutor. The eventual choice of language realisation for that function may turn out to be the same as that envisaged at this stage but it may also be different.

142

This procedure should enable one to handle the less obvious instances; only in those cases where the function seems to be positively neutral with regard to any of the possibilities, should no tone be assigned. Fourthly, the order of the micro-functions listed for each activity reflects (with the exception of items from section 1) the order of the inventory which has been worked through sequentially. Rearranging them to reflect their real order of occurrence within the activity seems possible or worthwhile only in the case of highly structured activities with reasonably predictable sequential development. Also, such rearrangement, if it is to be done at all, is better left until after the linguistic encoding stage, and in any case seems to be a matter more for the materials producer than the syllabus designer (cf. Bung, 1973b; and Candlin et al., 1976a). Fifthly, careful pruning of unnecessary tones, when reviewing initial specifications, will offset any tendency to over-mark a function during the first draft stage.

The following comments illustrate the kind of thinking behind the selection and marking of items in the above example.

Productive
1. Difficulty in deciding whether *obligation* or *liability* (or both) should be selected led to the choice of the former on the grounds that, being the broader term, it might also include the latter. This principle is likely to be applied wherever the choice between two or three similar micro-functions is not clear.
2. It may be worth mentioning that section 3.2 of the inventory was passed over since productively it will apply to the subsequent activities (see Chapter 6) but not to the one under present consideration. The point here is that one has to guard against the premature or misplaced specification of functions and not simply the irrelevant. This also applies to the specious or unnecessary assigning of attitudinal-tones.
3. The choice of attitudinal-tone for *accuse* is crucial if the participant is to avoid unnecessary confrontation. Using the profile of needs one can see that the social relationship between the customs officer and passenger is, in this activity, potentially authority—offender as well as actually official—public, and that the psychosocial environment is public, formal, and unsympathetic. With these factors in mind, by marking this function as [+ formal], [+ dispassionate] one seeks to ensure that the resultant language is appropriate for this

143

participant with this interlocutor. Increasing the double tone marking had been considered but, for reasons given at the end of the previous paragraph, this was not done. Here, the further marking of this function with, for example, [+ authoritative] would add little or nothing to the constraints provided by the tones already specified.

4. As might be expected with this kind of activity, many of the functions, nos. 6–13, come from the category of argument, the tone markings deriving from, inter alia, the investigator–subject relationship. Further, five of these subdivide into separate sociosemantic units. For example, in item 10 the customs officer has to be able to reject something said by the passenger in a correct and unequivocal way on one occasion (10.1), in a tone indicating doubt (10.2) on another, and regret (10.3) on a third. It might be worth noting that these are three different units of meaning, whereas item 12.1 is one unit where the three tones all operate at the same time to determine the manner of the contradicting.

5. The tone marking [+ unruffled] for *warn* indicates that one expects this function to be a response rather than an initiative. In fact it is the participant's reaction to the unacceptable pressure and blandishments of the interlocuter's advice [+ threatening] and invite [+ seductive] respectively. Items 4, 6, 7, 10.1 and 10.3 are responses to pressures of different kinds from the interlocutor, the tone markings reflecting the stranger–stranger, adult–adult social relationship, in an ethical, unhurried, formal, and reserved environment.

6. In item 8 the participant is an official seeking answers he requires from a member of the public, whereas in item 9 he is the investigator on the offensive against his subject.

7. The triple tone marking for *interpretation* caters for a basically unhurried situation where the participant is expected to show that he knows what he is talking about in his official capacity. Item 15 is subsumable under 14 but is listed separately since it may be required independently of 14. These functions come from section 6 of the inventory, which contains the potentially longest language realisations. The nature of these functions is such that they often subsume other functions.

8. In this activity, on the productive side, there is no sign of the tone [+ apologetic] ; and [+ courteous] has disappeared (without being replaced by [+ discourteous]) after being used in previous activities in this event. This is because the customs officer is arguing over a *discovered* item in an unsympathetic and reserved environment.

Receptive

1. Generally speaking the receptive side is more likely to contain single tone markings and more alternative or different ways of marking the same function than the productive side, since it is less easy to predict than to specify. Usually the participant has to be able to understand more alternative possibilities than he has to produce.

2. Items 3—6 constitute functions one or more of which the participant may have to understand if his interlocutor resorts to suasion rather than argument. If the passenger is in the wrong, such tactics would reflect the offender—authority social relationship specified in the profile. The triple tone marking for *beg* indicates that one has something more specific in mind than whatever may be expected for *suggest*. Item 5 is the result of one's deciding that the participant in this situation is more likely to receive a threat couched in the form of *advice* than as an open *threat*.

3. The blank marking at 7.1 indicates the stating of information in a positively neutral way, as distinct from 7.2 where the almost formulaic 'I'm afraid . . . ' is expected.

4. Unlike the official, who is expected to contain his feelings of irritation or even outrage towards the public, the member of the public sometimes displays his displeasure, the different forms of which mark out 8.2, 10.1, 11.2, and 12.1.

5. The selection of a particular item from its own subcategory of similar looking functions, such as those at 5.1.3 and 5.3 of the inventory, is not always straightforward. Firstly, there is the similarity between the two subcategories themselves, information denied and disagreement, to resolve,[2] and then there is the similarity within each group. In this example, the choice and markings at 11 and 12 predict the way one expects the passenger to react to the assessment, accusation, and certain questions of the customs officer. Together with the items at 1.2, 8, 9, and 10, these units reflect the (indignant) subject to (reserved) investigator relationship in an argumentative and unsympathetic environment.

6. The passenger's *explanation* will be in response to the customs officer's *question* and to his *contradict*. These items at 16, since they come from section 6 of the inventory, will be expected to subsume other micro-functions such as *disagree* or *deny* or *exempt* (without, of course, replacing their independent specification elsewhere). The

145

participant needs to be able to recognise and understand such functions and their tones, especially markings such as [+ wavering].

7. The complex unit of meaning at 13 is also something the participant must be able to understand. One expects that the partial *concession* is to be in respect of more than one aspect, but with the same tone marking combination of the midway [+ half-certain] and the very useful [+ qualifying]. Such a unit, as with 16.2, anticipates the possibility of the offender—authority relationship indicated in the profile.

8. The unit at 17 is the only instance (productive or receptive) where it has been felt necessary to specify a function from section 1 of the inventory. For the rest these semantic elements have appeared as tone markings from the certain—uncertain key continuum, perhaps overlapping a little into tones fron the resolute—irresolute continuum.

It will now be possible to look a little further at some of these items by turning to their language realisations.

LINGUISTIC ENCODING

Input: units of meaning.

Instruction: encode each unit of meaning, taking account of dialect and target level requirements, and referring back to the profile as necessary.

n.b. (i) use the same numbering for the language realisations as for the meaning units, listing separately for productive and receptive command

(ii) use slant lines to indicate alternative language forms for the same meaning unit

(iii) use diacritics only where necessary, viz. where significant intonation might otherwise be missed.

Language realisations

Productive

1. You will have to produce the receipt/clearance certificate.
2. I am sure that this is an original work of art.
    Your _____ falls into category B.
3. You have been discovered attempting to export this illegally.
4. I don't think you should continue in this way. It will not help your case.
    I hope you are not making an improper suggestion.

5.   Section _____ of the _____ Act forbids the exporting of _____.

6.1   I can assure you I am not mistaken. It's my business to recognise such items.

6.2   Look, I'm in charge here. You have to deal with me.

7.1   Yes, I do understand your point but that does not alter the matter. You still have to have a clearance certificate.

7.2   Shouting at me won't help. You still haven't explained it satisfactorily.

8.   Where did you get this from?
        Why did you not declare this item when I asked if you had anything to declare?
        Why did you not obtain a clearance certificate from the National Museum?
        Where is the receipt?
        Can you verify that?

9.1   Is this something one is likely to overlook?
        That's hardly likely, is it?
        A trader told you that and you believed him?

9.2   Where did you buy it?

10.1   I cannot accept that.
        We are not allowed to make exceptions.

10.2   I find that difficult to believe.

10.3   I'm afraid that's not possible.

11.   I accept that/Yes, that is in order.

12.1   If you thought that, why did you attempt to conceal it? The way it has been packed shows that you did.

12.2   No, it's not obscure, and in any case it is your responsibility to find out about these things. Ignorance of the law is no excuse.

13.   It might be a copy, as you suggest, but I doubt it. However, I will obtain a ruling from the Controller.

14.   The Act states that certain goods are not exportable except under special licence. These goods include certain objects of indigenous art, and the National Museum decides whether an object falls within the terms of the Act. This means that, in order to avoid any possible inconvenience with the Customs, you should have obtained a clearance certificate from the National Museum.

15.   For the purposes of the Act, objects of indigenous art fall into three categories: A. original and valuable; B. original and semi-valuable; C. other. A special licence is needed for category A and a clearance certificate for category B.

Receptive (example realisations)

1.1   I would like to see the Controller.

1.2   I insist on seeing the Controller.

2.1   I would have thought that was exempt/I assumed that it was not liable.

2.2   I'm sure it isn't liable.

3.   I'm terribly sorry I haven't got a clearance certificate but couldn't you possibly make an exception, just this once? Please!

4.   You could decide that it is a category C item.

5.   Well, you had better believe me. I happen to be a friend of _____ and I don't think he would be happy with the way you treat a visitor to your country.

6.   I wonder if you and I could come to some . . . arrangement.

7.1   I bought it from _____ in _____.

7.2   I'm afraid I've lost it.

8.1   Look, I *know* that isn't an original. In any case I still say it can't be worth anything.

8.2   How many more times do I have to tell you! I didn't know about this regulation/I did not think it was liable.

9.   You can't expect people to comply with an obscure regulation – which no one has mentioned to me until now.

10.1   How am I supposed to know that a clearance certificate is required for this?

10.2   How do you know that this is an original? Can't you be mistaken?

    Why should I accept your valuation?

10.1/2   Why/Why not?

11.1   No, I wasn't/That's not true.

11.2   I was not attempting to conceal it. How dare you suggest that!

11.3   No, it's not. Well, I don't think it is, is it?

12.1   That's ridiculous! Why on earth should I have a clearance certificate for a common piece of local craft?

12.2   You can't be serious! Anyone can tell this is a common copy.

13. Alright, it's possible I need a certificate, but I don't see how I could have got one.
    Even if it is an original, I wouldn't have thought it was worth anything.

14. Here is the receipt from _____, a reputable art and craft shop. You can see how much it cost, which shows that it belongs to category C.

15. I assumed it was not liable because it is only a copy.

16.1 It's packed like that to give it protection in transit/to prevent it damaging other articles in the case.
    I simply overlooked it.
    The trader/person I bought it from said it wasn't necessary to get a clearance certificate for non-original pieces of local art.

16.2 Oh dear! Well, you see, I did not pack this myself — a firm of packers did. Perhaps this is how they normally do things.

16.3 Nobody told me I had to have a clearance certificate for such items, well, not at least until a few days ago — and then it was too late to do anything about it, I'm afraid.

17.1 I expect I've got it somewhere in these papers.

17.2 I thought I put it in this folder. Or`did I?

The following comments illustrate the kind of thinking behind the selection of some of the language realisations. I begin with general observations about the dialect and target level constraints from the profile of needs (not shown in Chapter 6).

Dialect. The participant needs to be able to produce Standard Fantasian English, with the General Fantasian accent; and to understand Standard English and Standard Fantasian English, spoken mainly with RP or the General Fantasian accent. Some Fantasians use English as a lingua franca since the country is multilingual. It would of course be desirable if the participant were also able to cope with the regional accent of any major group of interlocutor with whom he has regular contact.

Target level. The following is the target level guide for the receptive and productive command of spoken English:

6.1 *Dimensions*			Rec.	Prod.
6.1.1 Size	— of utterance		3	2/4
6.1.2 Complexity	— "	"	5	3/4
6.1.3 Range	— "	functions/forms	2	2
6.1.4 Delicacy	— "	" "	5/6	5

149

6.1.5 Speed	— of communication	4/5	3
6.1.6 Flexibility	— " "	4	2

6.2 *Conditions*

Tolerance of:	Rec.	Prod.
6.2.1 error	2	3/4
6.2.2 stylistic failure	2	2
6.2.3 reference	3	3
6.2.4 repetition	4	—
6.2.5 hesitation	—	3

From this one can see that, on the *productive* side, the participant needs to control a narrow range of functions and forms involving a generally small size of utterance (although the latter may increase on occasion). However, the complexity of the utterances rises to middling while their delicacy can be fairly high. The tolerance of linguistic error is moderately high, compared with a fairly low tolerance of stylistic failure. He needs to speak quite fluently although a fairly low speed is acceptable. On the *receptive* side, he has to be prepared to cope with utterances of fairly high complexity and delicacy with a rather low tolerance level of their misunderstanding. However, such utterances are in general of fairly short length and from a restricted range; and he can get things repeated easily enough, which is helpful since his interlocutors will have different accents and may on occasion speak quite quickly.

Productive

1. At item 2, although both utterances are language realisations of assess [+ certain], it is interesting to note that the second becomes so by following item 15 whereas the first needs no such context since it has its own verbal indicator of conviction.

2. Without the [+ formal] tone the utterance at item 3 could read 'We've caught you red-handed trying to smuggle this _____ out of the country', and without the [+ dispassionate] it might include the speaker's culturally-determined view on the iniquity of the attempt.

3. The utterances at item 4 exemplify the target level specifications for complexity and delicacy. These are quite sophisticated ways of warning, stylistically appropriate to the social relationship and psycho-social environment discussed above, without being grammatically complicated.

4. Each of the three tones marking the function *assert* (6.1) can be
seen in its language realisations: [+ calm] in 'I can assure you . . . '
and the low pitch; [+ retorting] in the negation of the interlocutor's
10.2; and [+ authoritative] in the second sentence's reinforcing of
the assertion in the first. One might also note that the term 'assure'
here is being used to help make an assertion rather than an assurance.
5. The difference between the two realisations of *maintain* lies in
their attitudinal emphases. Patience emerges from 7.1, imperturb-
ability from 7.2.
6. All the questions listed at 8 are asked in a detached and patient
way. This distinguishes them from the very different kind of utterance at 9, where the rising nucleus on the first syllable of 9.2 makes
it into a suspicious query while scepticism is produced through the
fall—rise intonation of the three queries at 9.1. The relatively high
value for delicacy in the target level guide allows us to specify these
realisations.
7. The short utterances at 10 are typical of the *information denied*
subcategory, to be contrasted with the relatively much longer utterances at 12 which are to be found as realisations of functions in the
disagreement subcategory of the inventory.
8. The language realisations at 9, and 12—15, are at the upper end of
the target level specifications for size, complexity and delicacy. The
participant should be able to handle 14, especially as he is not
expected to be rapid in his speech. Item 15 is deceptively straightforward. It would be very satisfactory if the customs officers were
able to produce *interpretation* and *classification* of this order.

Receptive
1. In item 3 the [+ frantic] , [+ urging] marking required is realised
through the use and heavy stressing of 'terribly', 'possibly', 'just this
once', and 'Please!' (including its end position). This may be contrasted with the lack of an overt verbal indicator for the [+ hoping]
tone of item 4 where it is the choice of linguistic form for the function, including the rising intonation on the last word, which makes
this an appropriate realisation for a hopeful suggestion.
2. The [+ exasperated] tone of 8.2 is expressed through the introductory 'How many more times . . . '. One might note here that the
second sentence in the utterance is a *maintain* because of its position
in the discourse and not because of anything in the sentence itself.

The same point about discourse position applies to the second sentence of the utterance encoding *dispute* at 12.2.

3. The wavering denial of 11.3 is realised through its fall—rise intonation and question tag. Other ways of encoding irresolution can be seen at 17.2 and 16.3

4. It is worth noting the use of the attitudinal-tone [+ qualifying] from the 'dissenting' key. The participant needs to be able to realise when his interlocutor is conceding only part of his argument or conceding a point while continuing to dispute its application. In the language realisations at 13 the concession contained in the first clause is qualified by the second clause. According to the specification this unit of meaning is not only a partial concession but also a half-certain one. This tone is realised by the words 'even if' and 'it's possible'. This sociosemantic unit and its realisation exemplifies the higher levels of delicacy with which this participant has to cope.

5. Item 15 is worth a closer look. The utterance 'I assumed it was not liable because it is only a copy' might be regarded as a realisation of (A) conjecture [+ confident], or (B) exempt [+ suppositional], or (C) deduction [+ sanguine]. Without the clause of reason it would be either A or B, depending on what is being emphasised. However, with the clause of reason it is not so much a confident conjecture or suppositional exemption as the sanguine deduction that is required in this case.

6. In the nature of its function an *explanation* may consist of one or more subsumed constituent functions, and the size of utterance which realises it will vary from quite short to very long. In view of this target level guide value for size of utterance, the participant is not expected to deal with anything longer than 16.3.

In conclusion it should be pointed out that the above specification of language realisations (productive and receptive) is based on introspection* or native-speaker intuition, augmented by reference to authoritative sources and some familiarity with the situation. Until such time as the kind of bank of stylistic information mentioned in Chapter 2 becomes available (a distant prospect in view of the amount of research required), it will be necessary to use a mixture of

*Following the argument used by Wilkins (1972) who prefers a more 'subjective approach which can be of some immediate practical value' since 'research into the realisation of different communicative functions is a task that would occupy many linguists for many years'.

intuition, field observation or study, appropriate informants, and authoritative reference texts. Questionable cases can always be checked out empirically.

Finally, it should be emphasised that a specification of socio-semantic units and their language realisations, such as have been processed above, constitutes a *minimal set* for that particular activity and its keys. It is beyond the scope of this book to attempt a comprehensive specification, but it *is* suggested that such sets provide the materials writer with the necessary guideline in terms of needs-related functions and forms. This minimal set is intended to embody the essence of what is required; alternative realisations and additional items are a bonus.

NOTES

1 The number of such additions may be unnecessarily high while the operation of the model is unfamiliar. This should decrease to an acceptable level with experience in its use.
2 Which is done following Leech and Svartvik (1975) in which affirmation and denial are taken to be concerned with fact whereas agreement and disagreement have to do with judgement or opinion.

9

THE OPERATIONAL INSTRUMENT

This chapter consists of the model presented as a full operational instrument for specifying target communicative competence. The parts of this instrument have been set out and discussed in the preceding chapters.

The instrument enables its user to construct a profile of the communication needs of a particular participant or category of participant, and then to convert the profile into the needs-related specification of syllabus content.

Notes for the user
1. This instrument assumes that the user has read the preceding chapters on the processing model and its parts. This is essential. Here, therefore, there are no definitions, explanations, examples, references, etc.
2. The user is referred to Chapter 10 for examples of specifications or answers at each heading or subheading.
3. Where an item is not applicable to that particular participant, write N/A.

For the successful use of this operational instrument, the syllabus designer is strongly urged to refer to the appropriate chapter on each section of the model.

PART ONE
PROCESSING THE PROFILE OF COMMUNICATION NEEDS

0.0 PARTICIPANT

Give details of the participant's identity and language as follows:

0.1 Identity
0.1.1 Age   [specify either exactly or in broad terms]

0.1.2 Sex
0.1.3 Nationality
0.1.4 Place of residence

0.2 Language
0.2.1 Mother tongue
0.2.2 Target language
0.2.3 Present level/command of the target language:
zero/false beginner/elementary/lower intermediate/upper
intermediate/advanced
0.2.4 Other language(s) known
0.2.5 Extent of command (in broad terms) of 0.2.4

1. PURPOSIVE DOMAIN

1.1 ESP classification
Is the purpose for which English is required occupational or educational?
1.1.1 If *occupational*, will it be pre-experience or post-experience
ESP?
1.1.2 If *educational*, will it be discipline-based or school subject
ESP?
1.1.2.1 If discipline-based, will it be pre-study or in-study ESP?
1.1.2.2 If school subject, will it be independent or integrated
ESP?

1.2 Occupational purpose
1.2.1 *Specific occupation*
State the occupation for which English is required.
1.2.2 *Central duty*
Identify the central duty of that occupation (if different from
1.2.1).
1.2.3 *Other duties*
Identify other known duties, if any, for which English is needed.
1.2.4 *Occupational classification*
Using the framework provided, classify the occupation by matching, as appropriate, the type of worker on the vertical axis with
the field of work on the horizontal axis (e.g. technical officer in
industry).

Field of work

Type of worker	commerce/industry	public administration	liberal professions	science	armed forces	entertainment/the arts	utilities/services	?
	[i]	[ii]	[iii]	[iv]	[v]	[vi]	[vii]	[viii]
[a] manual worker: skilled/semi-skilled/unskilled								
[b] clerical officer/ administrative assistant								
[c] technical officer/ technical representative								
[d] manager/ senior administrator								
[e] professional practitioner								
[f] officer								
[g] artiste/sportsman								

Occupational classification framework

1.3 Educational purpose

1.3.1 *Specific discipline*
State the specific discipline or subject for which English is required.

1.3.2 *Central area of study*
Identify the central area of study in which the participant will be engaged.

1.3.3 *Academic discipline classification*
Select, as appropriate, from the following: mathematics/physical science/humanities/social science/biological science/medicine/ engineering/education.

2.0 SETTING

2.1 Physical setting: spatial

2.1.1 *Location*

2.1.1.1 *Country*

In what country does the participant need to use English?

2.1.1.2 *Town*

In what town does the participant need to use English?

2.1.1.3 *En route*

If English is required while en route, specify the appropriate setting:

in flight/on board ship/in train/on bus/in car.

2.1.2 *Place of work* (occupational)

In what occupational premises will the participant need English? Specify, as appropriate, from the following list, supplying the item where necessary:

2.1.2.1 hotel, restaurant, inn, cafe . . .

2.1.2.2 department store, shop, showrooms, market . . .

2.1.2.3 factory, workshop, work site, power station, laboratory . . .

2.1.2.4 company office, government office . . .

2.1.2.5 airport, docks, railway/bus station, post office . . .

2.1.2.6 school, university, research institute, conference room . . .

2.1.2.7 hospital, surgery, law court, church, bank . . .

2.1.2.8 barracks, camp, police station . . .

2.1.2.9 theatre, hall, recording/broadcasting studio, sports arena, night club . . .

2.1.2.10 private house . . .

and give the name of the place of work, if known.

2.1.3 *Place of study and study setting*

Give the name and type of the educational institution where the participant needs English:

2.1.3.1 university/college/institute/secondary school/primary school

For which of the following academic study settings is English required:

2.1.3.2 lecture room/theatre

2.1.3.3 classroom

2.1.3.4 laboratory/workshop

2.1.3.5 seminar/tutorial

2.1.3.6 private study/library

2.1.4 *Other places*

In what other places will the participant need English?

157

2.1.5 *Extent: size of institution*
Is the place where English will be used: small/medium/large?
2.1.6 *Extent: scale of use*
Does the participant need to use English:
internationally/nationally/locally?

2.2 Physical setting: temporal
2.2.1 *Point of time*
When is English required most?
2.2.2 *Duration*
For approximately how many hours per day/week is English
required?
2.2.3 *Frequency*
Is English required regularly/often/occasionally/seldom?

2.3 Psychosocial setting
What is the psychosocial setting in which the participant will use
English? Using the inventory of psychosocial environments, on each
applicable continuum select the appropriate element, modifying as
necessary (e.g. non-intellectual, usually noisy, fairly demanding).

Inventory of psychosocial environments

2.3.1	culturally similar	—	culturally different
2.3.2	age/sex discriminating	—	age/sex non-discriminating
2.3.3	intellectual/thinking	—	non-intellectual/unthinking
2.3.4	aesthetic/refined	—	non-aesthetic/unrefined
2.3.5	ethical*	—	non-ethical
2.3.6	sporty/recreational	—	non-sporty
2.3.7	religious/ritualistic	—	secular
2.3.8	political	—	apolitical
2.3.9	professional	—	non-professional
2.3.10	educationally developed	—	educationally undeveloped
2.3.11	technologically sophisticated	—	technologically unsophisticated
2.3.12	urban	—	rural
2.3.13	public	—	private
2.3.14	familiar physical	—	unfamiliar physical
2.3.15	familiar human	—	unfamiliar human
2.3.16	quiet	—	noisy
2.3.17	demanding	—	undemanding
2.3.18	hurried	—	unhurried
2.3.19	formal	—	informal

*By 'ethical' is meant constrained by moral considerations.

2.3.20 hierarchic	—	non-hierarchic/egalitarian
2.3.21 authoritarian	—	un-authoritarian/laissez-faire
2.3.22 entertaining/festive	—	serious
2.3.23 aggressive/argumentative	—	conciliatory/harmonious
2.3.24 reserved	—	unreserved
2.3.25 sympathetic	—	unsympathetic

(n.b. Information previously identified about the participant's identity, communicative purpose, and especially physical setting, points to the types of environment that apply in the particular case.)

3.0 INTERACTION

3.1 Position
State the participant's position (i.e. in which he enacts a particular role) by reference to §1.2 and §1.3 above.

3.2 Role-set
Identify the target language role-set (i.e. the different people with whom he will interact in English, by virtue of his 'position'), taking account of the physical setting, especially location and place of work/study.

3.3 Role-set identity
Identify particulars for each member/group of the target language role-set in terms of the following:

3.3.1 *Number*
Select as appropriate from: individual/small group/large group/mass

3.3.2 *Age-group*
Select as appropriate, modifying for degree or quantity if necessary, from: elderly/adult/adolescent/child/mixed

3.3.3 *Sex*
State: male/female/mixed, modifying if necessary (e.g. mostly male)

3.3.4 *Nationality*
State nationality, modifying if necessary (e.g. mainly British)

3.4 Social relationships
From the inventory of social relationships, determine those that are

159

Inventory of social relationships

Asymmetrical

3.4.1	superior	— subordinate	3.4.36 senior relative	— junior relative
3.4.2	senior	— junior	3.4.37 parent	— offspring
3.4.3	'primus'	— 'pares'		
3.4.4	chairman	— member		
3.4.5	winner	— loser		
3.4.6	evaluator/judge	— applicant/ contestant	*Symmetrical*	
3.4.7	authority	— offender	3.4.38 equal	— equal
3.4.8	government	— opposition	3.4.39 insider	— insider
3.4.9	official	— member of the public	3.4.40 colleague	— colleague
			3.4.41 group member	— group member
3.4.10	employer	— employee	3.4.42 team-mate	— team-mate
3.4.11	management	— worker	3.4.43 professional	— professional
3.4.12	investigator	— subject	3.4.44 native	— native
3.4.13	mentor/ supervisor	— charge	3.4.45 competitor	— competitor
			3.4.46 enemy	— enemy
3.4.14	society	— individual	3.3.47 neighbour	— neighbour
3.4.15	representative	— elector	3.4.48 intimate	— intimate
3.4.16	instructor/ authority	— learner	3.4.49 friend	— friend
			3.4.50 acquaintance	— acquaintance
3.4.17	adviser	— advisee	3.4.51 stranger	— stranger
3.4.18	therapist	— patient	3.4.52 outsider	— outsider
3.4.19	media	— public	3.4.53 adult	— adult
3.4.20	consultant	— client	3.4.54 child	— child
3.4.21	consumer	— producer	3.4.55 own generation	— own generation
3.4.22	buyer	— seller		
3.4.23	customer	— server	3.4.56 own class	— own class
3.4.24	insider	— outsider	3.4.57 spouse	— spouse
3.4.25	professional	— non-professional	3.4.58 parent	— parent
			3.4.59 offspring	— offspring
3.4.26	native	— non-native	3.4.60 relative	— relative
3.4.27	host	— guest	3.4.61 own sex	— own sex
3.3.28	benefactor	— beneficiary		
3.4.29	leader	— follower/ supporter		
3.4.30	artiste	— public		
3.4.31	star	— fan		
3.4.32	adult	— child/ adolescent		
3.4.33	older generation	— younger generation		
3.4.34	higher class	— lower class		
3.4.35	man/male	— woman/female		

160

implied by the role relationships (the interaction of 3.1 with each member/group of 3.2), taking account of identity, domain, and setting.

4.0 INSTRUMENTALITY

4.1 Medium
State the required medium and type of command by selecting from the following:
    4.1.1 spoken : receptive
    4.1.2 spoken : productive
    4.1.3 written : receptive
    4.1.4 written : productive

4.2 Mode
Specify the required mode of communication in terms of the following, as appropriate:
    4.2.1 monologue, spoken to be heard
    4.2.2 monologue, spoken to be written
    4.2.3 monologue, written to be read
    4.2.4 monologue, written to be read as if heard
    4.2.5 monologue, written to be spoken
    4.2.6 monologue, written to be spoken as if not written
    4.2.7 dialogue, spoken to be heard
    4.2.8 dialogue, written to be read
    4.2.9 dialogue, written to be read as if heard
    4.2.10 dialogue, written to be spoken
    4.2.11 dialogue, written to be spoken as if not written

4.3 Channel
Select the channel of communication, as appropriate, from the following:
    4.3.1 face-to-face [bilateral]
    4.3.2 telephone
    4.3.3 radio contact
    4.3.4 print [bilateral]
    4.3.5 face-to-face [unilateral]

4.3.6   public address system
4.3.7   radio [live relay]
4.3.8   television [live relay]
4.3.9   disc
4.3.10 tape [audio/video]
4.3.11 film
4.3.12 print [unilateral]

5.0 DIALECT

Taking account of the relevant variables, what dialects of English are required by the participant?

5.1 Regional
Input
State the relevant input information from the following derivational sources:
Setting
   Location   :
   Place   :
   Scale of use:
Interaction
   Role-set identity (nationality):
Dialect and accent
5.1.1 Which of the following (one or more) does the participant need to be able to understand/produce?
   Standard English/a national standard/a local dialect
   5.1.1.1 Where applicable, specify the national standard/local dialect, using the classification of regional dialect below.
5.1.2 Does the participant need to be able to understand/produce a general or a regional accent of English, or both?
   5.1.2.1 If general, specify RP/General American/General Indian/etc.
   5.1.2.2 If regional, state the localised accent for the specification at 5.1.1.1.

5.2 Social class
Input
State the relevant input information from the following derivational sources:

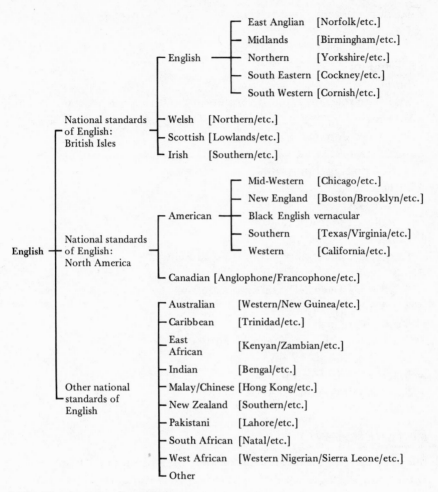

A classification of regional dialect

Purposive domain
   Occupational classification:
Interaction
   Role-set:
Dialect and accent
5.2.1 Which of the following (one or more) does the participant
need to be able to understand/produce?
   Upper Class English/Middle Class English/Working Class
   English

5.2.2 If relevant, specify the sub-class, e.g. Lower Working Class English

5.3 Temporal
Input
State the relevant input information from the following derivational sources:
Purposive domain
    Educational purpose:
    Occupational purpose:
Interaction
    Role-set:
    Role-set identity (age):
Dialect
Select, as appropriate, from the following:*
5.3.1 contemporary
5.3.2 early twentieth century
5.3.3 nineteenth century
5.3.4 eighteenth century
5.3.5 sixteenth—seventeenth century
5.3.6 late Middle English
5.3.7 early Middle English
5.3.8 Anglo-Saxon

6.0 TARGET LEVEL

Specify the target levels for the participant's command of English by completing each grid, where applicable, with values from its own scale. In assigning values, refer to relevant input information.
Input
Purposive domain
    Occupational purpose:
    Educational purpose:
Setting
    Place of study:
    Scale of use:
    Psychosocial environment:

*It is realised that, of the choices listed, only 'contemporary' is likely to be relevant for the vast majority of participants.

Interaction
   Role-set:
   Role-set age-group:
   Role-set nationality:
Instrumentality
   Medium:
   Mode:
   Channel:

Target level guide

	Medium			
	Spoken		Written	
6.1 Dimensions	Rec.	Prod.	Rec.	Prod.

   6.1.1 *Size* of utterance/text
   6.1.2 *Complexity* of utterance/text
   6.1.3 *Range* of forms/micro-
       functions/micro-skills
   6.1.4 *Delicacy* of forms/micro-
       functions/micro-skills
   6.1.5 *Speed* of communication
   6.1.6 *Flexibility* of communication

(n.b.: Size, here, is a matter of length; range, a matter of quantitative extent. Complexity (grammatical, etc.) includes discourse coherence and the capacity to handle redundancy, while delicacy refers to the level of specificity and detail. Speed is concerned with rapidity of flow, but can be extended to include deliberateness of speech; and flexibility covers the capacity to handle novelty or communication unrelated to the participant's own purposive domain, and adaptability to switching of subject, style, or interlocutor.)

Scale: *Value*
      1 = very low/very small
      2 = low/small
      3 = fairly low/fairly small
      4 = middling
      5 = fairly high/fairly large
      6 = high/large
      7 = very high/very large

	Medium			
6.2 Conditions	Spoken		Written	
Tolerance of:	Rec.	Prod.	Rec.	Prod.
6.2.1 error (linguistic)				
6.2.2 stylistic failure				
6.2.3 reference (to dictionary/ addressee, etc.)				
6.2.4 repetition (re-read/ask for repeat)				
6.2.5 hesitation (lack of fluency)				

Scale: *Value*

1	=	very low (tolerance of)		
2	=	fairly low	"	"
3	=	middling	"	"
4	=	fairly high	"	"
5	=	very high	"	"

7.0 COMMUNICATIVE EVENT

Input

State the relevant input information from the following derivational sources:

Purposive domain

    Occupational purpose:

    Educational purpose:

Setting

    Location:

    Place of work/study:

    Study setting:

    Other places:

    Size of institution:

Interaction

    Role-set:

Instrumentality

    Medium:

    Mode:

    Channel:

Communicative events
State the main and other communicative events that the participant is required to handle in English, and then specify for each event its activities and subject matter.*
Main: 7.1
Other: 7.2
 ⋮

Event 7.1
 Communicative activities
 7.1.1
 7.1.2
  ⋮

 Subject matter
 Referential vocabulary categories/Topics for above activities:
 [a]
 [b]
  ⋮

n.b. *Each* event is specified in this way.

8.0 COMMUNICATIVE KEY

Input
State the relevant input information from the following derivational sources:
Participant
 Identity:
Interaction
 Role-set identity:
 Social relationships:
Setting
 Psychosocial environments:
Instrumentality
 Command of medium:
Event
 Activities: all.
Communicative key
For each event, list the activities previously identified (in section 7),

*See Chapter 10 for examples.

Attitudinal-tone index

happy — unhappy	**happy** delighted, ecstatic, joyful	**unhappy** wretched, sad, heartbroken, sorrowful, suffering, harrowed
content — discontented	**content** contented, satisfied, complacent	**discontented** dissatisfied, disgruntled, grumbling, complaining, petulant
pleasant — unpleasant	**pleasant** agreeable, genial, amiable, appealing	**unpleasant** disagreeable, annoying, distressing, frightening, abrasive, spooky
cheerful — dejected	**cheerful** hearty, laughing, light-hearted, jaunty, gay, merry, jolly, festive, convivial	**dejected** gloomy, despondent, depressed, disappointed, melancholic, cheerless, depressing, sombre, disconsolate
frivolous — serious	**frivolous** flippant, levitous, joking, trivial, playful	**serious** earnest, grave, solemn, weighty
rejoicing — lamenting	**rejoicing** jubilant, gleeful, exultant, triumphant	**lamenting** tearful, mournful, plaintive, doleful, pathetic
entertaining — tedious	**entertaining** amusing, diverting, interesting	**tedious** dreary, dull, soporific, boring, monotonous
exciting — unexciting	**exciting** stirring, stimulating, dramatic, sensational	**unexciting** uneventful, dull, bored
humorous — humourless	**humorous** funny, amusing, comical, farcical, witty, droll, ridiculous	**humourless** unamusing, unfunny, uncomical, straight, serious

168

	sensitive/discriminating	**insensitive/indiscriminating**
sensitive/discriminating — insensitive/indiscriminating	**sensitive/discriminating** ...... delicate, aesthetic, discerning, subtle, sophisticated, fastidious, tactful	**insensitive/indiscriminating** vulgar, coarse, Philistine, undiscerning, naive, unsophisticated, raucous, tactless
hoping — hopeless	**hoping** ...... expectant, sanguine, optimistic, encouraging, wishful, hopeful	**hopeless** despairing, desperate, pessimistic, unhopeful
courageous — fearing	**courageous** ...... heroic, brave, bold, audacious, plucky, spirited, intrepid, fearless, undismayed	**fearing** afraid, panicky, dismayed, petrified, nervous, timid, apprehensive, cowardly, funky, diffident
cautious — incautious	**cautious** ...... wary, guarded, circumspect, tentative, careful, discreet	**incautious** reckless, heedless, unguarded, rash, wild, careless, indiscreet
caring — indifferent	**caring** ...... concerned, interested, enthusiastic, eager, keen, personal, anxious, worried, curious, fascinated	**indifferent** uncaring, unconcerned, uninterested, lukewarm, impersonal, unenthusiastic, incurious, nonchalant, apathetic, perfunctory
wondering — unastonished	**wondering** ...... marvelling, amazed, aghast, surprised, bewildered	**unastonished** unamazed, unsurprised, unimpressed, expectant, matter-of-fact
modest — prideful	**modest** ...... self-effacing, unassuming, humble, meek, bashful, retiring, demure, unboastful	**prideful** conceited, boastful, proud, snobbish, supercilious, patronising, condescending, pompous, ostentatious, arrogant
formal — informal	**formal** ...... ceremonious, punctilious, correct, detached, stiff, conventional	**informal** unceremonious, casual, familiar, intimate, chatty, relaxed, irregular

friendly — inimical	**friendly** sympathetic, cordial, amiable, intimate, warm	**inimical** unfriendly, unsympathetic, hostile, cold, disliking
courteous — discourteous	**courteous** chivalrous, polite, civil, urbane, dignified, gracious, gallant	**discourteous** ungallant, impolite, rude, off-handed, boorish, ungracious, brusque, abrupt, offensive
sociable — unsociable	**sociable** hospitable, welcoming, affable, approachable, loquacious, effusive, unreserved	**unsociable** inhospitable, unwelcoming, stand-offish, taciturn, sullen, sulky, aloof, reserved, preoccupied, ignoring
loving — hating	**loving** affectionate, tender, caressing, amorous, desiring, infatuated, adoring, erotic	**hating** antipathetic, loathing, rancorous, abhorring
unresentful — resentful	**unresentful** ungrudging, mild, unenvious, unjealous	**resentful** piqued, hurt, indignant, affronted, bitter, acrimonious, envious, jealous
pleased — displeased	**pleased** glad	**displeased** angry, cross, annoyed, infuriated, apoplectic, exasperated
benevolent — malevolent	**benevolent** benign, kind, obliging, altruistic, generous, charitable, pitying, compassionate	**malevolent** spiteful, vicious, malicious, unkind, uncharitable, cruel, sadistic, brutal, pitiless
forgiving — unforgiving	**forgiving** pardoning, merciful, condoning, placable	**unforgiving** retaliatory, revengeful, vindictive, implacable, merciless

patient ·
uncomplaining, forbearing, long-suffering, persevering, stoical, painstaking

grateful ·
thankful, appreciative, obliged, acknowledging

honest ·
candid, frank, ingenuous, straightforward, sincere, genuine, truthful, upright, fair, just

disinterested ·
impartial, unbiased, unprejudiced, dispassionate, unselfish, considerate, altruistic, generous, magnanimous

respectful ·
deferential, reverential obsequious, dutiful

admiring ·
regarding highly, appreciative, impressed

praising ·
complimentary, commendatory, laudatory, eulogistic, flattering, sycophantic

impatient
restless, over-eager, hasty, fretful, impetuous, unforbearing, unpersevering

ungrateful
unthankful, unmindful, unappreciative, taking for granted

dishonest
disingenuous, insincere, hypocritical, sanctimonious, cunning, devious, corrupt, perfidious, unfair, unjust

biased/selfish
prejudiced, nationalistic, chauvinistic, bigoted, egotistical, ungenerous, mercenary, avaricious, self-seeking, inconsiderate

disrespectful
lacking in deference, familiar, cheeky, impertinent, brash, presumptuous, irreverent

contemptuous
despising, disdainful, scornful, snobbish, cynical, derisive, mocking, sardonic, insulting, insolent

detracting
derogatory, pejorative, disparaging, defamatory, denigratory, sarcastic, satirical, uncomplimentary

patient – impatient

grateful – ungrateful

honest – dishonest

disinterested – biased/selfish

respectful – disrespectful

admiring – contemptuous

praising – detracting

171

approving — disapproving	**approving** . . . . favourable, supporting, assenting, well-inclined	**disapproving** unfavourable, critical, censorious, reproachful, intolerant, shocked, deprecating, admonitory
regretting — unregretting	**regretting** . . . . regretful, sorry, apologetic, contrite, remorseful, penitent, repentant	**unregretting** unapologetic, unrepentant, uncontrite, unpenitent, unashamed, brazen
temperate — intemperate	**temperate** . . . . moderate, sober, restrained, ascetic, austere	**intemperate** immoderate, drunken, unrestrained, sensual, hedonistic
pure — impure	**pure** . . . . clean, innocent, chaste, honourable, platonic, decent, edifying, printable prudish, puritanical	**impure** dirty, immoral, risque, obscene, porno-graphic, whorish, lecherous, lewd, licentious, depraved
pious — irreligious	**pious** . . . . religious, spiritual, worshipping, prayerful, devotional, invocatory, mystical	**irreligious** impious, secular, unbelieving, profane, blasphemous, idolatrous, diabolical
excitable — inexcitable	**excitable** . . . . impassioned, excited, agitated, tense, irascible, embarrassed, frantic, hysterical, disconcerted, hot-tempered	**inexcitable** impassive, phlegmatic, cool, imperturb-able, composed, calm, unruffled, placid, equable
willing — unwilling	**willing** . . . . desirous, ready, enthusiastic, helpful, cooperative	**unwilling** reluctant, unhelpful, uncooperative, disinclined, unenthusiastic
resolute — irresolute	**resolute** . . . . determined, firm, persistent, stubborn, obstinate, constant, adamant, militant	**irresolute** hesitating, vacillating, indecisive, capricious, half-hearted, wavering

inducive — **dissuasive**

inducive
persuasive, encouraging, provocative, inciting, urging, seductive, recommendatory

dissuasive
discouraging, damping, intimidating, cautionary, deprecatory, threatening, ominous

active — **inactive**

active
energetic, lively, businesslike, busy, industrious, studious, officious, efficient

inactive
lazy, languid, listless, leisurely, sleepy, soporific, fatigued, tranquil, sloppy, dilatory

concordant — **discordant**

concordant
harmonious, amicable, congenial, peaceful, soothing, pacificatory, conciliatory, placatory, mediatory, diplomatic

discordant
dissentient, quarrelling, argumentative, irascible, aggravating, bellicose, aggressive, contentious, polemical, undiplomatic

lenient — **severe**

lenient
gentle, mild, indulgent, tolerant, easy-going, permissive, accommodating

severe
harsh, stern, strict, intolerant, violent, forbidding, uncompromising

authoritative — **lacking in authority**

authoritative
official, commanding, dignified, majestic, imperious, dominant, self-assured, imposing, didactic, permitting

lacking in authority
unofficial, insignificant, undignified, anarchic, diffident, servile, unimposing

compelling — **uncompelling**

compelling
urgent, forceful, coercive, peremptory, bossy, insistent, authoritarian, demanding

uncompelling
unimportant, weak, feeble, unassertive, laissez-faire, innocuous

obedient — **disobedient**

obedient
compliant, submissive, docile, meek, dutiful, loyal

disobedient
insubordinate, rebellious, recalcitrant, naughty, contumacious, subversive, seditious, disloyal

certain — uncertain

certain . . . .
sure, unequivocal, unambiguous, confident,
believing, opinionated, dogmatic
trustful, convincing

uncertain
unsure, ambiguous, puzzled, vague,
doubting, sceptical, incredulous,
suppositional, distrustful, suspicious,
unconvincing

open — secret

open . . . .
plain, clear, public, revelatory,
undisguised, unreserved, blatant

secret
secretive, abstruse, cryptic, mysterious,
reticent, cabalistic, conspiratorial,
confidential, private

intelligent/thinking —
unthinking/unintelligent

intelligent/thinking . . . .
clever, wise, intellectual, shrewd,
rational, erudite, knowing, thoughtful
discreet

unthinking/unintelligent
stupid, unwise, foolish, unintellectual,
silly, irrational, fatuous, ignorant,
indiscreet

assenting — dissenting

assenting . . . .
agreeing, consenting, acquiescent,
concurring, admitting, confirmatory,
affirmative

dissenting
disagreeing, refusing, protesting,
querying, arguing, denying, retorting,
negative, qualifying

and opposite each activity specify those keys which the participant *needs* to be able to [i] produce (P), and [ii] recognise and understand (R), as applicable, in connection with that activity. The keys should be selected from the *left-hand* column of the attitudinal-tone index above, and the specification should be based on the input information above.

Event 7.1:

Activities	*Key (P)*	*Key (R)*
7.1.1		
7.1.2		
7.1.3		
⋮		

n.b. *Each* event is processed for communicative key in this way.

PART TWO

SPECIFYING THE SYLLABUS CONTENT

The profile of communication needs must now be interpreted in terms of language skills, functions and forms, which are required for its realisation. Where the syllabus content specification is to focus on micro-skills, the micro-functions will appear as parts of certain skills, e.g. in groups 26, 27, 47, 48, 49 and 50, selected from the taxonomy of language skills. Where, however, the syllabus content is to be specified mainly in terms of micro-functions and forms, parts of the profile of needs are converted into units of meaning before being realised as utterances or text.

LANGUAGE SKILLS

Input: the Profile of Needs, especially the information from communicative event and target level.

Instruction: From the taxonomy of language skills, select and specify the micro-skills required for each activity. Where necessary, modify the description of the skill to take account of the target level specification.

Activity:
>   *Skill no.*   *Description*
>   :   :
>   :   :

n.b. *Each* activity is processed for micro-skills in this way.

A taxonomy of language skills

1. Discriminating sounds in isolate word forms:
   - 1.1 phonemes, especially phonemic contrasts
   - 1.2 phoneme sequences
   - 1.3 allophonic variants
   - 1.4 assimilated and elided forms (esp. reduction of vowels and consonant clusters)
   - 1.5 permissible phonemic variation

2. Articulating sounds in isolate word forms:
   - 2.1 phonemes, esp. phonemic contrasts
   - 2.2 phoneme sequences
   - 2.3 allophonic variants
   - 2.4 assimilated and elided forms (esp. reduction of vowels and consonant clusters)
   - 2.5 permissible phonemic variation

3. Discriminating sounds in connected speech:
   - 3.1 strong and weak forms
   - 3.2 neutralisation of weak forms
   - 3.3 reduction of unstressed vowels
   - 3.4 modification of sounds, esp. at word boundaries, through
     - 3.4.1 assimilation
     - 3.4.2 elision
     - 3.4.3 liaison
   - 3.5 phonemic change at word boundaries
   - 3.6 allophonic variation at word boundaries

4. Articulating sounds in connected speech:
   - 4.1 strong and weak forms
   - 4.2 neutralisation of weak forms
   - 4.3 reduction of unstressed vowels
   - 4.4 modification of sounds, esp. at word boundaries, through
     - 4.4.1 assimilation
     - 4.4.2 elision
     - 4.4.3 liaison
   - 4.5 phonemic change at word boundaries
   - 4.6 allophonic variation at word boundaries

5. Discriminating stress patterns within words:
   - 5.1 characteristic accentual patterns
   - 5.2 meaningful accentual patterns

5.3 compounds

6. Articulating stress patterns within words:
   6.1 characteristic accentual patterns
   6.2 meaningful accentual patterns
   6.3 compounds

7. Recognising variation in stress in connected speech:
   7.1 variation of word accentual patterns for rhythmic considerations (e.g. accent shift in 'level-stress' words)
   7.2 variation of word accentual patterns for meaningful prominence
   7.3 non-stressing of pronouns
   7.4 differentiating phrases from compounds

8. Manipulating variation in stress in connected speech:
   8.1 variation of word accentual patterns for rhythmic considerations (e.g. accent shift in 'level-stress' words)
   8.2 variation of word accentual patterns for meaningful prominence
   8.3 non-stressing of pronouns
   8.4 differentiating phrases from compounds

9. Recognising the use of stress in connected speech
   9.1 for indicating information units;
       9.1.1 content words and form words
       9.1.2 rhythmic patterning
   9.2 for emphasis, through location of nuclear accent
   9.3 for contrast, through nuclear shift

10. Manipulating the use of stress in connected speech
    10.1 for indicating information units:
        10.1.1 content words and form words
        10.1.2 rhythmic patterning
    10.2 for emphasis, through location of nuclear accent
    10.3 for contrast, through nuclear shift

11. Understanding intonation patterns: neutral position of nucleus and use of tone, in respect of
    11.1 falling tone with declarative/moodless clauses
    11.2 falling tone with interrogative clauses beginning with a question word
    11.3 falling tone with imperative clauses
    11.4 rising tone with 'yes/no' interrogative clauses
    11.5 rising tone with non-final clauses
    11.6 fall—rise tone with any clause type
    11.7 rise—fall tone with any clause type
    11.8 multi-nuclear patterns
    11.9 tones with question-tags
    11.10 others

12. Producing intonation patterns: neutral position of nucleus and use of tone, in respect of

12.1 falling tone with declarative/moodless clauses
12.2 falling tone with interrogative clauses beginning with a question word
12.3 falling tone with imperative clauses
12.4 rising tone with 'yes/no' interrogative clauses
12.5 rising tone with non-final clauses
12.6 fall–rise tone with any clause type
12.7 rise–fall tone with any clause type
12.8 multi-nuclear patterns
12.9 tones with question-tags
12.10 others

13. Understanding intonation patterns: interpreting attitudinal meaning through variation of tone or nuclear shift, viz.
   13.1 rising tone with declarative/moodless clauses
   13.2 rising tone with interrogatives beginning with a question word, having the nucleus in
      13.2.1 end position
      13.2.2 front position
   13.3 same as 11.2 but nuclear shift to front position
   13.4 rising tone with imperative clauses
   13.5 falling tone with 'yes/no' interrogative clauses
   13.6 same as 11.4 but nuclear shift to front position
   13.7 others

14. Producing intonation patterns: expressing attitudinal meaning through variation of tone or nuclear shift, viz.
   14.1 rising tone with declarative/moodless clauses
   14.2 rising tone with interrogatives beginning with a question word, having the nucleus in
      14.2.1 end position
      14.2.2 front position
   14.3 same as 12.2 but nuclear shift to front position
   14.4 rising tone with imperative clauses
   14.5 falling tone with 'yes/no' interrogative clauses
   14.6 same as 12.4 but nuclear shift to front position
   14.7 others

15. Interpreting attitudinal meaning through
   15.1 pitch height
   15.2 pitch range
   15.3 pause
   15.4 tempo

16. Expressing attitudinal meaning through
   16.1 pitch height
   16.2 pitch range
   16.3 pause
   16.4 tempo

17. Recognising the script of a language:
   17.1 discriminating the graphemes
   17.2 following grapheme sequences (spelling system)
   17.3 understanding punctuation

18. Manipulating the script of a language:
   18.1 forming the graphemes
   18.2 catenating grapheme sequences (spelling system)
   18.3 using punctuation

19. Deducing the meaning and use of unfamiliar lexical items, through
   19.1 understanding word formation:
      19.1.1 stems/roots
      19.1.2 affixation
      19.1.3 derivation
      19.1.4 compounding
   19.2 contextual clues

20. Understanding explicitly stated information

21. Expressing information explicitly

22. Understanding information in the text, not explicitly stated, through
   22.1 making inferences
   22.2 understanding figurative language

23. Expressing information implicitly, through
   23.1 inference
   23.2 figurative language

24. Understanding conceptual meaning, especially
   24.1 quantity and amount
   24.2 definiteness and indefiniteness
   24.3 comparison; degree
   24.4 time (esp. tense and aspect)
   24.5 location; direction
   24.6 means; instrument
   24.7 cause; result; purpose; reason; condition; contrast

25. Expressing conceptual meaning, especially
   25.1 quantity and amount
   25.2 definiteness and indefiniteness
   25.3 comparison; degree
   25.4 time (esp. tense and aspect)
   25.5 location; direction
   25.6 means; instrument
   25.7 cause; result; purpose; reason; condition; contrast

26. Understanding the communicative value (function) of sentences and utterances
   26.1 with explicit indicators

26.2 without explicit indicators
 e.g. an interrogative that is a polite command; a statement that is in
 fact a suggestion, warning, etc. depending on the context; relationships
 of result, reformulation, etc., without 'therefore', 'in other words', etc.

27. Expressing the communicative value (function) of sentences and utterances
 27.1 using explicit indicators
 27.2 without explicit indicators

28. Understanding relations within the sentence, especially
 28.1 elements of sentence structure
 28.2 modification structure:
  28.2.1 premodification
  28.2.2 postmodification
  28.2.3 disjuncts
 28.3 negation
 28.4 modal auxiliaries
 28.5 intra-sentential connectors
 28.6 complex embedding
 28.7 focus and theme:
  28.7.1 thematic fronting; and inversion
  28.7.2 postponement

29. Expressing relations within the sentence, using especially
 29.1 elements of sentence structure
 29.2 modification structure:
  29.2.1 premodification
  29.2.2 postmodification
  29.2.3 disjuncts
 29.3 negation
 29.4 modal auxiliaries
 29.5 intra-sentential connectors
 29.6 complex embedding
 29.7 focus and theme:
  29.7.1 thematic fronting; and inversion
  29.7.2 postponement

30. Understanding relations between parts of a text through lexical cohesion
 devices of
 30.1 repetition
 30.2 synonymy
 30.3 hyponymy
 30.4 antithesis
 30.5 apposition
 30.6 lexical set/collocation
 30.7 pro-forms/general words

31. Expressing relations between parts of a text through lexical cohesion devices
 of

180

31.1 repetition
31.2 synonymy
31.3 hyponymy
31.4 antithesis
31.5 apposition
31.6 lexical set/collocation
31.7 pro-forms/general words

32. Understanding relations between parts of a text through grammatical cohesion devices of
    32.1 reference (anaphoric and cataphoric)
    32.2 comparison
    32.3 substitution
    32.4 ellipsis
    32.5 time and place relaters
    32.6 logical connecters

33. Expressing relations between parts of a text through grammatical cohesion devices of
    33.1 reference (anaphoric and cataphoric)
    33.2 comparison
    33.3 substitution
    33.4 ellipsis
    33.5 time and place relaters
    33.6 logical connecters

34. Interpreting text by going outside it
    34.1 using exophoric reference
    34.2 'reading between the lines'
    34.3 integrating data in the text with own experience or knowledge of the world

35. Recognising indicators in discourse for
    35.1 introducing an idea
    35.2 developing an idea (e.g. adding points, reinforcing argument)
    35.3 transition to another idea
    35.4 concluding an idea
    35.5 emphasising a point
    35.6 explanation or clarification of point already made
    35.7 anticipating an objection or contrary view

36. Using indicators in discourse for
    36.1 introducing an idea
    36.2 developing an idea (e.g. adding points, reinforcing argument)
    36.3 transition to another idea
    36.4 concluding an idea
    36.5 emphasising a point
    36.6 explanation or clarification of point already made
    36.7 anticipating an objection or contrary view

37. Identifying the main point or important information in a piece of discourse, through
    37.1 vocal underlining (e.g. decreased speed, increased volume)
    37.2 end-focus and end-weight
    37.3 verbal cues (e.g. 'The point I want to make is . . . ')
    37.4 topic sentence, in paragraphs of
        37.4.1 inductive organisation
        37.4.2 deductive organisation

38. Indicating the main point or important information in a piece of discourse, through
    38.1 vocal underlining (e.g. decreased speed, increased volume)
    38.2 end-focus and end-weight
    38.3 verbal cues (e.g. 'The point I want to make is . . . ')
    38.4 topic sentence, in paragraphs of
        38.4.1 inductive organisation
        38.4.2 deductive organisation

39. Distinguishing the main idea from supporting details, by differentiating
    39.1 primary from secondary significance
    39.2 the whole from its parts
    39.3 a process from its stages
    39.4 category from exponent
    39.5 statement from example
    39.6 fact from opinion
    39.7 a proposition from its argument

40. Extracting salient points to summarise
    40.1 the whole text
    40.2 a specific idea/topic in the text
    40.3 the underlying idea or point of the text

41. Selective extraction of relevant points from a text, involving
    41.1 the coordination of related information
    41.2 the ordered rearrangement of contrasting items
    41.3 the tabulation of information for comparison and contrast

42. Expanding salient/relevant points into summary of
    42.1 the whole text
    42.2 a specific idea/topic in the text

43. Reducing the text through rejecting redundant or irrelevant information and items, especially
    43.1 omission of closed-system items (e.g. determiners)
    43.2 omission of repetition, circumlocution, digression, false starts
    43.3 compression of sentences or word groups
    43.4 compression of examples
    43.5 use of abbreviations
    43.6 use of symbols denoting relationships between states, processes, etc.

44. Basic reference skills: understanding and use of
    44.1 graphic presentation, viz. headings, sub-headings, numbering, inden-
         tation, bold print, footnotes
    44.2 table of contents and index
    44.3 cross-referencing
    44.4 card catalogue
    44.5 phonetic transcription/diacritics

45. Skimming to obtain
    45.1 the gist of the text
    45.2 a general impression of the text

46. Scanning to locate specifically required information on
    46.1 a single point, involving a simple search
    46.2 a single point, involving a complex search
    46.3 more than one point, involving a simple search
    46.4 more than one point, involving a complex search
    46.5 a whole topic

47. Initiating in discourse:
    47.1 how to initiate the discourse (elicit, inform, direct, etc.)
    47.2 how to introduce a new point (using verbal and vocal cues)
    47.3 how to introduce a topic (using appropriate micro-functions such as
         explanation, hypothesis, question)

48. Maintaining the discourse:
    48.1 how to respond (acknowledge, reply, loop, agree, disagree, etc.)
    48.2 how to continue (add, exemplify, justify, evaluate, etc.)
    48.3 how to adapt, as result of feedback, esp. in mid-utterance (amplify,
         omit, reformulate, etc.)
    48.4 how to turn-take (interrupt, challenge, inquire, dove-tail, etc.)
    48.5 how to mark time (stall, 'breathing-space' formulae, etc.)

49. Terminating in discourse
    49.1 how to mark boundaries in discourse (verbal and vocal cues)
    49.2 how to come out of the discourse (excuse, concede, pass, etc.)
    49.3 how to conclude a topic (using appropriate micro-functions such as
         substantiation, and verbal cues for summing up, etc.)

50. Planning and organising information in expository language (esp. presentation
    of reports, expounding an argument, evaluation of evidence), using rhetorical
    functions, especially
    50.1 definition
    50.2 classification
    50.3 description of properties
    50.4 description of process
    50.5 description of change of state

51. Transcoding information presented in diagrammatic display, involving
    51.1 straight conversion of diagram/table/graph into speech/writing

51.2 interpretation or comparison of diagrams/tables/graphs in speech/ writing

52. Transcoding information in speech/writing to diagrammatic display, through
  52.1 completing a diagram/table/graph
  52.2 constructing one or more diagrams/tables/graphs

53. Recoding information (expressing/understanding equivalence of meaning)
  53.1 within the same style (e.g. paraphrasing to avoid repetition)
  53.2 across different styles (e.g. from technical to lay)

54. Relaying information
  54.1 directly (commentary/description concurrent with action)
  54.2 indirectly (reporting)

LANGUAGE MICRO-FUNCTIONS AND ATTITUDINAL-TONES

Input: the profile of needs

Instruction:* Interpret the profile in terms of required units of meaning by

(1) converting each activity into micro-functions selected from the inventory of micro-functions

(2) marking each micro-function, as far as possible, with one or more attitudinal-tones selected from the attitudinal-tone index.

n.b. (i) tones separated by a comma jointly constrain the function.

(ii) the productive and receptive command of these units of meaning should be listed separately for each event.

Event 7.1

Activity	Micro-function	Productive Attitudinal-tone
7.1.1	1.	
	2.	
	3.	
	⋮	
7.1.2		
⋮		

n.b. For *each* event, the activities and their keys are processed into units of meaning in this way.

---

*See Chapter 8, pp. 142–3, for five points of procedure.

An inventory of micro-functions
(a modified form of Wilkins, 1976)

Note: the items listed at a subcategory are not intended to be exhaustive.

1. *Scale of certainty*	*Cross-references**
Impersonalised	§ 292–301

1.1 Affirmation

1.2 Certainty
   e.g. He is certain to be there.
      He must have known the answer beforehand.
      It has to come out here.

1.3 Probability
   e.g. It is likely that he will be there.
      He should be free in a minute.
      It ought to be a good programme.

1.4 Possibility
   e.g. He is not certain to be there.
      It is possible that the bus will be late.
      It may be a good programme.

1.5 Nil certainty
   e.g. He is certain not to be there.
      It is not possible to see him now.
      He can't have known the answer beforehand.

1.6 Negation

Personalised   § 302–6

1.7 Conviction
be + convinced, positive, sure, certain, confident,
know, believe
   e.g. I am certain that he will be there.
      I am convinced that he knew the answer beforehand.
   [cf. the examples in 1.2 above for the difference
between 'impersonalised' and 'personalised']

1.8 Conjecture
think, reckon, consider, expect, daresay, be of the
opinion, presume, suppose, assume, trust, hope,
surmise, guess, imagine, anticipate, foresee, predict,
prophesy
   e.g. I think he will be there.
      I expect he will be free in a minute

1.9 Doubt
doubt, wonder, be + sceptical, doubtful, dubious
   e.g. I doubt whether he will be there.
      I am not convinced that he is telling the truth.

1.10 Disbelief
above verbs + negative

*The references are to sections in Leech and Svartvik (1975).

e.g. I don't believe he will be there.
    I am convinced that he is not telling the truth.

2. *Scale of commitment*
    2.1　Intention　　　　　　　　　　　　　　　　　§ 334–8; 325; 355
        volition, will, unwilling; wish, want, desire, choice,
        inclination, prefer; mean, intention, contemplate,
        plan, propose; promise, undertake, assure, guarantee
        e.g. I'll pick you up at the station.
            I'd like to see the manager.
    2.2　Obligation　　　　　　　　　　　　　　　　§ 341–3
        obligation, necessity (social), onus, liability, duty,
        allegiance, responsibility, conscientiousness
        e.g. They must pay up by the end of the week.
            He ought to stop and help.
            I have to go now.
            You will have to produce the receipt.

3. *Judgement and evaluation*
    3.1　Valuation
        3.1.1 assess, judge, estimate, value; rank, place, grade
        3.1.2 misjudge, prejudge, overestimate
    3.2　Verdiction
        pronounce, rule, find, award
        3.2.1 Committal
            condemn, convict, proscribe, sentence
        3.2.2 Release
            release, exempt, acquit, discharge, let off, excuse;
            pardon, forgive, exculpate, exonerate, absolve,
            reprieve; conciliate, reconcile, extenuate
            e.g. I acquit you of this charge.
                You are free to go.
                It wasn't your fault.
    3.3　Approval　　　　　　　　　　　　　　　　§ 330
        approve, think well, appreciate, give credit, value;
        commend, praise, applaud; deserve, merit, entitle
    3.4　Disapproval
        disapprove, frown upon, deprecate, deplore; remon-
        strate, complain, allege, impute, accuse, charge;
        blame, reproach, disparage, reprimand, denounce,
        condemn
        e.g. You are to blame.
            It's your fault.
            I take strong exception to your behaviour.

4. *Suasion*　　　　　　　　　　　　　　　　　　　§ 350
    4.1　Inducement
        persuade, propose, suggest, advise, recommend;

186

advocate, exhort, beg, urge, incite
e.g. (for suggesting [S] , and advising [A])
(1) I suggest that we go to the zoo. [S]
(1) I advise you to take the job. [A]
(2) Let's go to the zoo. [S]
(2) I think you should take the job. [A]
(3) Perhaps the zoo is open. [S]
(3) Why don't you take the job? [A]

4.2 Compulsion   § 345–7; 344
command, order, dictate, direct, compel, force,
oblige; prohibit, forbid, disallow

4.3 Prediction   § 300; 355; 351
predict, warn, caution, menace, threaten,
instruct, direct, invite

4.4 Tolerance (i.e. no hindrance offered to a proposal)   § 340
allow, tolerate, grant, consent to, agree to, permit,
authorise

5. *Argument*

5.1 Information

5.1.1 Stated/asserted   § 272; 274
state, inform, tell, express, report, describe,
publish, know; proclaim, declare, assert,
emphasise, affirm, maintain; argue, advocate,
claim, contend, protest
e.g. I don't want to appear dogmatic but I
     was not responsible.

5.1.2 Sought   § 244–58
question, query; request   § 348–9; 363
e.g. Would you mind shutting the window?
     Could you shut the window?
     If you shut the window, we'll soon get warm.
(all three examples are requests)

5.1.3 Denied   § 273; 275
deny, refute, disclaim, protest; oppose, refuse,
decline, reject; disprove, confute, negate

5.2 Agreement   § 279; 281–2
agree, concur, assent, acquiesce, consent; confirm,
corroborate, endorse, support, ratify, approve

5.3 Disagreement   § 280
disagree, demur, dissent; dispute, contradict,
repudiate
e.g. That's nonsense.
     I would disagree with you.
     I see things rather differently.

5.4 Concession   § 212; 361

concede, grant, admit, yield, defer, allow, submit;
renounce, withdraw, abjure, abandon, retract,
resign; confess, apologise

6. *Rational enquiry and exposition*
   6.1 proposition, hypothesis; corollary, presupposition   § 284—7
   6.2 substantiation, verification, justification, proof
   6.3 supposition, conjecture, assumption   § 305—6
   6.4 implication, inference, deduction, illation, conclusion,
       generalisation   § 372
   6.5 interpretation; demonstration, explanation   § 373
   6.6 classification, definition; illustration, exemplification
       e.g. Thyme is a kind of herb used in cooking.
       The atomicity of an element is the number of
       atoms contained in one molecule of the element.
       (Both examples are definitions)

7. *Formulaic communication*
   7.1 greeting, farewell   § 358—60
   7.2 acknowledgement, thanks; regret, apology   § 361; 363
   7.3 good wishes, congratulations   § 362
   7.4 solicitude, condolence, commiseration   § 362
   7.5 attention signals   § 254
       e.g. go on, mm.

LANGUAGE FORMS

Input: units of meaning.

Instruction: encode each unit of meaning, taking account of dialect
and target level requirements, and referring back to the profile as
necessary.

n.b. (i)   use the same numbering for the language realisations as for
the meaning units, listing separately for productive and receptive command

(ii)   use slant lines to indicate alternative language forms for the
the same meaning unit

(iii) use diacritics only where necessary, viz. where significant
intonation might otherwise be missed.

Activity: 7.1.1

Productive

Meaning
unit no.   *Language realisation**
7.1.1.1
    2
    3
    ⋮

n.b. For *each* activity, the units of meaning are realised as language forms in this way. Then repeat procedure for receptive command.

*See Chapter 10 for examples

10

THE INSTRUMENT APPLIED

In this final chapter the operational instrument (Chapter 9) is applied to two different and highly typical kinds of participant. Example A is concerned with the post-experience subcategory of English for occupational purposes, in this case a head waiter/receptionist who knows his job but not the English needed for it. Example B concerns the in-study, discipline-based subcategory of English for educational purposes, in this case a university agricultural science student who needs English for part of his studies which he has already begun.

In both examples profiles will be constructed of the communication needs of each participant (Part one). Then, in the syllabus content specification (Part two) the exemplification will be restricted to the activities of the major event in both cases. It is hoped that this will be sufficient to show in detail the application of the operational instrument.

EXAMPLE A

PART ONE: THE PROFILE OF COMMUNICATION NEEDS

0. PARTICIPANT

0.1 Identity
    0.1.1 Age: 30–40
    0.1.2 Sex: male
    0.1.3 Nationality: Spanish
    0.1.4 Place of residence: from Valencia

0.2 Language
    0.2.1 Mother tongue: Spanish

190

0.2.2 Target language: English
0.2.3 Present level/command of target language: very elementary
0.2.4 Other language(s) known: German
0.2.5 Extent of command: very elementary

1.0 PURPOSIVE DOMAIN

1.1 ESP classification
    1.1.1 Occupational – post-experience

1.2 Occupational purpose
    1.2.1 Specific occupation: hotel employee
    1.2.2 Central duty: head waiter
    1.2.3 Other duties: relief receptionist
    1.2.4 Occupational classification: administrative assistant, and
        skilled manual worker, in services

1.3 Educational purpose
    N/A

2.0 SETTING

2.1 Physical setting: spatial
    2.1.1 Location
        2.1.1.1 Country: Spain, Ibiza
        2.1.1.2 Town: Es Cana
    2.1.2 Place of work:
        2.1.2.1 tourist hotel, specifically restaurant and reception
    2.1.3 Place of study
    N/A
    2.1.4 Other places: none
    2.1.5 Extent – size of institution: small
    2.1.6 Extent – scale of use: international

2.2 Physical setting: temporal
    2.2.1 Point of time: at any time in tourist season
    2.2.2 Duration: most of the day
    2.2.3 Frequency: regularly

2.3 Psychosocial setting
2.3.3 non-intellectual
2.3.4 semi-aesthetic
2.3.5 public
2.3.14 familiar physical
2.3.15 unfamiliar and familiar human
2.3.16 often noisy
2.3.18 hurried
2.3.29 generally formal
2.3.20 hierarchic (status conscious)
2.3.22 often entertaining
2.3.23 sometimes argumentative/conciliatory

3.0 INTERACTION

3.1 Position
Head waiter; receptionist

3.2 Role-set
(a) Customers in restaurant
(b) Hotel residents
(c) Reservation seekers

3.3 Role-set identity
For 3.2(a) and (b):
3.3.1 Number: individuals and small groups
3.3.2 Age-group: mainly adult, some adolescent
3.3.3 Sex: mixed
3.3.4 Nationality: mainly British, some Americans
For 3.2(c):
3.3.1 Number: individuals
3.3.2 Age-group: adult
3.3.3 Sex: mixed
3.3.4 Nationality: mainly British, some Americans

3.4 Social relationships
3.4.9 official to member of the public
3.4.23 server to customer
3.4.26 native to non-native

3.4.27 host to guest
3.4.32 adult to adolescent
3.4.35 male to female
3.4.51 stranger to stranger
3.4.53 adult to adult

4.0 INSTRUMENTALITY

4.1 Medium
4.1.1 spoken: receptive
4.1.2 spoken: productive
4.1.3 written: receptive
4.1.4 written: productive

4.2 Mode
4.2.7 dialogue, spoken to be heard
4.2.8 dialogue, written to be read

4.3 Channel
4.3.1 face-to-face [bilateral]
4.3.2 telephone
4.3.4 print [bilateral]

5.0 DIALECT

5.1 Regional
Input
Setting
    Location: Spain, Ibiza, Es Cana
    Place: tourist hotel/restaurant
    Scale of use: international
Interaction
    Role-set identity (nationality): mainly British, some Americans
Dialect and accent
5.1.1 understand and produce Standard English
5.1.2 understand RP and General American; produce Spanish
      approximation to RP

5.2 Social class
N/A

5.3 Temporal
Input
Purposive domain
   Occupational purpose: hotel employee
Interaction
   Role-set: (a) customers; (b) residents; (c) reservation seekers
   Role-set identity (age-group): (a) and (b) mainly adult, some adolescent; (c) adult
Dialect
5.3.1 contemporary

6.0 TARGET LEVEL

Input
Purposive domain
   Occupational purpose: hotel employee; head waiter; relief receptionist
Setting
   Scale of use: international
   Psychosocial environment: non-intellectual; semi-aesthetic; public; familiar physical; unfamiliar and familiar human; often noisy; hurried; generally formal; hierarchic; often entertaining; sometimes argumentative/conciliatory
Interaction
   Role-set: (a) customers in restaurant; (b) hotel residents; (c) reservation seekers
   Role-set age-group: (a) and (b) mainly adult, some adolescent; (c) adult
   Role-set nationality: (a), (b) and (c) mainly British, some Americans
Instrumentality
   Medium: spoken, receptive and productive; written, receptive and productive
   Mode: dialogue, spoken to be heard; dialogue, written to be read
   Channel: face-to-face (bilateral); telephone; print (bilateral)

Target level guide

6.1 Dimensions

	Medium			
	Spoken		Written	
	Rec.	Prod.	Rec.	Prod.
6.1.1 *Size* of utterance/text	2	2	3	2
6.1.2 *Complexity* of utterance/text	3/4	3	4	3
6.1.3 *Range* of forms/micro-functions/micro-skills	3	2	2	2
6.1.4 *Delicacy* of forms/micro-functions/micro-skills	5	4/5	4	3
6.1.5 *Speed* of communication	5	4	2/1	2/1
6.1.6 *Flexibility* of communication	4	3	2/1	2/1

6.2 Conditions

	Medium			
	Spoken		Written	
Tolerance of:	Rec.	Prod.	Rec.	Prod.
6.2.1 error (linguistic)	3	4	2/1	3
6.2.2 stylistic failure	3	2	4	2
6.2.3 reference (to dictionary/addressee, etc.)	3	3	5	5
6.2.4 repetition (re-read/ask for repeat)	2	—	5	—
6.2.5 hesitation (lack of fluency)	—	2	—	5

7.0 COMMUNICATIVE EVENT

Input
Purposive domain
    Occupational purpose: head waiter; relief receptionist
Setting
    Location: Ibiza
    Place of work: tourist hotel, specifically restaurant and reception
    Size of institution: small
Interaction
    Role-set: customers in restaurant; hotel residents; reservation
    seekers

Instrumentality
  Medium: spoken, receptive and productive; written, receptive and productive
  Mode: dialogue, spoken to be heard; dialogue, written to be read
  Channel: face-to-face [bilateral]; telephone; print [bilateral]
Communicative events
Main : 7.1 Head waiter attending to customers in restaurant
Other: 7.2 Receptionist dealing with table reservations
       7.3 Head waiter/receptionist dealing with residents'/customers' enquiries (e.g. concerning sight-seeing and local events)
       7.4 Receptionist answering correspondence on room reservations
Event 7.1
  Communicative activities
  7.1.1 Attending to customers' arrival
  7.1.2 Attending to customers' order
  7.1.3 Serving the order
  7.1.4 Attending to customers' complaints and well-being
  7.1.5 Attending to the bill
  7.1.6 Attending to customers' departure
  Subject matter
  Referential vocabulary categories for activities 7.1.1 to 7.1.6:
  [a] food (generic and specific)
  [b] drink (generic and specific)
  [c] cooking
  [d] utensils (generic and specific)
  [e] tobacco
  [f] money/bill
  [g] cloakroom
  [h] service
[n.b. Events 7.2, 7.3, and 7.4 would also be specified in this way]

8.0 COMMUNICATIVE KEY

Input
Participant
  Identity: 30—40 years old; male; Spanish
Interaction
  Role-set identity: number — individuals and small groups; age-

group — mainly adult, some adolescent; sex — mixed; nationality
— mainly British, some Americans
Social relationships: official to member of the public; server to
customer; native to non-native; host to guest; adult to adolescent;
male to female; stranger to stranger, adult to adult
Setting
Psychosocial environments: non-intellectual; semi-aesthetic; public;
familiar physical; unfamiliar and familiar human; often noisy;
hurried; generally formal; hierarchic (status conscious); often enter-
taining; sometimes argumentative/conciliatory
Instrumentality
Command of medium: productive and receptive
Event
Activities: all
Communicative key
Event 7.1: Head waiter attending to customers in restaurant

Activities	*Key (P)*	*Key (R)*
7.1.1 Attending to	formal	hoping
customers' arrival	courteous	formal
	sociable	uncertain
	regretting	dissenting
	resolute	
7.1.2 Attending to	discriminating	dejected
customers' order	caring	discriminating
	patient	caring — indifferent
	respectful	formal — informal
	regretting	courteous
	willing	grateful
	inducive	willing — unwilling
	dissuasive	irresolute
	active	compelling
	obedient	assenting
7.1.3 Serving the order	assenting	temperate
7.1.4 Attending to	pleasant	content
customers' com-	caring	discontented
plaints and well-	formal	cheerful
being	courteous	dejected
	regretting	displeased
	concordant	impatient

Activities	Key (P)	Key (R)
		praising
		disapproving
7.1.5 Attending to the bill	sensitive	courteous — discourteous
	formal	resentful — unresentful
	courteous	regretting
	patient	resolute
	grateful	compelling
	regretting	certain — uncertain
	inexcitable	
7.1.6 Attending to customers' departure	pleasant courteous assenting	formal — informal courteous praising

n.b. *Each* event is processed for communicative key in this way.

PART TWO: THE SYLLABUS CONTENT

LANGUAGE MICRO-FUNCTIONS AND ATTITUDINAL-TONES

Input: the profile of needs
Event 7.1

Productive

Activity	Micro-function	Attitudinal-tone
7.1.1	1. intention	[+ formal]
	2. prohibit	[+ polite], [+ regretting]
	3. direct	[+ polite]
	4. request	[+ courteous]
	5. explanation	[+ polite], [+ firm]
	6. greeting	[+ correct], [+ welcoming]
7.1.2	1. suggest	[+ personal], [+ deferential], [+ encouraging]
	2. advise	[+ personal], [+ deferential]
	3. predict	[+ cautionary], [+ deferential]
	4. describe	[+ discriminating], [+ patient]
	5. affirm	[+ lively], [+ compliant]
	6. question	[+ helpful], [+ efficient]
	7. confirm	[+ efficient]

	8.	explanation	[+ concerned], [+ apologetic]
	9.	definition	[+ discriminating]
7.1.3	1.	question	[+ confirmatory]/—
7.1.4	1.	intention	[+ personal], [+ apologetic]
	2.	excuse	[+ polite], [+ regretting], [+ placatory]
	3.	affirm	[+ agreeable]
	4.	question	[+ concerned], [+ contrite]
	5.	solicitude	[+ agreeable], [+ caring], [+ correct]
7.1.5	1.	release	[+ tactful], [+ gracious]
	2.	state	—
	3.	query	[+ tactful], [+ formal]
	4.	request	[+ formal], [+ polite]
	5.	apology	[+ contrite]
	6.	verification	[+ forbearing], [+ composed]
	7.	thanks	[+ acknowledging]/[+ appreciative]
7.1.6	1.	hope	[+ agreeable]
	2.	question	[+ confirmatory]
	3.	farewell	[+ courteous]
	4.	acknowledgement	[+ courteous]

Receptive

Activity	Micro-function	Attitudinal-tone
7.1.1	1. state	[+ formal]
	2. query	[+ doubting], [+ protesting]
	3. request	[+ hoping], [+ formal]
	4. greeting	[+ formal]
7.1.2	1. want	[+ fastidious]
	2. intention	[+ semi-formal], [+ sure]
	3. approve	[+ discerning]
	4. command	[+ peremptory]/[+ polite]
	5. question	1. [+ interested]/[+ half-interested]
		2. [+ fastidious]
	6. request	[+ formal]
	7. decline	[+ acknowledging]
	8. agree	1. [+ enthusiastic]
		2. [+ reluctant], [+ acquiescent]

	9.	concur	[+ vacillating]
	10.	demur	[+ vacillating]
	11.	defer	[+ willing]
	12.	obligation	[+ disappointed] , [+ reluctant]
7.1.3	1.	affirm	—
	2.	assent/decline	[+ restrained]
7.1.4	1.	release	[+ disappointed]
	2.	complain	[+ exasperated] , [+ unforbearing]
	3.	reproach	[+ annoyed] , [+ censorious]
	4.	express	[+ contented] /[+ complimentary]
	5.	question	[+ restless]
	6.	request	[+ convivial]
	7.	assent/decline	[+ dissatisfied]
7.1.5	1.	command	[+ polite]
	2.	question	—
	3.	query	1. [+ polite] , [+ mild]
			2. [+ mild] , [+ uncertain]
			3. [+ indignant] , [+ unequivocal]
	4.	request	[+ urgent]
	5.	disagree	1. [+ mild] , [+ firm]
			2. [+ adamant]
			3. [+ annoyed] , [+ insistent]
	6.	concede	[+ apologetic] /[+ off-handed]
7.1.6	1.	approve	[+ complimentary] /[+ laudatory]
	2.	request	[+ courteous]
	3.	farewell	[+ formal] /[+ informal]

n.b. For *each* event, the activities and their keys are processed into units of meaning in this way.

LANGUAGE FORMS

Input: units of meaning

Productive

Meaning unit number	Language realisation
7.1.1.1	I will bring the menu.
2	I'm afraid we are full/closed.
3	Please follow me/Will you sit here, please.

4 May I take your coat, sir/madam?

5 It is necessary to book, I'm afraid. All these tables are reserved./We close at _____.

6 Good morning/afternoon/evening, sir/madam.

7.1.2.1 May I suggest the _____?/Would you care to try the _____? It is a very typical local dish.

2 May I recommend the _____?
I think you would like the _____.
Our house speciality is the _____. I don't think you will be disappointed.

3 You may find the _____ too hot/spicy.

4 It's peppery/hot/spicy/cold/_____. (Yes, it is/No, it isn't.)
It's hotter/milder/more _____ than _____.
It's not as _____ as _____.
It's like _____.
It's deep fried/shallow fried/grilled/boiled/stewed/baked/roasted/braised/_____ in batter/butter/wine_____.
There is garlic/_____ in it. (Yes, it does/No, it doesn't.)
It's a dry/medium dry/medium sweet/sweet _____ wine.

5 I'm coming, sir/I'll be with you in a moment, sir.

6 Yes, certainly, sir. What would you like?
What vegetables would you like?
How would you like your steak?
Would you like something to begin with/some dessert or cheese/some coffee/a drink first?
Would you like some wine with the meal? I will bring the wine list.

7 (numeral) _____, (numeral) _____, etc.

8 I'm very sorry but the _____ is finished/not available.
I'm afraid it has been popular today/I'm afraid there is a shortage of _____ at the moment.

9 It's made of _____, _____, _____.
It's a kind of _____.

7.1.3.1 _____ for you, sir/madam?/The _____?

7.1.4.1 I'm very sorry, I will get it immediately.
I'm very sorry, I will bring a hot/cold/fresh/clean/_____ one.

2 I'm sorry but we are very busy/short-staffed today. We will be as quick as we can.

3	`Certainly, sir/madam.
4	Would you like to try something else? We really are very sorry.
5	Is everything all right? How is your _____, sir/madam?
7.1.5.1	That's perfectly all right, sir/madam.
2	That is the wine/cover charge/_____. Yes, it is/No, it isn't.
3	Are you sure about that, sir/madam? Didn't the lady/gentleman there have _____?
4	Would you mind checking it again, please?
5	I'm so sorry. Please excuse me.
6	This is for the _____ which the lady/gentleman here had. You had (numeral) _____. I'm afraid I still make the total _____.
7	Thank you/Thank you very much, sir/madam.
7.1.6.1	I hope you enjoyed the meal.
2	Your coat, sir/madam?
3	Goodbye/Good day/Good night, sir/madam. We hope to see you again.
4	Thank you, sir/madam.

Receptive

7.1.1.1	I have booked a table for (numeral). The name is _____.
2	Full? But what about those empty tables?/Closed? Why? It's only _____.
3	Do you have a table for (numeral), please? We have not booked, I'm afraid.
4	Good morning/Good afternoon/Good evening.
7.1.2.1	I would like my steak rare/medium/well done. I would like my Martini very dry, please.
2	I'm going to have the _____./The _____ for me, please.
3	That sounds fine/delicious/interesting. Yes, I'll have that.
4	Waiter!/Waiter.
5.1	What do you suggest/advise? What is _____? What is the _____ like?
2	Is it peppery/hot/spicy/mild/thick/thin/light/heavy/heavy cold? How is it cooked? Is the _____ fried/_____?

Does it have garlic/_____ in it?

Are the peas/_____ fresh or frozen/tinned?

6   Could we order, please?

Could I/we have a drink first/some more coffee/some cigarettes/a brandy/the menu/_____?

7   Not for me, thank you.

8.1   Oh, yes, I'll have that!

  2   Well, all right, I'll try it./Yes, I suppose so.

9   Yes, I'll try that . . . Wait a minute, let me think about that for a moment.

10   No, I don't think I'll try that . . . Or shall I?

11   All right, I'll follow your suggestion.

12   Oh, dear! What a pity. In that case I'll have to have the _____.

7.1.3.1   Yes, please.

   3   Just a little . . . that's enough, thank you./Not for me.

7.1.4.1   It doesn't matter.

   2   I/we have been waiting for _____ for my/our order. I am not prepared to wait any longer.

   3   The _____ is cold/bad/dirty/not cooked enough/too _____/_____.

This bottle is corked/warm/nowhere near cold enough.

There is an insect/_____ in my food.

   4   Yes, thank you./Very nice./Splendid!

   5   What has happened to my/our order?

   6   Could we have some more of this excellent _____?

   7   Yes, I think we'd better./No, I've had enough.

7.1.5.1   The bill, please.

   2   What's this?

Is service included?

   3   1. I think there is a mistake in the bill.

       2. I'm not sure what this is for.

       3. How on earth did you arrive at this figure?

   4   Could we have the bill, please? I'm in a hurry.

   5   1. I can't agree with your addition. I make it _____.

       2. We did not have this./No, he/she did not have this. Only one of us had the _____.

       3. Look, how many more times do I have to tell you. We only had one/_____ _____.

6   My mistake, I'm sorry about that.
         Ah, yes, I'd forgotten about that.

7.1.6.1   Yes, we did. We enjoyed the meal very much./That was one of the best meals I've had in Ibiza. I particularly enjoyed the _____.

2   Would you bring my/our coat(s), please.

3   Goodbye/Goodnight/Bye/Cheerio.

n.b. For each activity of each event, the units of meaning are realised as language forms in this way. Here, therefore, the activities and keys for events 7.2, 7.3, and 7.4 would in turn be processed into units of meaning before being realised as language forms.

These sample language realisations constitute the *essence* of the utterance that is required for the realisation of that particular unit of meaning. That utterance may turn out to be a little longer because of the need for continuity, coherence, feedback, etc., in communication, and because of the redundant nature of much of natural discourse. It is not the purpose of the model to predict the totality of required language forms (a clearly impossible aim) but to specify those forms that are central to the successful realisation of the activities for which English is required.

EXAMPLE B

Introductory note
In the profile of needs one takes account of the fact that although this type of participant apparently needs English only for reading, the classroom activity in English lessons usually involves some writing in English and a degree of listening and speaking. It should be noted that when this participant is reading books or articles in English his note-taking is in most cases done in Spanish except when he deliberately wants to recover a part of the English text verbatim. However, for certain kinds of reading activity in the English lessons he will be expected to produce written responses in English. It is this that we have in mind when assigning values in the written productive column of the target level guide on page 209 below. In that guide the values shown in the spoken receptive and productive columns reflect the minimal oral interaction in English which may be expected between student and teacher during English lessons.

Although the target level guide is therefore completed for all four columns, since the spoken medium and to a lesser extent the written productive one are only minor requirements here (and we exemplified the spoken medium in Example A above), the syllabus specification will here be confined to the receptive command of the written medium.

PART ONE: THE PROFILE OF COMMUNICATION NEEDS

0.0 PARTICIPANT

0.1 Identity
    0.1.1 Age: 18–21
    0.1.2 Sex: mixed, mostly male
    0.1.3 Nationality: Venezuelan
    0.1.4 Place of residence: Caracas

0.2 Language
    0.2.1 Mother tongue: Spanish
    0.2.2 Target language: English
    0.2.3 Present level/command of target language: elementary
    0.2.4 Other languages known: none
    0.2.5 Extent of command: N/A

1.0 PURPOSIVE DOMAIN

1.1 ESP classification
    1.1.2 educational – discipline-based
        1.1.2.1 In-study

1.2 Occupational purpose
N/A

1.3 Educational purpose
    1.3.1 Specific discipline: agriculture
    1.3.2 Central area of study: cattle breeding
    1.3.3 Other areas of study: animal husbandry; animal physiology
    1.3.4 Academic discipline classification: biological science

2.0 SETTING

2.1 Physical setting: spatial
    2.1.1 Location
        2.1.1.1 Country: Venezuela
        2.1.1.2 Town: Caracas
    2.1.2 Place of work: N/A
    2.1.3 Place of study and study setting
        2.1.3.1 university
        2.1.3.2 classroom
        2.1.3.4 laboratory
        2.1.3.6 private study/library
    2.1.4 Other places: bookshop
    2.1.5 Extent — size of institution:* small
    2.1.6 Extent — scale of use: international

2.2 Physical setting: temporal
    2.2.1 Point of time: in English classes and private study at first;
        increasingly in private study as course progresses
    2.2.2 Duration: 5—10 hours per week
    2.2.3 Frequency: regularly, in term time; more variable frequency
        during vacation

2.3 Psychosocial setting
    2.3.3 intellectual
    2.3.9 quasi-professional
    2.3.13 private and public
    2.3.14 familiar physical
    2.3.16 generally quiet
    2.3.17 demanding
    2.3.18 mainly unhurried
    2.3.19 fairly formal

3.0 INTERACTION

3.1 Position
    Student

---

*This refers to the size of the actual physical environment in which the target language is used, in this case the student's own room, library, laboratory, and classroom.

3.2 Role-set
authors/writers of books/articles; English language teacher

3.3 Role-set identity
3.3.1 Number: individual
3.3.2 Age-group: adult
3.3.3 Sex: mixed
3.3.4 Nationality: mostly American and British

3.4 Social relationships
3.4.16 learner to instructor/authority
3.4.26 non-native to native
3.4.39 insider to insider
3.4.43 professional to professional
3.4.53 adult to adult

4.0 INSTRUMENTALITY

4.1 Medium
4.1.1 spoken:receptive
4.1.2 spoken: productive
4.1.3 written: receptive
4.1.4 written: productive

4.2 Mode
4.2.3 monologue, written to be read
4.2.7 dialogue, spoken to be heard
4.2.8 dialogue, written to be read

4.3 Channel
4.3.1 face-to-face [bilateral]
4.3.4 print [bilateral]
4.3.12 print [unilateral]

5.0 DIALECT

5.1 Regional
Input
Setting

Location: Venezuela, Caracas
Place: university library, classroom, laboratory, bookshop
Scale of use: international
Interaction
Role-set identity (nationality): mostly American and British
Dialect and accent
Understand and produce Standard English dialect, understand General American or RP accent, produce Spanish approximation to either.

5.2 Social class
N/A

5.3 Temporal
Input
Purposive domain
Educational purpose: agriculture student
Interaction
Role-set: authors, English language teacher
Role-set identity (age-group): adult
Dialect
5.3.1 contemporary

6.0 TARGET LEVEL

Input
Purposive domain
Educational purpose: student of agriculture, especially cattle breeding, also animal husbandry and animal physiology
Setting
Place of study: university
Scale of use: international
Psychosocial environment: intellectual; quasi-professional; private and public; familiar physical; generally quiet; demanding; mainly unhurried; fairly formal
Interaction
Role-set: authors; English language teacher
Role-set age-group: adult
Role-set nationality: mostly American and British

Instrumentality
  Medium: spoken — receptive and productive; written — receptive
  and productive
  Mode: monologue, written to be read; dialogue, spoken to be
  heard; dialogue, written to be read
  Channel: face-to-face [bilateral]; print [bilateral] and [unilateral]

Target level guide

6.1 Dimensions

| | *Medium* | | | |
| | Spoken | | Written | |
	Rec.	Prod.	Rec.	Prod.
6.1.1 *Size* of utterance/text	2	1	7	1/3
6.1.2 *Complexity* of utterance/text	2	1	6	3
6.1.3 *Range* of forms/micro-functions/micro-skills	2	1	4	2
6.1.4 *Delicacy* of forms/micro-functions/micro-skills	1	1	5	3
6.1.5 *Speed* of communication	3	2	3/5	2
6.1.6 *Flexibility* of communication	1	1	2	1

6.2 Conditions

| | *Medium* | | | |
| | Spoken | | Written | |
Tolerance of:	Rec.	Prod.	Rec.	Prod.
6.2.1 error (linguistic)	4	5	1	2
6.2.2 stylistic failure	5	5	4	4
6.2.3 reference (to dictionary/addressee, etc.)	5	5	3	3
6.2.4 repetition (re-read/ask for repeat)	5	—	5	—
6.2.5 hesitation (lack of fluency)	—	5	—	—

7.0 COMMUNICATIVE EVENT

Input
Purposive domain
  Educational purpose: student of agriculture, especially cattle breed-
  ing, also animal husbandry and animal physiology

The instrument applied

Setting
    Location: Venezuela, Caracas
    Place of study: university
    Study setting: private study/library, classroom, laboratory
    Other places: bookshop
    Size: small
Interaction
    Role-set: authors of books/articles; English language teacher
Instrumentality
    Medium: written — receptive (major); written — productive,
    spoken — receptive and productive (minor)
    Mode: monologue, written to be read; dialogue, spoken to be
    heard; dialogue, written to be read
    Channel: print [unilateral] ; print [bilateral] ; face-to-face [bilateral]
Communicative events
Main : 7.1 Agriculture student studying reference material (standard
        textbooks/manuals/articles, etc.) in English, in university
        library/laboratory/private study
Other: 7.2 Agriculture student reading the current literature (new
        books/periodicals, etc.) in own discipline and related fields, in
        English, in library/bookshop
        7.3 University student taking English lessons to develop his
        ability to understand agricultural science material written in
        English
Event 7.1
    Communicative activities
    7.1.1 reading intensively for all the information in the text
    7.1.2 reading for specific information to carry out an assignment
    7.1.3 reading to find out the writer's position on a particular issue
    (and, where relevant, to evaluate experimental data)
    7.1.4 reading for the main information in a text (note-taking in
    Spanish or English; writing up notes, in Spanish)
    ⋮
    Subject matter
    (Topics in cattle breeding, also in animal husbandry and animal
    physiology, would be listed here)
Event 7.2
    Communicative activities
    7.2.1 reading as routine check on new information of possible

relevance to student's particular areas of study

7.2.2 reading to keep abreast of developments

7.2.3 reading to assess desirability of text for intensive study

7.2.4 reading extensively in search of information wanted, but from unknown sources

 ⋮

Subject matter

(Topics in agriculture, and related fields in biological science, would be listed here)

Event 7.3

 Communicative activities

 7.3.1 written question and answer work on the text

 7.3.2 oral interaction with the teacher on the text

 7.3.3 group work (at this stage only in Spanish) on the text and questions

 ⋮

 Subject matter

 (Topics in any relevant field of study or related area of interest stylistically compatible with § 1.3.4 above)

8.0 COMMUNICATIVE KEY

Input

Participant

 Identity: 18–21 year old; mixed sex; mostly male; Venezuelan

Interaction

 Role-set identity: number — individual; age-group — adult; sex — mixed; nationality — mostly American and British

 Social relationships: learner to instructor/authority; non-native to native; insider to insider; professional to professional; adult to adult

Setting

 Psychosocial environments: intellectual; quasi-professional; private and public; familiar physical; generally quiet; demanding; mainly unhurried; fairly formal

Instrumentality

 Command of medium: mainly receptive

Event

 Activities: all

211

The instrument applied

Communicative key
Events 7.1, 7.2, and 7.3

Activities	*Key (receptive)*
All,* except for 7.3.2;† and especially 7.1.3 and 7.2.3	cautious — incautious
	caring — indifferent
	formal — informal
	honest — dishonest
	disinterested — biased
	approving — disapproving
	inducive — dissuasive
	concordant — discordant
	authoritative — lacking in authority
	certain — uncertain
	intelligent/thinking — unthinking/unintelligent
	assenting — dissenting

PART TWO: THE SYLLABUS CONTENT

LANGUAGE SKILLS

Input: the profile of needs
Activity: 7.1.1

Skill No.	Description
19.	Deducing the meaning and use of unfamiliar lexical items, through
	19.1 understanding word formation, especially roots and prefixes
	19.2 contextual clues
20.	Understanding explicitly stated information
22.	Understanding information in the text, not explicitly stated, through
	22.1 making inferences
24.	Understanding conceptual meaning, especially

*In written discourse activities such as these it seems to make more sense to specify the keys for the activities taken as a whole. Then, if any particular activity is especially concerned with the keys, this can be stated (as here).

†Since the spoken medium will not be dealt with in the syllabus specification (see the introductory note, above, to this Example B), this activity will not be handled here.

24.1 quantity and amount

24.2 definiteness and indefiniteness

24.3 comparison; degree

24.4 time (esp. present tense and aspect)

24.5 location; direction

24.6 means; instrument

24.7 cause; result; purpose; reason; condition; contrast

26. Understanding the communicative value of a sentence/piece of text

    26.1 with the less common explicit indicators for the main sub-categories of micro-function (see the inventory of micro-functions)

    26.2 without explicit indicators for these micro-functions

28. Understanding relations within the sentence, especially

    28.2 premodification, esp. long noun phrase, and postmodification

    28.4 modal auxiliaries

    28.5 intra-sentential connectors

30. Understanding relations between parts of a text through lexical cohesion devices, especially

    30.2 synonymy

    30.3 hyponymy

    30.4 antithesis

    30.7 pro-forms

32. Understanding relations between parts of a text through grammatical cohesion devices of

    32.1 reference (cataphoric as well as anaphoric)

    32.2 comparison

    32.3 substitution

    32.4 ellipsis

    32.5 time relaters

    32.6 logical connecters, esp. less common ones

34. Interpreting text by going outside it:

    34.3 integrating data in the text with own experience or knowledge of the world

51. Transcoding information presented in diagrammatic display, involving

    51.2 interpretation or comparison of diagrams/tables/graphs in writing (Spanish)

Activity: 7.1.2
Basic to this activity, at the level indicated in the profile, is
46. Scanning to locate specifically required information on
    46.4 more than one point, involving a complex search
    46.5 a whole topic
In addition, when the required information or each part of it is
located, whether certainly or only tentatively, selected skills from
those listed above for activity 7.1.1 will be needed, viz:
19, 20, 22.1, 24, 26, 28, 30, 32, 34.3, and 51.2; and possibly also
41. Selective extraction of relevant points from a text, involving
    41.3 the tabulation of information for comparison and contrast
Activity: 7.1.3
For this activity one would select in particular:
26. Understanding the communicative value of the text
    26.1 and 26.2 with and without explicit indicators in respect of
    the following micro-functions (taken from the inventory of
    micro-functions):
        26.1/2.1 certainty, probability, possibility, nil certainty; con-
                viction, conjecture, doubt, disbelief
        26.1/2.2 inclination, prefer
        26.1/2.3 assess, estimate; pronounce; approve, praise; dis-
                approve, impute, disparage
        26.1/2.4 advise, advocate; predict, warn
        26.1/2.5 assert, emphasise, advocate, deny; agree, corrobor-
                ate; disagree, repudiate; concede
        26.1/2.6 substantiation, justification; conclusion
    and the following attitudinal-tones (derived from the keys
    specified in the profile of needs, as relevant to this activity):
    cautious, tentative, rash; enthusiastic, indifferent; frank, dis-
    ingenuous; impartial, generous, biased; favourable, support-
    ing, unfavourable, critical; encouraging, provocative, dis-
    couraging; diplomatic, aggressive, polemical; sure, unequivocal,
    dogmatic, half-certain, unsure, ambiguous, sceptical; acqui-
    escent, concurring, qualifying, dissenting, querying
28. Understanding relations within the sentence, especially
    28.2 disjuncts
    28.4 modal auxiliaries
    28.7 focus and theme
35. Recognising indicators in discourse for

35.2 reinforcing an argument

36.7 anticipating an objection or contrary view

39. Distinguishing the main idea from supporting details, by differentiating

    39.3 a process from its stages

    39.4 category from exponent

    39.5 statement from example

    39.6 fact from opinion

    39.7 a proposition from its argument

41. Selective extraction of relevant points from a text, including

    41.1 the coordination of related information

Activity: 7.1.4

For this activity one would select in particular:

35. Recognising indicators in discourse for

    35.1 introducing an idea

    35.5 emphasising a point

37. Identifying the main point or important information in a piece of discourse, through

    37.4 topic sentence, in paragraphs of inductive and deductive organisation

39. Distinguishing the main idea from supporting details, by differentiating

    39.1 primary from secondary significance

    39.2 the whole from its parts

40. Extracting salient points to summarise (later, in Spanish)

    40.1 the whole text

    40.2 a specific idea/topic in the text

43. Reducing the text through rejecting redundant or irrelevant information and items, and through

    43.5 use of abbreviations

    43.6 use of symbols denoting relationships between states, processes, etc.

    (n.b. This limited application of this skill category is possible in English. The writing up of any such notes, after the reducing, is of course likely to be done in Spanish.)

44. Basic reference skills: understanding and use of

    44.1 graphic presentation, viz. headings, subheadings, numbering, indentation, bold print

44.2 table of contents and index*
45.   Skimming to obtain
45.1 the gist of the text

n.b. *Each* activity for each event is processed for micro-skills in this way.

*It might be worth pointing out that for activity 7.2.4 one would also need to specify skills 44.3 and 44.4 from this group, and skill 45.2 from the following group

EPILOGUE

This book has not dealt with those variables which are concerned with that dimension of course design which is subsequent to syllabus specification. These variables, which are constraints upon the implementation of the syllabus specification, include:

1. *Socio-political*
   attitude of government; status of English (optional/compulsory, medium/subject); expectations of institution/society; decisions on timing (viz. when to start); etc.
2. *Logistical*
   number of trained teachers; accommodation; amount/suitability of equipment; extant materials; money; etc.
3. *Administrative*
   quantity, intensity, and mode of instruction; time-table; etc.
4. *Psycho-pedagogic*
   learner's motivation and expectations; traditional styles of learning; etc.
5. *Methodological*
   recommended language learning strategies and language teaching techniques; order of items and organisation into teaching units; selection, adaptation, and production of suitable materials; etc.

These implementational constraints are, of course, significant in the modification of syllabus specifications and production of materials, but that is the next stage in course design and should not take place until after the output from the operational instrument has been obtained.

In the course of this work a number of lines of further research for the extension of the model or the refinement of some of its categories have been indicated or become apparent. Furthermore there is an evident need for research to evaluate the reliability of a certain aspect of the model. This concerns those parts of the operational instrument where decisions have to be made according to the subjective judgement of the user of the instrument. There is a need here for empirical validation in order to establish the reliability of this part of the decision making process.

This book has been concerned with language syllabus design. More specifically, the contention has been that, where the purpose for which the target language is required can be identified, the syllabus specification is directly derivable from the prior identification of the communication needs of that particular participant or participant stereotype. This syllabus specification is the target communicative competence, and the contention made here is that in the design of ESP syllabuses it is not only highly desirable but perfectly possible to begin with the learner and work systematically forward to the syllabus specification that represents the target communicative competence. In the model that has been presented, the systematic processing of the profile of communication needs for the particular participant input is prerequisite to the syllabus specification output. It follows logically that syllabus specification is prerequisite to the production of materials for the realisation of the syllabus. Finally, a point worth stressing is that this sociolinguistic model for specifying communicative competence makes it possible for the user to be confident of the relevance and appropriateness of the resultant syllabus content in the design of courses in English for specific purposes.

REFERENCES AND BIBLIOGRAPHY

Allen, J.P.B. (1975) 'English, science and language teaching: the "Focus" approach'. *Edutec/Languages for Special Purposes*, No. 9.

Allen, J.P.B. and H.G. Widdowson (1974) *English in physical science*. Teacher's edn. Oxford University Press. (English in Focus.)

Allen, W. Stannard (1954) *Living English speech*. Longman.

Austin, J.L. (1962) *How to do things with words*. Oxford, Clarendon Press.

Banton, M. (1965) *Roles*. Tavistock.

Bates, Martin and Tony Dudley-Evans (1976) *Nucleus: English for science and technology*. Longman.

Bell, R.T. (1976) *Sociolinguistics*. Batsford.

Bernstein, Basil (1971) *Class, codes and control*, Vol. 1. Routledge and Kegan Paul.

Birdwhistell, R.L. (1970) *Kinesics and context*. University of Pennsylvania Press.

Bloom, B.S., J.T. Hastings and G.F. Madaus (1971) *Handbook on formative and summative evaluation of student learning*. McGraw-Hill.

Briere, Eugène J. (1971) 'Are we really measuring proficiency with our foreign language tests?' *Foreign Language Annals*, Vol. 4, No. 4.

Bright, J.A. and G. McGregor (1970) *Teaching English as a second language*. Longman.

Brown, R. and M. Ford (1961) 'Address in American English'. *Journal of Abnormal Social Psychology*, Vol. 62.

Brown, R. and A. Gilman (1960) 'The pronouns of power and solidarity'. In Sebeok, T. ed. *Style in language*. MIT Press.

Brumfit, C.J. (1977) 'The teaching of advanced reading skills in foreign languages, with particular reference to English as foreign language'. *Language Teaching and Linguistics: Abstracts*, Vol. 10, No. 2. (A survey article.)

Bung, K. (1973a) *The specification of objectives in a language learning system for adults*. CCC/EES (73) 34. Strasbourg, Council of Europe.

(1973b) 'The foreign language needs of waiters and hotel staff'. CCC/EES (73) 16. Strasbourg, Council of Europe.

Campbell, Robin and Roger Wales (1970) 'The study of language acquisition'. In Lyons, John, ed. *New horizons in linguistics*. Penguin.

Candlin, C.N. (1976) 'Communicative language teaching and the debt to pragmatics'. In Rameh, C. ed. *Semantics: theory and application*. Georgetown University Round Table on Languages and Linguistics, 1976. Georgetown University Press.

Candlin, C.N., J.H. Leather and C.J. Bruton (1974) 'English language skills for overseas doctors and medical staff: work in progress'. Reports 1—4 and Appendices 1—2. Linguistics Section, Department of English, University of Lancaster.

Candlin, C.N., C.J. Bruton and J.H. Leather (1976a) *Doctor—patient communication skills*. Chelmsford, Medical Recording Service Foundation.

(1976b) 'Doctors in casualty: applying communicative competence to components of specialist course design'. *IRAL*, Vol. 14, No. 3.

Candlin, C.N., J. Michael Kirkwood and Helen M. Moore (1975) 'Developing study skills in English'. *English for academic study*. British Council, English Teaching Information Centre.

Carroll, J.B. (1961) 'Fundamental considerations in testing for English language proficiency of foreign students'. In *Testing the English proficiency of foreign students*. Center for Applied Linguistics.

Carroll, J.B. and R. Freedle, eds. (1972) *Language comprehension and the acquisition of knowledge*. Winston.

Chamberlain, R. (1976) 'ESP: the communication skills in English project at King Faisal University, Dammam'. ETIC Archives. Mimeo.

Chomsky, N. (1965) *Aspects of the theory of syntax*. MIT Press.

(1970) 'Remarks on nominalisation'. In Jacobs, R. and P. Rosenbaum, eds. *Readings in English transformational grammar*. Ginn.

Cicourel, A. (1972) *Cognitive sociology*. Penguin Education, 1973.

Communication Skills in English (1976) Materials developed for the projects of this name at King Abdul Aziz and King Faisal universities, Saudi Arabia. Mimeo.

Cooper, M.D. (1975) 'A report on the University of Malaya ESP project'. 11th Regional Seminar, 1975, SEAMEO Regional English Language Centre. Mimeo.

Cooper, Robert L. (1968) 'An elaborated language testing model'. *Language Learning*. Special Issue No. 3 on problems in foreign language testing.

Corder, S. Pit (1973) *Introducing applied linguistics*. Penguin Education.

Coulthard, Malcolm (1975) 'Discourse analysis in English — a short review of the liberature'. *Language Teaching and Linguistics: Abstracts*, Vol. 8, No. 2 (A survey article.)

Coulthard, R.M. and C.M. Ashby. 'Doctor—patient interviews'. University of Birmingham. (Working papers in discourse analysis, 1.) Mimeo.

Crystal, David (1971) 'Stylistics, fluency, and language teaching'. In *Interdisciplinary approaches to language*. Centre for Information on Language Teaching and Research.

Crystal, David and Derek Davy (1969) *Investigating English style*. Longman.

Davies, Alan (1973) 'Textbook situations and idealised language'. In Candlin, C.N. ed. 'The communicative teaching of English'. AILA/BAAL Seminar, 1973. University of Lancaster. Mimeo.

Davies, Alan and H.G. Widdowson (1974) 'Reading and writing'. Chapter 6 in Allen, J.P.B. and S. Pit Corder, eds. *The Edinburgh course in applied linguistics*, Vol. 3. Oxford University Press.

220

Dudley-Evans, A., C.C. Shettlesworth and M.K. Phillips (1975). 'Aspects of the writing and teaching of EST courses: the Tabriz materials'. *ELT Documents*, No. 2. 1975.

Early, P.B. (1976) 'English-language teaching in the Republic of Croatia, Yugoslavia: some recent developments'. *ELT Documents*, No. 1, 1976.

ELTDU (1973) (English Language Teaching Development Unit.) *English in flight: a course for air hostesses*. Oxford University Press.

(1978) (English Language Teaching Development Unit.) *Basic English for science*. Oxford University Press.

Ervin-Tripp, Susan (1964) 'An analysis of the interaction of language, topic and listener'. In Argyle, M. ed. *Social encounters*. Penguin Education, 1973.

(1972) 'On sociolinguistic rules: alternation and co-occurrence'. In Gumperz and Hymes, eds. *Directions in sociolinguistics: the ethnography of communication*. Holt, Rinehart.

Ewer, J.R. and G. Latorre (1967) 'Preparing an English course for students of science'. *English Language Teaching*, Vol. 21, No. 3.

(1969) *A course in basic scientific English*. Longman.

Fawcett, Robin (1973) 'Language functions and language variation in a cognitive model of communication'. In Candlin, C.N. ed. 'The communicative teaching of English'. AILA/BAAL Seminar, 1973. University of Lancaster. Mimeo.

Ferguson, C.A. (1959) 'Diglossia'. In Giglioli, ed. *Language and social context*. Penguin, 1972. (Reprinted from *Word*, Vol. 15.)

Fillmore, Chalres J. (1968) 'The case for case'. In Bach, Emmon and Robert T. Harms, eds. *Universals in linguistic theory*. Holt, Rinehart.

Fishman, Joshua A. (1966) 'The implications of bilingualism for language teaching and language learning'. In Valdman, A. ed. *Trends in language teaching*. McGraw-Hill.

(1970) *Sociolinguistics: a brief introduction*. Rowley, Mass., Newbury House.

(1971) 'The relationship between micro- and macro-sociolinguistics in the study of who speaks what language to whom and when'. In Pride, J.B. and J. Holmes eds. *Sociolinguistics*. Penguin Education, 1972.

Fishman, Joshua A., ed. (1968) *Readings in the sociology of language*. The Hague, Paris, Mouton.

Fodor, J. and M. Garrett (1966) 'Some reflections on competence and performance'. In Lyons, J. and R. Wales eds. *Psycholinguistic Papers*. Edinburgh University Press.

Frake, C.O. (1961) 'The diagnosis of disease among the Subanun of Mindinao'. *American Anthropologist*, Vol. 63, No. 1.

Freeman, Sarah and Jo McDonough (1975) 'English for science at the University of Essex: the Venezuelan scheme: materials development and methodology'. *ELT Documents*, No. 2. 1975.

Freihoff, Roland and Sauli Takala (1974) *A systematic description of language teaching objectives based on the specification of language use situations*. Abridged version, Jyväskylä, University of Jvyäskylä, Language Centre.

Giglioli, Pier Paolo (1972) *Language and social context*. Penguin.

References and bibliography

Gimson, A.C. (1970) *An introduction to the pronunciation of English*. 2nd edn. Edward Arnold.

Goffman, E. (1964) 'The neglected situation'. In Giglioli, ed. *Language and social context*. Penguin, 1972. (Reprinted from *American Anthropologist*, Vol. 66.)

(1971) 'Relations in public'. In Argyle, M. ed. *Social encounters*. Penguin Education, 1973.

Goodman, K. (1967) 'Reading: a psycholinguistic guessing game'. *Journal of the Reading Specialist*, 6.

(1971) 'Psycholinguistic universals in the reading process'. In Pimsleur, P. and T. Quinn, eds. *The psychology of second language learning*. Cambridge University Press.

Greene, Judith (1972). *Psycholinguistics*. Penguin Education.

Gregory, Michael (1967) 'Aspects of varieties differentiation'. *Journal of Linguistics*. Vol. 3, No. 2.

Gumperz, John J. (1970) 'Sociolinguistics and communication in small groups'. In Pride, J.B. and J. Holmes, eds. *Sociolinguistics*. Penguin Education, 1972.

Gumperz, John J. and Dell Hymes, eds. (1964) 'The ethnography of communication'. *American Anthropologist*, Vol. 66, No. 6, Part 2. (Special publication.) Menasha, Wisc., American Anthropological Association.

(1972) *Directions in sociolinguistics: the ethnography of communication*. Holt, Rinehart.

Habermas, J. (1970) 'Towards a theory of communicative competence'. In Dreitzel, H. ed. *Recent Sociology*, No. 2. Collier-Macmillan.

Halliday, M.A.K. (1963) 'Intonation systems in English'. In McIntosh, A. and Halliday, M.A.K. eds. *Patterns of language*. Longman, 1966.

(1967) *Intonation and grammar in British English*. Mouton.

(1970a) 'Language structure and language function'. In Lyons, John, ed. *New horizons in linguistics*. Penguin.

(1970b) *A course in spoken English: Intonation*. Oxford University Press.

(1971) 'Language in a social perspective'. In *Explorations in the functions of language*. Edward Arnold, 1973.

(1972) 'Towards a sociological semantics'. In *Explorations in the functions of language*. Edward Arnold, 1973.

(1975) *Learning how to mean: explorations in the development of language*. Edward Arnold.

Halliday, M.A.K. and Ruqaiya Hasan (1976). *Cohesion in English*. Longman.

Harris, David (1969). *Testing English as a second language*. McGraw-Hill.

Harvey, A.M., M. Horzella and G. Latorre (1977) 'Materials production for ESP — some first principles'. In Moody and Moore, eds. *English for specific purposes: an international seminar*. The British Council, Bogota, Colombia.

Hasan, Ruqaiya (1968) *Grammatical cohesion in spoken and written English*. Part 1. Communication Research Centre, Department of General Linguistics, University College London, and Longman.

(1971) 'Syntax and semantics'. In Morton, J. ed. *Psycholinguistics*. Logos Press.

222

Hawkey, Roger (1977) *Consultancy Report on English for Specific Purposes for Instituto Universitario Politecnico Experimental Ciudad Guayana.* The British Council, London.

Heaton, J.B. (1975) *Studying in English.* Longman.

Hymes, Dell (1962) 'The ethnography of speaking'. In Fishman, ed. *Readings in the sociology of language.* The Hague, Paris, Mouton, 1968. (Reprinted with revision from Gladwin, T. and W.C. Sturtevant, eds. *Anthropology and human behaviour.* Washington, DC, Anthropological Society of Washington, 1962.)

(1969) 'Sociolinguistics and the ethnography of speaking'. In Ardener, E. ed. *Social anthropology and language.* Tavistock, 1971.

(1971) 'On communicative competence'. In Pride and Holmes, eds. *Socioonguistics.* Penguin, 1972. (Excerpts from the paper published 1971, Philadelphia, University of Pennsylvania Press.)

(1972) 'Models of the interaction of language and social life'. In Gumperz and Hymes, eds. *Directions in sociolinguistics.* Holt, Rinehart. (A revision of 'Models of the interaction of language and social setting', *Journal of Social Issues,* Vol. 23. 1967.)

(1974) 'Toward ethnographies of communication: the analysis of communicative events'. In Giglioli, ed. *Language and social context.* Penguin, 1972.

Hymes, Dell, ed. (1974) *Language in culture and society: a reader in linguistics and anthropology.* Harper and Row.

Isaacs, R.H., ed. (1968) *Learning through language.* Teachers' Book and Pupils' Book. Dar es Salaam, Tanzania Publishing House.

Jackson, J.A. ed. (1972) *Sociological studies, 4 — Role.* Cambridge University Press.

Jakobovits, Leon A. (1970) *Foreign language learning: a psycholinguistic analysis of the issues.* Rowley, Mass., Newbury House.

Jakobson, Roman (1960). 'Closing statement: linguistics and poetics'. In Sebeok, T. ed. *Style in language.* MIT Press.

Johnson, Keith (1976) 'The production of functional materials and their integration within existing language-teaching programmes (with special reference to the secondary school syllabus of Croatia, Yugoslavia)'. *ELT Documents,* No. 1. 1976.

Jones, Keith and Peter Roe (1975) 'Designing English for science and technology (EST) programmes'. In *English for academic study.* British Council, English Teaching Information Centre.

Jones, Randall and Bernard Spolsky, eds. (1975) *Testing language proficiency.* Center for Applied Linguistics.

Joos, Martin (1961) *The five clocks.* Harcourt Brace.

Jordan, R. and A. Matthews (1976). 'Working papers on English for academic purposes'. University of Manchester. Mimeo.

Jupp, T.C. (1977) 'Developing skills and resources for teachers in an ESP situation'. In Moody and Moore, eds. *English for specific purposes: an international seminar.* The British Council, Bogota, Colombia.

References and bibliography

Jupp, T.C. and Susan Hodlin (1975) *Industrial English: an example of theory and practice in functional language teaching.* Heinemann Educational.

Kachru, Braj B. (1976) 'Models of English for the third world: white man's linguistic burden or language pragmatics'. *TESOL Quarterly*, Vol. 10, No. 2.

Katz, J. and Postal, P. (1963) *An integrated theory of linguistic descriptions.* MIT Press.

Kingsbury, R. (1971) 'A proposed model for critical discussion and study of a possible unit/credit system in modern language teaching for adults in Europe'. In *Modern languages in adult education.* CCC/EES (71) 135. Strasbourg, Council of Europe.

Kirkwood, J.M. (1973a) 'Towards an integrated programme for advanced students of Russian'. *Audio-Visual Language Journal*, Vol. 11, No. 3.

(1973b) 'Analysing the linguistic and cultural content of foreign language textbooks — an application of variety theory'. *IRAL*, Vol. XI, No. 4.

Knowles, D. (1975) 'A report on the design and operation of an orientation and English language course for prospective technicians on the Arun Gas Field, Aceh, Indonesia'. 11th Regional Seminar, 1975, SEAMEO Regional English Language Centre. Mimeo.

Labov, William (1969) *The study of non-standard English.* Champaign, Ill., National Council of Teachers of English.

(1970) 'The study of language in its social context'. In Giglioli, ed. *Language and social context.* Penguin, 1972.

Lackstrom, John, Larry Selinker and Louis Trimble (1972) 'Technical rhetorical principles and grammatical choice'. In International Congress of Applied Linguistics, Copenhagen, 1972. *Proceedings*, Vol. 3. Heidelberg, Groos, 1974. Also appears in *TESOL Quarterly*, Vol. 7, No. 2. 1973.

Laver, J. (1970) 'The production of speech'. In Lyons, J. ed. *New horizons in linguistics.* Penguin.

(1973) 'Neurolinguistic strategies in speech performance'. Mimeo.

Laver, John and Sandy Hutcheson, eds. (1972) *Communication in face to face interaction.* Penguin Education.

Lawrence, Mary S. (1972) *Writing as a thinking process.* Ann Arbor, Mich., University of Michigan Press.

Leech, Geoffrey N. (1974) *Semantics.* Penguin.

(1976) 'Metalanguage, pragmatics, and performatives'. In Rameh, C. ed. *Semantics: theory and application.* Georgetown University Round Table on Languages and Linguistics, 1976. Georgetown University Press.

Leech, Geoffrey N. and Jan Svartvik (1975). *A communicative grammar of English.* Longman.

Le Page, R.B. (1975) 'Sociolinguistics and the problem of "competence" '. *Language Teaching and Linguistics: Abstracts*, Vol. 8, No. 3. (A survey article.)

Lockwood (1972) *Introduction to stratificational linguistics.* Harcourt Brace.

Lyons, John (1968) *Introduction to theoretical linguistics.* Cambridge University Press.

(1970) *Chomsky*. Fontana/Collins.

Mackay, Ronald (1974) 'Teaching the information gathering skills'. *RELC Journal*, Vol. 5, No. 2.

Mackay, Ronald and Beverly Klassen (1975) 'An operational framework for the classification of reading comprehension exercise types'. Research and Development Unit Report No. 3. *CELE*, National University of Mexico. Mimeo.

Maclean, Joan (1975) *English in basic medical science*. Oxford University Press. (*English in focus*.) (With recordings.)

Macmillan, M. (1971) 'Teaching English to scientists of other languages: sense or sensibility'. In *Science and technology in a second language*. Centre for Information on Language Teaching and Research.

Merton, R. (1957) *Social theory and social structure*. Free Press.

Moody, H.L.B. and J.D. Moore, eds. (1977) *English for specific purposes: an international seminar*. The British Council, Bogota, Colombia.

Moore, J.D. (1977) 'The preparation of rhetorically focussed materials for service courses in English'. In Moody and Moore, eds.

Moore, J.D. et al. (1977) *Reading and thinking*. University of Los Andes, Colombia.

Morrow, K. and K. Johnson (1976) *Communicate: the English of social interaction*. Centre for Applied Language Studies, University of Reading.

Mountford, Alan (1975) *English in workshop practice*. Oxford University Press. (*English in focus*.) (With recordings.)

(1976) 'ESP: the communication skills in English project at King Abdul Aziz University, Jeddah'. ETIC Archives. Mimeo.

Munby, John (1968) *Read and think: training in intensive reading skills*. Longman.

(1973) 'Extensive reading skills'. Chapter 8 in Williams, D.J. *English teaching in the primary school*. Evans.

(1977a). 'Processing profiles of communication needs'. In Moody and Moore, eds. *English for specific purposes: an international seminar*. The British Council, Bogota, Colombia.

(1977b) 'Applying sociocultural variables in the specification of communicative competence'. In Saville-Troike, M. ed. *Linguistics and anthropology*. Georgetown University Round Table on Languages and Linguistics, 1977. Georgetown University Press.

Munby, John and C.J. Brumfit (1975) 'A problem-solving approach to the development of intensive reading skills'. *IATEFL Newsletter*, 40.

Newberry, R.C. (1974) 'English language support for the teaching of mathematics and science in Singaporean primary schools'. *ELT Documents*, No. 4. 1974.

Oller, John W. and Jack C. Richards, eds. (1973) *Focus on the learner: pragmatic perspectives for the language teacher*. Rowley, Mass., Newbury House.

Paulston, Christina Bratt and Mary Newton Bruder (1976) *Teaching English as a second language: techniques and procedures*. Winthrop.

References and bibliography

Plaister, Ted (1976) *Developing listening comprehension for ESL students.*
Prentice-Hall.

Pride, J.B. and Janet Holmes, eds. (1972) *Sociolinguistics: selected readings.*
Penguin Education.

Quirk, R., S. Greenbaum, G. Leech and J. Svartvik (1972) *A grammar of contemporary English.* Longman.

Richterich, R. (1972) 'A model for the definition of adult language needs'.
CCC/EES (72) 49. Strasbourg, Council of Europe. (Also in *Systems development in adult language learning.* Strasbourg, Council of Europe, 1973.)

Rivers, Wilga (1968). *Teaching foreign language skills.* University of Chicago Press.

(1971) 'Linguistic and psychological factors in speech perception and their
implications for teaching materials'. In Pimsleur, P. and T. Quinn, eds. *The
psychology of second language learning.* Cambridge University Press.

(1973) 'From linguistic competence to communicative competence'. *TESOL
Quarterly*, Vol. 7, No. 1.

Robinson, W.P. (1972) *Language and social behaviour.* Penguin Education.

Roget/Dutch, A. (1966) *Thesaurus of English words and phrases.* Penguin.

Savignon, Sandra J. (1972) 'Teaching for communicative competence: a research
report'. *Audio-visual Language Journal*, Vol. 10, No. 3.

Schegloff, Emanuel A. (1968) 'Sequencing in conversational openings'. In
Gumperz and Hymes, eds. *Directions in sociolinguistics.* Holt, Rinehart,
1972. (Reprinted from *American Anthropologist*, Vol. 70, No. 6.)

Searle, John R. (1965) 'What is a speech act?' In Giglioli, ed. *Language and social
context.* Penguin, 1972.

(1969) *Speech acts: an essay in the philosophy of language.* Cambridge University Press.

Selinker, Larry, Louis Trimble and Robert Vroman (1974) 'Presupposition and
technical rhetoric'. *English Language Teaching*, Vol. 29, No. 1.

Selinker, Larry, R.M. Todd Trimble and Louis Trimble (1976) 'Presuppositional
rhetorical information in EST discourse'. *TESOL Quarterly*, September
1976.

Shaw, A.M. (1975) 'Approaches to a communicative syllabus in foreign language
curriculum development'. Unpublished PhD thesis. University of Essex.

Shuy, Roger, W., ed. (1973) *Sociolinguistics: current trends and prospects:*
report of the twenty-third Annual Round Table Meeting on Linguistics
and Language Studies. Washington, DC, Georgetown University Press.

Sinclair, J.McH., I. Forsyth, R.M. Coulthard, and M. Ashby (1972) 'The English
used by teachers and pupils: final report to SSRC'. Department of
English Language and Literature, Birmingham University.

Sinclair, J.McH. and R.M. Coulthard (1975). *Towards an analysis of discourse.*
Oxford University Press.

Spicer, A. et al. (1977) *The initial training of teachers of modern languages in
colleges and departments of education.* Leeds, E.J. Arnold.

Spolsky, Bernard (1971). 'Reduced redundancy as a language testing tool'. In
Pimsleur, P. and T. Quinn, eds. *The psychology of second language learning.* Cambridge University Press.

Spolsky, Bernard and others (1968) 'Preliminary studies in the development of techniques for testing overall second language proficiency'. *Language Learning*, Special Issue No. 3 on problems in foreign language testing. 1968.

Strevens, Peter (1971) 'The medium of instruction (mother-tongue/second language) and the formation of scientific concepts'. *IRAL*, Vol. 9, No. 3

(1972) *British and American English*. Collier-Macmillan.

(1976) 'Problems of learning and teaching science through a foreign language'. *Studies in Science Education*, No. 3. 1976.

(1977a) *New orientations in the teaching of English*. Oxford University Press.

(1977b) 'Special-purpose language learning: a perspective'. *In Language Teaching and Linguistics: Abstracts*, Vol. 10, No. 3.

Swales, John (1971) *Writing Scientific English*. Nelson.

(1973) 'Introducing teachers to English for science and technology'. *ELT Documents*, No. 6. 1973.

Trim, J.L.M. (1970) 'Definition of language contents on modern language courses at the university level — introduction to discussion, and appendix', at Skepparholmen Symposium. CC/ESR/LV (71) 19. Strasbourg, Council of Europe.

(1971) 'Towards a situational definition of language contents — a schematic inventory of language roles, activities and uses'. In *Modern language learning in adult education*. CCC/EES (71) 135. Strasbourg, Council of Europe.

(1973) 'Draft outline of a European unit/credit system'. In *Systems development in adult language learning*. Strasbourg, Council of Europe, 1973.

Trimble, R.M. Todd and Louis Trimble (1977) 'The development of EFL materials for occupational English'. In Moody and Moore, eds. *English for specific purposes: an international seminar*. The British Council, Bogota, Colombia.

Trudgill, Peter (1974) *Sociolinguistics*. Penguin.

Turner, Roy, ed. (1974) *Ethnomethodology*. Penguin Education.

Upshur, John A. (1971) 'Productive communication testing: progress report'. In Pimsleur, P. and T. Quinn eds. *The psychology of second language learning*. Cambridge University Press.

Valette, R. (1971) 'Evaluation of learning in a second language'. In Bloom, Hastings and Madaus. *Handbook on formative and summative evaluation of student learning*. McGraw-Hill.

Valette, R. and R. Disick (1972) *Modern language performance objectives and individualization*. Harcourt Brace.

Van Ek, J.A. (1975) *Systems development in adult language learning: the threshold level*; with an appendix by L.G. Alexander. Strasbourg, Council of Europe.

Ward, Ida C. (1929) *The phonetics of English*. Heffer.

White, Ronald V. (1974) 'Communicative competence, registers, and second language teaching'. *IRAL*, Vol. 12, No. 2.

(1975) 'The language, the learner and the syllabus'. *RELC Journal* Vol. 6, No. 1.

227

Widdowson, H.G. (1971) 'The teaching of rhetoric to students of science and technology'. In *Science and technology in a second language.* Centre for Information on Language Teaching and Research.

(1973) 'Directions in the teaching of discourse'. In Corder and Roulet, eds. *Theoretical linguistic models in applied linguistics.* Brussels, AIMAV; Paris, Didier, 1973.

(1975) 'EST in theory and practice'. In *English for academic study.* British Council English Teaching Information Centre.

(1976) 'Gradual approximation'. Mimeo (held in ETIC Archives).

(1977a) 'The communicative approach and its application'. In Moody and Moore, eds. *English for specific purposes: an international seminar.* The British Council, Bogota, Colombia.

(1977b) 'Approaches to discourse' in Gutknecht, C. ed. *Grundbegriffe und Hauptstromungen der Linguistik.* Hamburg, Hoffmann und Campe.

Wilkins, D.A. (1972) 'The linguistic and situational content of the common core in a unit/credit system'. In *Systems development in adult language learning.* Strasbourg, Council of Europe, 1973.

(1973) 'Grammatical, situational and notional syllabuses'. *ELT Documents,* No. 6. 1973.

(1974) 'A communicative approach to syllabus construction in adult language learning'. In *Modern languages in adult education.* EES/Symposium 57, 10. Strasbourg, Council of Europe.

(1976) *Notional syllabuses.* Oxford University Press.

(1977) 'Proposal for level definitions'. Appendix C in Trim, J.L.M., *Report on some possible lines of development of an overall structure for a European unit/credit scheme for foreign language learning by adults.* CCC/EES (77) 19. Strasbourg, Council of Europe.

Wingard, P.G. (1971) 'English for scientists at the University of Zambia'. In *Science and technology in a second language.* Centre for Information on Language Teaching and Research.

Wootton, A. (1975) *Dilemmas of discourse.* Allen and Unwin.

Worsley, P. et al. (1970) *Introducing sociology.* Penguin Education.

Yorkey, Richard C. (1970) *Study skills for students of English as a second language.* McGraw-Hill.

INDEX

activity, differentiated from act, skill, function, 41, 46–7, 101, 116
antonymy: relationship of, in index of attitudinal tones, 39, 103
argument, in inventory of micro-functions, 138–9, 187–8
attitudinal tones: communicative key and, 103; index of, 104–10, 168–74, (comments) 39, 103, 111, 139; marking of micro-functions for, 48, 140–6; see also communicative key

certainty: scale of, inventory of micro-functions, 136–7, 185
channel, 78–9; classification of communicative, 80, (example) 79
cohesiveness, in symmetrical social relationships, 73–4; types of relationship involving, 74–5
commitment: scale of, in inventory of micro-functions, 137, 186
communication needs processor (CNP), to obtain communication needs profile, 31, 32–4, 39–40; summary of variables in, 34–9; see also communicative event, communicative key, dialect, and target level (a posteriori variables), and instrumentality, interaction, participant, purposive domain, and setting (a priori variables)
communication needs profile, 24, 31, 32, 33, 34, 39–40, 49; interpreted in terms of language skills required for its realisation, 40, 116, 133; interpreted in terms of micro-functions required for its realisation, 31, 133–5, 139–40; method of obtaining, in model, 154–68; must precede syllabus specification, 24, 40, 218
communicative activities, components of communicative event, 37–8, 98–9; distinguished from acts, skills, functions, 37–8, 41, 46–7, 101, 116; not ready for

verbal or non-verbal realisation until processed, 46–7, 115n, 133
communicative competence: and a theoretical framework, 6, 22–7; Hymes' formulation of, 15; model for specifying, see model; specification of difference from variety analysis, 30, 32
communicative event (activities and subject matter), 37–8, 98–102; derivational sources for, 99, 100–1; in CNP, 32, 33; information required on, 166–7, (example) 99–100, 195–6; see also communicative activities, subject matter
communicative key, 38–9, 102–3, 111–15; derivational sources for, 102–3, 113–14; in CNP, 32, 33; information required on, 167, 175, (example) 196–8; specifying for communicative activity, 111–13; psychosocial setting and, 64; role conflict and, 68; social relationships and, 70; use of term, 102; see also attitudinal tones
communicative value (function), 47; of sentences and utterances: understanding and expressing, as language skills (26–7), 127, 179–80
competence: positions on, of Chomsky, 7–9, 20–1, of Habermas, 10–12, 20–1, of Halliday, 12–14, 21–2, of Hymes, 13, 14–16, 21–2, related viewpoints, 16–19
contextual meaning of an utterance, depending on position in discourse, 26, 43, 45

dialect, 36–7, 83–4; in CNP, 32, 33, 34; information required on, 162–4, (example) 89–91; regional, 84–7; social-class, 87–9, 97; temporal, 84
dialogue, as mode of communication, 76–7, 78, 81
discourse: identifying, indicating, extracting, and expanding main points in, as language skills (37–9), 121, 129, 182; initiating, maintaining, and terminating, as language skills (47–9), 122, 130–1, 183; recog-

231